HERMANN BE(
Sanskrit, becomi
University of Be_
languages, he wrote extensively on religious and philosophical subjects, including Buddhism, Indology,
Christianity, Alchemy and Music. In 1911, he heard a
lecture by Rudolf Steiner and was inspired to join the
Anthroposophical Society, where he soon became a valued co-worker.
In 1922, he helped found The Christian Community, a movement for
religious renewal. His many books are gradually being translated from
the original German and published in English.

THE MYSTERY OF MUSICAL CREATIVITY

The Human Being and Music

Hermann Beckh

Translated by Alan and Maren Stott
Edited by Neil Franklin, Katrin Binder and Alan Stott

TEMPLE LODGE

Temple Lodge Publishing Ltd.
Hillside House, The Square
Forest Row, RH18 5ES

www.templelodge.com

Published in English by Temple Lodge 2019

From the author's unrevised handwritten manuscript discovered after his death, transcribed by Helga & Ingrid Paul and Dr Katrin Binder

A CIP catalogue record for this book is available from the British Library

ISBN 978 1 912230 38 9

Cover by Morgan Creative featuring 'Fingal's Cave' by Thomas Moran
Typeset by DP Photosetting, Neath, West Glamorgan
Printed and bound by 4Edge Ltd., Essex

Contents

Introduction

*'... meine Seele hatte ein intimes Verhältnis zum Tönenden der Welt, zu dem, was die
ewige Harmonie im Innersten aller Dinge ist.'*
Hermann Beckh, 'Aus meinem Leben', in Gundhild Kačer-Bock 1997, p. 87.

*'... my soul had an intimate relationship to what sounds in the world, to that which
lives most inwardly as the eternal harmony in everything.'*
Hermann Beckh, 'From my Life', in Gundhild Kačer-Bock 2016, p. 82.

A year before his death, Hermann Beckh (1875–1937) began penning
The Language of Tonality (Leominster 2015), regarded by some as his
crowning achievement. He was able to check the proofs when they
arrived, although he suffered considerable pain from his final illness
and hardly slept. Through the help of friends, the book was published
posthumously in Stuttgart (1938). Just over a year before his death,
Beckh had written:

> Initially the *lectures on music* demand my whole concentration. I hope in
> my suffering condition I am still able to succeed at least satisfactorily with
> these lectures. They are important for me in so far as they give me the
> theme for the *next book* that I now intend to write. The theme is simply the
> cosmic rhythm in the musical keys. This really lives in me; this is my
> theme (letter 26 Jan. 1936. Tr. A. S., emphases added).

Now that the manuscript of a book on music has come to light, it seems
that with 'lectures on music' the author was referring to this *other book*
on music, *Das Geheimnis des musikalischen Schaffens: der Mensch und die
Musik.* On his sick-bed, it appears, the Professor was preparing two
books. Knowing his end was approaching, Beckh left revising the
manuscript of *Das Geheimnis des musikalischen Schaffens: Der Mensch und
die Musik* in order to concentrate on finalizing his expanded account of
tonality.

The author's pioneer intuitions on music, to which he refers in these
lectures, was first published as a monograph (Foreword dated Breitbrunn, July 1922); Eng. tr. *The Essence of Tonality* (Leominster [2]2011).
Shortly after this, Rudolf Steiner (1861–1925) gave a tremendous lecture
on musical inspiration in Dornach (2 Dec. 1922, in GA 283),[1] perhaps in
response to Beckh's lectures, though it seems the lectures he did attend
in Stuttgart were more likely held in 1923.[2] Steiner also said of Beckh's
studies on language:

> Beckh ventures into provinces which I have not had the opportunity of
> investigating myself. And there is a great deal in what Beckh says about
> them.

In his lecture, Steiner gives what amounts to the esoteric basis of the
musical arts. The meditation that is given would appear to accompany
the musical organism known as the circle of fifths, the 'tone-zodiac'
Beckh intuited. Steiner describes it in cosmic terms. Beckh's monograph and his later book could not have received a richer confirmation
and stimulus for further research than this single, unique lecture,
which purposely avoids supplying information for schematic thinking.
Beckh's diagrams — as his descriptions demonstrate — are intended to
be regarded as *Imaginations*, pictures indicating qualities, relationships,
analogies and movement. Like the circle of fifths itself, they too are not
to be reduced to something only schematic.

The 'beautiful and mature book', as years later (1959) his colleague
Emil Bock[3] (1895–1959) calls *The Language of Tonality*, 'forms a wonderful concluding and summarizing cadence to his [Beckh's] rich
creative work'. Had Bock known of the *other* musical study written
down at that time, he would no doubt have included it in his appreciation. Certainly, Bock, himself a prolific author, acknowledged, 'An
abundance of books came into existence whose significance perhaps
will only be properly appreciated in the future'. In his summary of
Beckh's contribution, Bock points out:

> A fundamental musical attitude runs through everything that he wrote
> on the gospels and also what he thought and wrote on what has remained
> alive in the East of the early wisdom of humanity.

'Das Geheimnis des Musikalische Schaffens'

The manuscript of the assembled lectures entitled *Das Geheimnis des
musikalischen Schaffens: Der Mensch und die Musik; — The Mystery of
Musical Creation: The Human Being and Music*, with Beckh's literary
estate, passed to his mother, who survived him. Later the Ms spent
some decades in a drawer in America; finally it came to light and went
to Australia. An article from the literary remains, 'The Mystery of the
Night in Richard Wagner' (included here as Appendix One), devoted
to Wagner and Novalis and concentrating on *Tristan and Isolde*, had
already appeared in the original German in the posthumous volume of

essays and articles.[4] But not until recent times did a substantial part (six chapters in fact, Nos. 1–5, and 11), from *Der Mensch und die Musik* appear in three instalments in the journal *Die Europäer*.[5] For the present complete edition the remaining chapters have been transcribed into letterpress from the Professor's script, written in Sütterlin, and the whole translated into English.

The resulting text lays good claim to illustrate Beckh's lecturing style, his comprehensive knowledge of music and its spirituality, with profound awareness of the contexts. *The Human Being and Music* forms a significant supplement to *The Language of Tonality*. Viewed in the order they were written, however, one could also call *The Language of Tonality* (1937) a comprehensive excursion from the survey of the musical field, *The Human Being and Music* (1936). Beckh turns his attention to the raw material of musical perception. He discusses the sighing wind, the billowing wave, the song of the birds, and soul-experience — in particular the theme of *longing*. He characterizes musical development, examines chosen musical works, for him representing the peak of human creativity as such, and on this solid basis he looks to a possible future. So, strictly speaking, the title of this book is correctly worded. The author:

- does not write as a musical *specialist* and then turn to universal *human* concerns;
- he writes from universal, human concerns and reveals music as of *special concern to everyone*.

Beckh writes as a universal scholar from the cosmic context to the individual situation, and from there seeks again the re-won cosmic context. In this respect, this book's educational form — uniting heaven and earth — belongs to the tradition of Goethe and particularly the early Romantic poet, Novalis [1772–1801], that Johannine spirit with whom Beckh felt particularly at home.

Accounts exist (see Appendix 2) of the popularity of his lectures, where, at the piano, Beckh would share his enthusiasm for music, regardless of the clock: 'Everyone gained something,' reports August Pauli. The same estimation applies to this book recording the content of those lectures; Beckh has something to say for everyone. Indeed, as others point out, Beckh's artistic, musical personality informs all of his work, including the pioneer work on the origins of language, for which he is most known. To complement the usual 'pragmatic etymology' that investigates the historical developments and comparisons, Beckh's work blazes a trail for 'genetic etymology' (a distinction made by Novalis) of what the sounds of speech teach. Beckh's musical ear and perceptive mind penetrated the meaning of the speech-sounds themselves. He does it even more thoroughly and consistently than the composer Josef Matthias Hauer (1883–1959), whose manifesto *Deutung des Melos* ('*Interpreting Melos*') appeared in 1923,[6] to which Steiner refers in his 1924-lectures on eurythmy, the new art of 'visible singing' (GA 278) — to which Beckh frequently refers.

Today, almost one hundred years on, the Professor's musicality may seem even more important than his astonishing memory and vast range of knowledge. This included mastery of numerous languages, including six ancient and six modern. Beckh's musical approach is fundamental to all his work on world spirituality. An initial attempt to assist further research to justify this claim would seem timely. To this end, this translation appears as part of the *Collected Works* in English, while a more scholarly edition is being prepared. The author's faint pencilled corrections and additions (mostly for his own use) still need to be deciphered, and links followed up to his other pioneer works.

Spirituality and music

It should be remembered that Beckh worked and taught during the difficult inter-war years of the twentieth century. He alludes to this in Chapter 3 and at the end of Chapter 10:

> Much that exists today can be felt as earthly chaos and earthly darkness. But this passing through the darkness and the chaos of the present may be necessary for that which will come, for the gaining, or re-gaining, of the higher, starry element in music with new means of expression. Especially where chaos reigns in the earthly element the ground is being created for the working-in of the starry forces.

After decades researching world spirituality, Beckh felt he could trace causes and cures for today's issues. Beckh was drawn to the story of humanity's emerging consciousness and its development. This he saw as essential for the task of renewal — to appreciate the past in order to take an informed step forwards. Despite his academic brilliance appreciated by his colleagues and superiors at Germany's premier university, Beckh was not content to remain a specialist. With his comprehensive knowledge, he recognized in Rudolf Steiner a world-teacher.[7] Comprehensive knowledge had found a contemporary focus. For his part, Steiner recognized Beckh's calibre. It seems likely[8] we owe the existence of several lecture-cycles by Dr Steiner, as well as individual lectures and addresses from him, to Beckh's presence in the audience.

Prof. Beckh's decision in 1921 to devote the rest of his life to develop spiritual science, or anthroposophy, was the next logical step on a path utterly committed to bona fide research both material and spiritual (see footnote 6). Behind the respective disciplines of research he clearly saw the human story as a development of consciousness. It would appear that Beckh quite likely took the widest, most inclusive canvas available to the questing human being; references to mythology and creation stories are consequently strictly relevant. That inner story is also told in music. Beckh unfolds the story of music he knew, set within the wider historical background of world spirituality that, he shows, prepared both the form and content of the art of music. Spirituality — the inner story — appeared to him inherently musical, focussed, incarnational. The phenomena he uncovered lies more in the experience *between the notes* than what is recorded — and has to be recorded — in the score. The results originate from a *meditative deepening of the experience of music*, out of which it was born in the first place, transmitted from composer to player and listener. To appreciate this creative process, the author, as a pioneer in such studies, had to have recourse to a less familiar terminology where strictly necessary.

In the autobiographical account of his childhood, *Sun before Seven*, the writer and poet Ian Dall[9] records his early struggle to learn the piano:

> You always got the same sound from the same note, but somehow between these sounds it seemed to me there must lie other sounds beautiful and weird, which were a part of music, but which the piano could not play. I knew this, because I heard these sounds in my head coming out of nowhere when I looked at pictures of the sea and caves on the shores of Scotland. And there were sounds, too, in the top of the *ombú* [large, herbaceous tree-like plant], and under the bridge, and in the eaves and keyholes during a *pampero* [a strong, cold, dry wind blowing from southern Patagonia to the Rio de la Plata], and cries which people made selling things in the streets as well as in the birds' cries and the frogs. You could not possibly get any of these sounds on the piano. So the piano was disappointing.

This perception of the 'between' is precisely the *pons asinorum* of cutting-edge research. Rather than argue the obvious answer of the professional musician, Beckh's achievement is to combine both views, neither to lose the spontaneous, creative context, nor to lose an holistic relationship. Consequently Beckh can remain firmly grounded and well-balanced in company with his 'cosmic' concept of the 'sound-ether'. The human inner world Beckh saw emerging in history comes 'down to earth' in the musical system; its present form is mapped by musicians in the sounding circle of musical keys, the well-known 'circle of fifths'. This closed system, nobody's invention, available to and used by everyone, is consequently in no way an abstract 'theory' to be proved, but a reality to be investigated. For other researchers, it is known as the traditional zodiac circle, the 'cosmic rhythm'. The two, the Professor teaches in *The Language of Tonality*, are in reality one and the same. This universal scholar, moreover, had earlier revealed the archetypal human story in his two-volume work expounding the 'cosmic rhythm' in the Gospels of Mark and John (1928 and 1930. Eng. trans. 2015). 'Cosmos' means 'order' as opposed to 'chaos'; it is also used in the sense of 'universal'. In Beckh's definition, the term 'cosmic' is 'the revelation of the spirit within the earthly realm' (*Language of Tonality*, p. 59), which, to repeat, has to do with qualities, relationships, analogies and movement.

Beckh saw that the battle for the spirit, our humanity, is taking place particularly tangibly in the musical realm. Research in inner listening involves taking concrete steps to develop consciousness, essential (Beckh claimed) to balance our one-sided civilization. Beckh takes up the main composer reviled by Hauer; he shows how Richard Wagner (1813-83) was indeed artistically sensitive precisely to that spiritual perception Hauer himself championed. Beckh intimately knew every bar of this music; his account of Wagner's use of tonality is, I believe, scrupulous. In the following chapters, by concentrating on Wagner's acknowledged masterpiece *Tristan and Isolde* with some concluding remarks on Wagner's final creation, *Parsifal*, Beckh attempts to demonstrate in detail how the artistic event in both music and poetry really does reflect and recreate tangible advances in human consciousness.

To correct any false impressions with his choice of composer, Beckh (Lecture 8) is the first to admit:

> It does *not* mean that, if the 'starry quality in music' is one day sought in the musical style of the future, this will be undertaken in Wagner's musical style. On the contrary, the musical style of the future will cer-

tainly be another. It should be recognized that Wagner's musical style is a unique event in the history of music ... Wagner's musical style is not to be repeated and not to be continued. For this reason, though, it is important not to deny it, but rather to gain knowledge and insights from this unique, perhaps so far most interesting phenomenon of music history. These insights can be made fruitful also without any imitation for the musical developments of the future.

Beckh's account of music also climaxes in Bruckner's symphonies. The author justifies as his main field of enquiry the music of 'Bach to Bruckner'. His few restrained comments about twentieth-century developments are clearly suggestions within the context prepared from Lecture 1 onwards.

Polarity amongst musicians?

Of course, intellectual 'moonshine' exists as well as the 'esoteric' sort; but both being beside the point serves only to highlight the existence of bona fide research. The issue, rather more than any reaction, will inevitably extend beyond artistic matters. Nothing here need be swept aside today, but political and other controversy is simply not the subject of Beckh's research. His intention is to help the individual develop those forces that *alone can cope* with such 'issues' that are even threatening the basis of civilization. Technology, efficiency, one-sided professionalism including an over-insistence on 'evidence', may all be necessary, but as such they are all proving themselves to be sadly insufficient. Spiritual substance and spiritual advance have to be present as well. This is why — particularly in his lecture 'Anthroposophy and University Knowledge' (see footnote 6) — Beckh insists, and in his life-decisions upheld, a consciousness of spiritual categories, ultimately the creative archetypes themselves (his 'theme'), before empirical ones. Beckh is read for his insight; his knowledge is taken for granted.

Fingal's Cave on Staffa, in the Inner Hebrides, Scotland, was an image not only for Ian Dall but also for August Strindberg, who is studied in these lectures. Felix Mendelssohn (1809–1847) burst into tears upon his first view of the sea. *The Hebrides Overture*, op. 26, was written after his visit to Fingal's Cave, as we know from a letter (1 Aug. 1829) to his family, where he quotes the opening theme. For Mendelssohn, music is 'too definite for words' (Letter to Marc-André

Souchay, October 15, 1842). The poet William Wordsworth, nevertheless, inspired generations in the nineteenth and twentieth centuries with his 'Ode: Intimations of Immortality from Recollections of Early Childhood' (1804/07, final version 1815). He records:

> ...
> Hence in a season of calm weather
>   Though inland far we be,
> Our souls have sight of that immortal sea
>   Which brought us hither,
>   Can in a moment travel thither,
> And see the children sport upon the shore,
> And hear the mighty waters rolling evermore.
>
> Then sing, ye birds, sing, sing a joyous song!
> ...

The poet, the playwright and the composer do not delude themselves by sensory sounds and sights, but, on the contrary, are inspired by their sensory experience to write poetry, plays and music (cf. Chapter 11). Sensory experience may provide the occasion; 'recollections in tranquillity' fashion it into art. Even in daily discourse meteorological words, even 'atmosphere' itself, carry more than one meaning. The point here is that 'wind and waves' are an esoteric shorthand.[10] Our sensory environment is a parable. In Professor Beckh's own case an experience as a five-year-old in the mountains fuelled his later vocational career.[11] This experience, convincing him of pre-existence, unleashed an overwhelming compassion for suffering humanity. The event comes anterior to the exercise of his prodigious memory and other gifts that helped him as a polymath to fulfil that life's vocation. The five-year-old saw:

> ... behind my relatives, all the other people whom I had not known in life, people in general, and an incredible pain about human beings laid hold of me, a warm compassion which I, although personally very compassionate, had never known in this encompassing greatness in everyday life. And the feeling of this incredible compassion, this pain with humanity, this urge to help and to direct one's whole life towards an active, helping human work was also later on — I did experience this a couple more times in later years — always connected with this experience. But these feelings are also those which then send us back from the consciousness of cosmic widths into the narrow consciousness of the day. The soul recognizes: you cannot and may not remain on that shore. What is experienced there does but show you the

task which here, on this side of the sensory world, amongst your fellow man, you have in fact to fulfil; it shows you why you have become a human being. Yet of course in my child development I was not so far that I could have carried this fully consciously into my everyday life.

A university department today empirically researches 'life before life';[12] the critic's task here, however, is artistic — that is, to explore the inner relationship of early perception to creativity.[13] More immediately, it is well known that exemplary musicians exist who claim the prerogative of the profession to speak only of notes and rests; poetic descriptions are perhaps only admitted as 'aids'. We may explain that the drama of Beethoven's *Piano Sonata*, op. 57, 'Appassionata', stems from the tension between 'tonic harmony directly adjacent to that of the flattened supertonic' already in the very first bars, or, with Prof. Donald Tovey[14] of 'the death of the hero' in the last movement, or again, like Prof. Hermann Beckh, speak of 'billowing storms of passion' to characterize the tragic musical development — these approaches, not mutually exclusive, are actually already present in Tovey's classic analyses. Is it not a truism to point out that the storms in the gospels and the storm in *King Lear* are about much more than getting wet — similarly Beckh's 'wind and waves'? 'Elementary'? — certainly, but musical and spiritual issues reach deep, under the veils that hide the spirit in nature. It is easy to hoodwink ourselves.

In these pages (Chapter 5) Beckh mentions that in *Theosophy* ([GA 9], III, iii), Rudolf Steiner speaks of *'ein Meer von Tönen* — an ocean of musical sounds' in a passage devoted to 'cosmic music'. In this text, Steiner 'for the sake of simplicity' does not pursue this observation in his descriptions of the supersensory realm. In the present book, Beckh, like Steiner, always committed to independent research, takes up the challenge. The opinion that conventional scholars are in the right and that Steiner's and Beckh's comprehensive approach is misguided, the Professor himself answers here in his expositions, which reach a climax in the final chapters. As already mentioned (see footnote 6), in his historic yet still topical lecture to the University of Berlin (1921), Beckh raises his voice for independent research as a vital element in civilization. At all events, a reassessment is due.

Die-hard, practical musicians, insisting on what their training taught them, limit the art of music to the arrangement of organized sounds. To the best of their ability, they play 'what is written'. Though the author explains with his customary utmost clarity, his division of 'primary' and 'secondary music' is ignored and thus dismissed. It is extremely doubtful whether composers themselves would behave in such a debonair manner today—indeed, players are frequently expected to exercise more imaginative freedom than was the rule in living memory. Even for us lesser mortals, creation is far more than a matter of re-arrangements, a 'twelve-note game', a game of counters. Beckh's guiding-star is that Johannine spirit, Novalis; the spiritual-scientific *Fragmente* of the poet-miner speak to him more of creativity and music than the theories and reactionary opinions of the music critic of the *Neue Freie Presse*. Eduard Hanslick (1825–1904) distrusted what he thought were 'extra-musical' associations. For Novalis, however, 'every disease is a musical problem; every cure is a musical solution'. The natural man must radically change, echoes Rudolf Steiner,[15] speaking in a therapeutic context: 'Out you go! For music alone is human.' This goal of full humanity pursuing the middle way of T A O is precisely Mozart's testament in his final masterpiece *The Magic Flute* (cf. the name TAminO—'More than a Prince, he is a human being!').[16]

With his 'cosmic' concepts, Beckh is certainly in good company as he conducts spiritual-scientific research into the 'magic' world of human music for which we all passionately care. The cosmic sources have already been apprehended by musicians, he claims; they are not cate-gories separate from 'music history'. Beckh discusses other composers, yet chose to enter into specific details with Wagner's acknowledged masterpiece, so dear to the composer's and his own heart. In these chapters, Beckh investigates what *Tristan and Isolde* attempts to say as a complete work of art. Only after writing this music drama, he also points out elsewhere, could Wagner have written his final consummate work, *Parsifal*: 'Without this *Tristan* A♭-major, the *Parsifal* A♭-major could never have been created' (*Tonality*, p. 239). They belong together (Lecture 7).

Today, we have moved on from the rather parochial 'social divide' of the *followers* of Brahms and those of Wagner. In those days, it is worth noting, to the 'absolute' musician Bruckner, Wagner was 'the Master'. Today, if Beckh is finding his rightful place in the history of artistic thinking, his vision—more accurately 'audition'—of the creative source, or, in other words, the Goethean, holistic approach the Pro-fessor consistently followed, is likely to be the essential and valuable thing about his contributions. Indeed, musicians already know that music itself does not exist exclusively *for them*; faithful from first note to the last, for musicians performance is an act of sharing with whoever has ears to hear. It is essentially no different with all the subjects to which Beckh turned his enquiring and productive mind. 'This manner of "being musical" can also be revealed in quite other spheres than in "only musical" pursuits,' Beckh claims in the pages that follow.

Specifically for those coming after, the universal scholar Prof. Dr Hermann Beckh himself lived his own advice, giving stimuli for further reflection in all the subjects to which his seminal mind turned its attention—the sign not only of a universal scholar, but also of a born educator.

Future prospects

The musical system as pursued in the West in particular has been further researched since Beckh's day. The mathematical basis is well known for the various divisions of the octave standing behind the musical scales down the ages. We need no time-machine when our ears can attune to human experience from the earliest times inherent in the early scales; prospects of possible future developments are also indicated. Here the outstanding researchers Hermann Pfrogner and Heiner Ruland—who acknowledge Beckh's tone-zodiac—should be mentioned, who have built on the researches of Bela Bartok, Kathleen Schlesinger, and other pioneers. Pfrogner is an authority on twentieth-century developments because he places them in a world-historical context (*Lebendige Tonwelt*, 1982, and *Zeitwende der Musik*, 1986, Eng. tr. '*Music's Turning Point of Time*', forthcoming). Pfrogner also voiced his concern with regard to the challenge of musically preparing the future—we may *know* the new musical scales from their mathematical basis that reflects the developing human constitution, but are not yet ourselves actual citizens of the future epochs. Careful not to fabricate compositions, we can, however, as for any other meaningful human activity, humbly *prepare* the future—our own. Moreover, this Professor insists, a start *has* to be made, with steady, meditative inner listening, working—as Beckh also maintains—'out of the "I"', the self-reflecting personality. The matter, then, is not simply a matter of tuning, but of inwardly recognizing and meditatively 'owning' the new scales involving variable tuning, if a new chapter in musical composition is to be prepared here and now. If this points to the crux of the matter—the future of tonality—then it is worth mentioning.

Music as an extended activity, as Beckh's life also shows, explores spiritual contexts, even the central concerns of humanity. Neither pursuing exotic 'aural delights' nor indulging in questionable antics that include speculative systems, it remains to be seen whether bona fide research and artistic projects in the twenty-first century develop out of the 'middle way' of full humanity. On this path, and with the present work that came to the light of day in the twenty-first century, Beckh may become an inspiring companion. His work reads like a spiritual adventure, itself a music drama, owing something to Goethe's holistic vision, the poetic prose of Novalis, and Steiner's essential insights—how else could it have been written? A correlation of world spirituality with stimuli for musical development produces more than a passing enthusiasm. Professor Hermann Beckh, a master and by all accounts one of the world's great 'originals', may yet stimulate developments of lasting value in the near future.

The Translation

This translation aims to render in English what Prof. Beckh wrote. Yet, following accepted practice, in order to respect the author's meaning in another language, it does not slavishly transliterate every passage. As is customary, editorial additions appear in square brackets [ ]; footnotes, intending to be helpful, are marked as additions. Capitals have been used for technical terms: Mystery, Imagination, Inspiration and Intuition, the Earth, and so on. *Geheimnis*, a term frequently used, is translated 'Mystery'. Bona fide research of the 'open secret', the 'daily miracle'—for example, the study of speech, right into the *sounds of speech* that are our access to the primordial language[17]—is a domain of spiritual science, or anthroposophy, whose methods are artistic at the same time. This is Beckh's consistent viewpoint, and why his work is distinctive in any subject to which he devotes his attention. In earlier times 'the Mysteries' or 'Mystery centres' were the only centres of learning. Today, advance in exact pictorial (Imagination), musical (Inspiration) and fully authentic awareness (Intuition) sums up the pursuit of developing spiritual science. The philosophical and cognitive basis is outlined in: Rudolf Steiner, *A Theory of Knowledge implicit in Goethe's World Conception* [GA 2], and other basic texts noted in Beckh's text. The subject of study is 'what is'.

Frequent use of abbreviated titles is avoided. *Tristan and Isolde* is the title Wagner gave to the main work discussed here. For passages of

Wagner's libretti I have consulted in particular the website: www.rwagner.net, the ENO opera guides, and Stewart Spenser's splendid translation *Wagner's Ring of the Nibelung* (London: Thames & Hudson 1993). As in other translations of Prof. Beckh, I have divided those sentences that are over-long by the standards of today's German, and added more paragraph breaks, even bullet-points for lists. Thereby, I trust, Beckh's lecturing style is not essentially disturbed. Beckh's own lecture-divisions have been retained, though the text is often continuous; his original 'Contents' page (included here) has been rewritten and completed. In the text, references to the author's other works have also been retained, the bibliographical details updated.

Beckh's entire work is all of a piece. The references are not relatively irrelevant; they belong to the specifics of a comprehensive vision the author tries his best to communicate. Like that seminal thinker, the romantic poet, S.T. Coleridge, Beckh's grasp of Logos philosophy was secure — but Coleridge did not have an exact training in law behind him. Don't be misled; charming stories of the absent-minded German professor are what is irrelevant when it comes to what he has to say — as little as the laudanum Coleridge took initially as a narcotic pain-killer — but from his addiction he *did* finally manage to free himself — has to do with what *he*, another polymath, had to say (cf. Owen Barfield, *What Coleridge Thought*. Barfield Press 2014).

My special thanks go to the musician Gotthard Killian, owner of Beckh's manuscript, and Danaë Killian, PhD, MMusPerf, BA(Mus), AMusA, DipCA who made the scans and helped clarify some details; to Helga and Ingrid Paul (Ulm) and Edzard Klemm for preparing a substantial part of the text published in *Die Europäer*. (Perseus Verlag not only published some original text, but also reissued Beckh's *Der Hingang des Vollendeten*, with a Postscript by Thomas Meyer, Basel, 2011.) Dr Katrin Binder completed the professional transcription; very knotty problems were confirmed as illegible by local readers of Sütterlin script. My bi-lingual wife Maren Stott, M.A. Eu., helped with the initial draft, which as always was improved with editorial help from Neil Franklin, Ph.D. All these helpers, together with our most cordial and helpful publisher, Sevak Gulbekian and his team, mercifully do not count the many hours they sacrifice for the day of seeing Beckh's *Complete Works* appear in English translation. As always, all surviving blemishes 'I acknowledge as mine'.

Alan Stott, Stourbridge, Epiphany 2016.

Beckh's contents list of eight chapter headings:

[This page of the Ms contains deletions and several pencil additions, not all of which are legible. There is evidence of two systems of chapter division, where one system is discontinued. The further divisions in the Ms amounting to 15 chapters, where clear, have been retained in the text, though these divisions, too, might conceivably have been revised.]

1. The polarity of the musical element: the airy and the sound-etheric (the earthly and the cosmic element).
2. The two elements as the soul and the spirit of music.
3. The two elements in the music from Bach to Beethoven and Chopin.
4. The two elements of music as 'wind and wave': Strindberg's *The Dream Play*.
5. The union of both elements in the theme of longing in *Tristan and Isolde*.
6. The realm of expression of the musical element. The starry content and mystery of music; its relationship to initiation, to the Mystery [of human life].
7. The mystery content of the musical element in Richard Wagner.
8. The mystery content of absolute music in Anton Bruckner (with an excursus on instrumentation).

It should not be forgotten that this work was left incomplete and written in most distressing circumstances. It was, after all, a draft and very much a work in progress, and this is particularly the case in Chapter 15 where several words are illegible: a most moving testament to Beckh's indefatigable devotion to the Mysteries and to music.

1. The Polarity of the Musical Element: the Airy and the Sound-Etheric (the Earthly and the Cosmic Element)

'Our soul has to be air because it knows of music and delights in it. Musical sound is substance of air, air-soul, the propagating movement of the air is an emotional state of the air through the musical sound. In the ear the musical sound arises anew.'
Novalis, *Fragmente*, No. 2053.

With these words,[18] [the early Romantic, German poet and thinker] Novalis [1772–1801], touches on deep mysteries of the musical element, its relationship to the world and to the human being. These secrets are accessible to us today through anthroposophical spiritual science.

The relationship of musical sound to the air is obvious. Physically the acoustic side of music is an oscillation of the air, 'sound-waves'. We are used in physics to imagining the essence of light as wave-movement. And with the singing human voice as well as with musical instruments — especially with wind instruments, but not only with these — the relationship of musical sound to the element of air becomes clear.

And yet the saying of Novalis basically speaks of something else. 'Musical sound is substance of air, air-soul' — this is still something more than the movement of the air and vibrations of physical sound of the physical imagination. Here something is said of the relationship of musical sound — and the element of air in the sound — to the element of soul. Moreover, in Novalis' saying, much is said in contrast to the physical way of imagining. The propagating movement of the air is 'an emotional state of the air *through the musical sound*'. Consequently, in the meaning of these words, it is not at all the air that produces musical sound. That actual musical element has deeper backgrounds and subterranean bases, lying deeper in the spiritual element of the world. This deeper, original, *primary*, antecedent musical element affects only *secondarily*, following the air; it reaches over the element of air, taking it as its medium, a conveying agent.

If the physical manner of observation is complemented through one deriving from a theory of knowledge, as understood by the science of today, then this theory of knowledge of today will show the phenomenon of musical sound as somehow coming about in the sense-organ of the human ear in connection with the brain. The meaning of another of Novalis' sayings goes beyond this: 'In the ear the musical sound arises *anew.*' For if it arises *anew*, then it would have had to have existed beforehand in a different way. To search and bring nearer to our understanding this primary element of musical sound, which Novalis means as a deeper hidden, original element, will be the content of the observations here.

Today we link music and the musical element in a much too one-sided way with the ear. Whoever can distinguish with the ear very fine differences of oscillations of pitch, quarter-tones, even sixth-tones, we usually regard as particularly musical individuals. Yet another category of 'being musical' exists, which the professional musician does not necessarily possess in the strongest degree. It has not only to do with the sense [of hearing], but the soul, with the spirit, with the whole human being. Such a 'being musical', quite apart from a mere musical ear, perhaps at the expense of this ability, we find in a high degree with Richard Wagner [1813–83], who consequently in such a unique way also knew how to connect music with the whole problematic and dramatic cosmic-depths of human consciousness. This manner of 'being musical' can also be revealed in quite other spheres than in 'only musical' pursuits. And Novalis as *poet and thinker* lived in a unique way in the musical element as understood here. His whole spirituality was as if born out of the cosmic element of music.

In the *Hymns to the Night* of Novalis, there are places where a spiritual feeling for the musical keys can be felt as directly stimulated. And in the prose writings, such as *The Apprentices of Sais* and *Heinrich von Ofterdingen*, the musical primal grounds of the world seem to be heard joining in everywhere. Novalis himself writes in *Sais*:

> He who speaks truly is imbued with eternal life, and His scripture appears to us to be miraculously affiliated with authentic mysteries, for it is in accord with the symphony of the cosmos.

Like a billowing sea, cosmic music surges in these words, in the words and poetry of Novalis in general. His language is woven from these elements of cosmic music, whereas Goethe's no less admirable language is formed more out of the element of light, of cosmic light. In this sense we can distinguish people, artistically creative people, into two camps. In the one the light element, the 'eye' predominates, in the other the element of musical sound, the 'ear'. This is not at all to say that every creative musician belongs without more ado to the latter group. The powerful forming of Bach's music can appear to us woven out of cosmic light, like a cosmic architecture of light. Bach, the musician, was in a certain sense a man of light, a visual person, like Goethe ... This does not exclude, also with him, especially in the great Preludes [e.g. of 'The 48', the *Well-tempered Clavier*], that we feel as if surrounded by the sea of cosmic music, whereas especially in the Fugues, the other element characterized above is more evident.

* * *

Thus we would have to distinguish two elements of music:

- the one more earthly, bound to the ear and the element of air, the air-breath;
- the other, the more hidden, revealed to the higher soul-forces, is anchored in deeper cosmic grounds and sub-conscious depths. It is what in a picture we have already called the 'billowing sea of cosmic music'.

The one would be the more earthly, the other the cosmic element of music. That which is bound to the air and the ear is but the secondary element, the other, hidden element, the primary source and actual element of music.

In perceiving the one we are more in the earthly-physical realm, in perceiving the other we are somehow released from the earthly-physical, outside it. This is indeed one of the most significant characteristics of music, of the resonance, of the waving (*Wogen*) of sound in general, that it produces an effect on us, pulling us out of the merely earthly element. Consequently, the ritual use of music, of sound in general, of the deep undefined sounding in ancient times, [and] of church bells in earlier Christian times.

The ethers and the elements

Anthroposophical spiritual science employs the concept of the etheric, of the ether, for this higher essential element that is wrested from the physical. Not the hypothetical ether of recent physics [today redundant] that is still too much bound towards the physical, but a reality that is only revealed to us to the degree we have begun to free our consciousness itself out of the fetters of the physical. In Rudolf Steiner's book[19] *Knowledge of the Higher Worlds: How is it attained?* [GA 10] the path is described step by step to realise these goals in a way that corresponds to the consciousness and culture of humanity today. As the rigidity of the stone pictures the physical, the life of the plant is a picture of the etheric — although the plant in the visible and tangible part of its being, naturally takes part in the physical world. That one *only* sees the physical of the plant is not even correct.

It is, moreover, only the use of the differentiation gained here in the musical realm, in the world of sound in general, when anthroposophical spiritual science employs the concept of the *sound-ether*. It takes it for the higher, anterior, primary element of music, and of sound in general, which is revealed to the hidden forces of consciousness, for another realm already touched on in these observations, the concept of the *light-ether*, as this term is used in spiritual science. It speaks of two further kinds of ether: the *warmth-ether* revealed in warmth phenomena, the element of fire; the *life-ether* revealed in the phenomena of life.

- The *warmth-ether* is seen as the lowest, placed closest to the element of the earth.
- The *life-ether* is seen as the highest kind of etheric, whereas
- *light-ether* and *sound-ether* stand in the middle; the light-ether belongs more to the lower etheric level, the sound-ether to the upper, highest etheric level.

In relationship to the four elements of the earthly (firmness), watery (liquid), airy (gaseous), fiery, which are received in an earlier spiritual science — not to be confused with the 'elements' of chemistry today (which are rather what the physicist calls 'aggregate conditions of matter') — these four kinds of ether behave in such a way that to the lowest element, the highest ether corresponds and to the highest element the lowest ether. The life-ether as the highest ether relates to the earth; the warmth-ether relates to the element of fire; the light-ether to the air; the sound-ether to the water.

The sound-ether and life-ether, as 'the higher kinds of ether', are also the ones that are more removed from the human being in his earthly state. With the element of life this is immediately obvious. With the sound-ether, as the hidden, higher primary element of music, this has become clear from our whole exposition. The revelation of the lower kinds of ether, of the light-etheric and the warmth-etheric, are closer and more accessible to the human being in the earthly element (although the ether as such always remains something 'super sensory').

Thus the higher kinds of ether, life-ether and sound-ether, are more related to the eternal and immortal; the lower kinds of ether to the mortal side. We have often pointed to the relationship existing in the biblical story of Paradise between the 'Tree of Life' and the 'Tree of Knowledge',[20] which after his Fall became for man the Tree of Death. The 'Tree of Life', unobtainable to man who had entered mortality, would correspond from the etheric aspect, to the life-ether and sound-ether. 'The Tree of Knowledge' would correspond to the lower kinds of ether nearer to man's mortality and earth-knowledge. During the course of this study, it will become clear how far this relates directly to musical phenomena.

An earlier spiritual science conceived the earthly element, 'Mother Earth', and the watery element, as the female elements; air and fire as the masculine. From the aspect of the etheric, the elements of light and warmth would belong accordingly to the masculine, the lower kinds of ether, whereas the higher kinds, sound and life, would be feminine.

Regarding the relationships of the elements and kinds of ether — details in Günther Wachsmuth[21] — what is immediately important for the present study is the one of water, of the watery condition to the sound-ether. The picture already used here of the billowing sea of cosmic music for the higher element of sound, for the 'sound-ether' as understood in anthroposophy, points in this direction. Purely from the earthly element, the revelation of music as sound is known in the surging of the sea, in the roar of the waterfall, in the surging of water in general, in the melody of the fountain, in the murmuring of the brook, in the trickling spring. It is well known how on the water, for example, during a boat-trip, the sound is carried quite differently. The acoustic on the water is quite different, more alive. In the Egyptian temple-scene in his mystery-drama *The Soul's Awakening* [Scene 8], in the musicality of the words Rudolf Steiner poetically brings out this relationship of the element of water to the sound-ether as the cosmic, spheric element of music.

The Representative of the Water Element (Theodosius-Torquatus):

Der Schein ersteht zum Sein dir anders nicht,
Als wenn des Weltenwassers Wellenschlag
Dich mit dem Sphärenton durchdringen kann.
Im Weltenwasser such' das Sein als Welle,
Verbinde, was du findest, deinem Schein;
Im Wagen wird es dir das Sein gewähren.

Semblance will not arise into existence
Unless the wave-beat of the cosmic ocean

Can penetrate thee with its spheric tone.
  In cosmic ocean seek reality as wave:
  Bind to thy semblance that which thou dost find;
  In surging, it will grant to thee existence.
  (*Tr. Ruth and Hans Pusch*)

Anthroposophical spiritual science also points out important things for the knowledge of music and its cosmic backgrounds, when it calls the sound-ether also the chemical-ether. Novalis meant the same with his expression '*chymische Musik* — chymical music', appearing in the important *Fragment* on the mysteries of music quoted at the head of the present chapter. The terms 'colour-ether' and 'number-ether' can also be found. What is meant, is that this reality which forms in the etheric the background of life in the sound, is at the same time the decisive factor in the grouping and chemical relationships of matter. Spiritual science searches to bring this knowledge — directly gained only through supersensory research — to general understanding by pointing to the phenomena of what are called the 'Chladni sound-figures'. Fine grains of sand, evenly spread on a metal plate are stimulated through the sound evoked by a violin bow drawn along the side of the plate. They order themselves into certain geometrical figures. If one correctly understands how here the physical experiment is a *picture* for super-physical processes in the border region of spirit and matter, then one can increasingly feel into the whole tangible meaning of the 'creative cosmic word' of which the beginning of John's Gospel speaks. It is revealed in all that governs matter and chemical-physical processes, right into the formation of stones, right into the depths of the bedrock.[22]

Between sound, the musical element, and the power in world-becoming governing the combination of substances, a mysterious connection exists, accessible to spiritual research. The sound-ether at the same time is the chemical-ether. In the little book, *Alchymy: The Mystery of the Material World*[23] we wish here to point out how for the alchemist of the Middle Ages the forming of substances was accompanied by certain soul-experiences, a certain soul-drama. This sought its expression in the musical element and could find it there. Some contemporary works were mentioned; access to their understanding is given through this 'chymical' aspect. Also to the fact that one such alchemist, the Frenchman Nicolas Flamel [1330–1418] in the fourteenth century, called his work *Musique chimique*, 'chymical music'.

A point of view connecting the chemical realm with the musical, moreover, lies in the *secret of numbers*, as it dominated Pythagorean teaching. The relationship of oscillations of the various musical sounds can be expressed in numbers, and so can the relationships of combinations of substances in the numbers of the chemical formulae. These certainly mean something, even if we do not see the final reality in the atoms and molecules. Thus the sound-ether and chemical-ether are sometimes called 'number-ether' by Rudolf Steiner. In the musical element the harmony of numbers, as it were, sounds; in the combination of substances it is revealed in the visible, tangible world. Likewise, in the world between the visible, but not the tangible, it exists in the band of colour of the rainbow. Dr Steiner shows in the 'forms of the Mysteries',[24] how the cosmogonic primal secrets of the metals are revealed here. This allows the 'colour-ether' to appear as the 'chemical-ether', which among the natural elements corresponds to water. From the outer revelation of nature it is known how the rainbow appears especially in the watery element, in the foggy, nebulous substance of the atmosphere, in the swirling masses of water, and also in the fine, dispersing veil around waterfalls. In the words of Maria and Astrid in Scene 7 of *The Portal of Initiation*, Steiner inserts many secrets of the connection sound-ether, colour-ether and chymical-ether.

As a kind of leitmotif at the head of these observations, *'Our soul has to be air because it knows of music and delights in it'* (*Fragmente* No. 2053, ed. Kamnitzer), Novalis, in the parenthetical remarks in his Introduction, uses the term 'chymical music ...'. In another *Fragment* (No. 499) he speaks of 'chymical acoustic'. To the reader unprepared through spiritual science, this manner of expression is incomprehensible. It is only understandable to the depths of a 'Johannine thinking', which is so characteristic of Novalis. In the book *John's Gospel: The Cosmic Rhythm – Stars and Stones*,[25] it is shown how aspects of cosmic music and the cosmic word are linked in John's Gospel itself with the alchymical (chymical) aspects of metamorphosing the Earth, of the transubstantiation of the Earth. Again, Novalis is the poet and thinker in whom chymical-musical viewpoints of John's Gospel are called to life again in more recent times. In his *Fragmente*, that are so instructive concerning musicality, he has given the subject conceptual expression. All this allows us to understand how such remarkable words as those of 'chymical music' and 'chymical acoustic' could have found their way into the *Fragmente* of Novalis.

The insight that the sound-ether, the etheric, is the primal element of music, is also expressed in anthroposophy, when it is said that music lives inwardly in the etheric realm.[26] It has to be considered here, in order to arrive at an imagination of the etheric, that it is necessary to rise beyond the physical context, out of the accustomed spatial concepts, and learn to live in the *element of the flow of time*. Thus the 'etheric body of plants' is revealed precisely in their metamorphosis in time, in their passing through the various stages of development from seed, shoot, leaf, flower, fruit, seed, and so on. For an obdurate, physical and spatial consciousness this imagination is not achieved without more ado. This consciousness basically cannot grasp the concept of time; it is not attainable to the physical and spatial categories of the intellect bound to the brain.

To the person of today, time remains an inconceivable mystery for the intellect bound to the physical brain. Where, nevertheless, can s/he gain access to this mystery? In that art to which it belongs, for it actually has nothing to do with the physical and spatial world—the art of *music* that lives completely in time. Obviously, to perform a piece of music the *room* (theatre, concert hall, etc.) and the physical musical instruments are necessary. Rudolf Steiner points out that all true musical instruments—[with a joke] he makes a special case for the piano[27]—are cosmic Imaginations manifesting in physical and spatial form. Music, however, the piece of music as such, is something existing purely in the Ideal world, in the course of time. On hearing a piece of music, people today live completely in that element of time to which they cannot find a conscious relationship with their understanding. Music is indeed the only case where in a certain sense they come to a tangible concept of the otherwise inconceivable concept of time, even if this conceiving initially takes place beneath the threshold of consciousness. In listening to a significant piece of music, one can also say, the person of today understands everything, or at least much or some of that which otherwise is veiled to his momentary consciousness. Out of this, the popularity of music for people today can perhaps partly be explained. Rudolf Steiner has also said that music amongst all the arts is the one to which people relate most immediately today.[28]

If we made ourselves aware of this relationship of music to the element of time, and on the other hand time to the etheric element, then we also can gain an increasing relationship to the statement that music inwardly lives in the human etheric body. This whole introduction has shown in what sense the etheric, the sound-ether, is the primary, *cosmic* element of music—the breath of air is its secondary, *earthly* element. This also corresponds completely to the fact that we understand in and with the physical only the earthly-physical, the *earth*. We understand with feeling the super-earthly, the cosmic and starry element, only with that part of our being which itself is raised out of the physical.

'In the physical body,' says Rudolf Steiner, 'the earth lives, and in the ether-body the starry world.' Whether I say more abstractly, 'the cosmic', or more tangibly, 'the starry world', is actually the same: the cosmic *is* the world of the stars. Thus the starry element basically lives where the musical element lives in the etheric, in the ether-body. Modern astronomy – whose high achievements in mathematics should in no way be questioned – in its way of going into the cosmic realm with earthly-physical and mathematical concepts, actually extinguishes this *experience* of the stars. To a not inconsiderable degree, it has caused the crisis in the consciousness of humanity, with effects going right into physical manifestation.

The true experience of the stars, still divined by poets, threatens to disappear increasingly from human consciousness today. In early Egypt[29] there still existed a musical astronomy and astrology. People still possessed or looked for the experience of the sounding of the spheres. Recalling the relationship of the 'higher kinds of ether', sound-ether and life-ether, to the biblical 'Tree of Life' (mentioned above), we can also say, the true original, primary cosmic element of music is the *sounding cosmic starry Tree of Life*, the harmony of the spheres connected to the cosmic life.

2. The Two Elements as the Soul and the Spirit of Music

It is possible and proves fruitful for looking at the music element itself to search in the Bible for those two elements in music to which we have come in our observations, the more cosmic and spiritual, and the more earthly element. It will be shown that right into the problems of modern compositions we can gain practical aspects. 'Music is basically the human being,' Steiner said in *Eurythmy as Visible Singing*.[30] Thus we find a connection between what in the Bible are the two stories of creation in Genesis and the two elements of music.

The two Biblical Creation Stories

An earlier theology has always baulked at the contradiction that meets us at the beginning of the Bible with the creation of man. In the first chapter of Genesis we already read of the creation of man by the Elohim, created in the image of God, then at the beginning of Chapter 2 a Yahweh-creation of man out of the dust of the Earth. These narrations were thought incompatible. An explanation of the apparent contradiction was attempted through philology out of the flowing together of various literary, documentary sources. Even if it is true that things have flowed into the Bible from various sources, for a spiritual consideration of the sacred text an inspiration of the whole exists, a 'larger historical' context of which Novalis speaks (*Fragmente* No. 993). Such a context is found by anthroposophy between the first and second chapters on creation. Chapter 1 speaks of the creation of the spiritual human beings of the primordial beginning, in Chapter 2 of the earthly human being. In Genesis 1 the human being is created in God's image of the spiritual creative Power itself in a higher spiritual element. Only in Genesis 2 is the human being clothed, which is initially still to be thought of as a very fine substance of earthly matter. Only here is the human being fashioned as earthly man out of the element of earth. The one, higher human being, the image of God, is the inner kernel of the other (more on this whole question, see Hermann Beckh, *Our Origin in the Light*, Chapters 1 & 2).

The two archetypal elementary sources of man behave very similarly to the two elements of music: right into the musical element we can follow the contrast between the two chapters of creation and the relationship between them.

The primary cosmic element of music we called, in anthroposophical terms, the sound-ether. Do we find something of the sound-ether in the Bible? We know this already as the sounding, musical side of the creative, cosmic Word which is mentioned at the beginning of John's Gospel, but not least in the beginning of the Biblical story of creation, 'God said, Let there be ... and there was ...'. In the most tangible sense, anthroposophical spiritual science finds [cf. Rudolf Steiner, *Genesis*. GA 122] the revelation of the activity of the sound-ether (which is consequently also called the 'chemical-ether') right into the chemical and physical substance-building, into the grouping and dividing of substances. In Genesis 1:6 and 7, through the word of the Creator the 'waters over the dry land' are separated from the 'waters under the earth' — 'waters' is here to be understood still everywhere as the 'primal waters' of a higher etheric. (We mentioned above the relationship of the watery especially to the sound-ether, and also to the chemical element; the liquid condition plays the well-known important role.) All this still lies over the earthly element in a higher spiritual element.

We then step on the earthly-physical ground. Comparing the conditions with those prevalent today, this is still to be thought of as very fine etheric substance, where in the second chapter of creation it is mentioned how the previously still pure spiritual man is now formed into earthly man out of earthy substance. At the same time with this imprint of the element of earth, of 'the dust of the earth', the element of the air, the breath of air is breathed into him. The well-known Gen. 2:7 says, 'the Lord God formed man from the dust of the ground, and breathed into his nostrils the breath of life; and the man became a living being (the correct translation would run: '... formed him out of earthly dust'), and he blew into him the living breath into his nostrils. And so man became a living soul.' In [transcribed] Hebrew: *vayyitser Yahveh Elohim eth-haadam aphar min-haadamah veyyipah b'aphayu nesh'mah hayyim vayehi haadam l'nephesh hayyah.*

Through the course of these observations it will become ever clearer how in this famous verse, besides and with everything else it contains, there are also archetypal questions of music. We can recognize provisionally that, as in Genesis 1, regarding the sound-ether the primal cosmic element of music was touched on, whereas in Chapter 2, in the 'earthly creation' of the human being the second, the earthy element can be found. All this is more important than we can initially overview.

Genesis 2:7 has to do with the earthly development of the human being, with nothing less than the Fall out of the spiritual into the earthly element, not yet with that later Fall into sin, which is the actual deeper estrangement of the human being from his spiritual origin. But it is already a prerequisite for it and carries it in itself as a later possibility. The creation of woman 'out of Adam's rib' later narrated in the same chapter (Gen. 2:21ff.), the 'separation of male and female' (which in the spiritual human being of Chapter 1, if we understand v. 27 correctly, are still connected) is a further step on the descent, a further preparation of the later Fall of man. The earthly raiment of the human being is still a fine etheric one (the beginnings, too, of the earthly element still lie in the etheric), transparent for the spiritual airy rays. The human being still lives in Paradise, in a world of light of his origin that he only leaves completely in the Fall of man.

And yet with the breath of air and with the earthly element, even if still fine and dust-like, the seed of the later estrangement is laid in him. With these two elements in particular, air and earth, the possibility of dying, of earthly death, has been implanted into man. The possibility of dying in the Fall of man becomes reality. As the first breath signifies the beginning of life, the last breath signifies death. If the breath of air implanted into the human being from the heights of divine life has left the earthly sheath, then the latter falls back into the dust from which it came.

The Human Soul-Air

The famous verse, Genesis 2:7, describes the connection of the air-breath with the element of earth in earthly man, of the breathing-in of the breath of air at the same time with the impression of the earthly dust. The concluding clause is particularly meaningful, 'and he became a living soul'. The human being of Genesis 1 was the image of God, was immortal spirit, for as such spirit is eternal. With the earthly air and with the earthly dust the element of death is planted into him. The process of life and death – and earthly substance is mortality, is death as such – depends on the air-breath. But the *soul* now implanted into man with the earthly air and earthly dust is in itself neither mortal nor immortal. Placed between the spirit, the eternal element and the earthly sheaths, the mortal part, it partakes of both; the soul becomes the bearer of the whole critical human destiny. From above the immortal spirit wants to pull it towards itself. But from below the sinking into death of matter threatens. It is in no way predetermined that the soul can only follow *one* of the two ways.

It is especially the *soul* in which the adversary of humanity seeks and finds its point of attack: the 'Fall of man' as told in Genesis 3 takes its starting point in the human soul. Consequently, it is right to say: the possibility of death implanted into man with the breath of air and earthly dust is also connected to the fact that man, who hitherto was only spirit and as a spirit-being was immortal, now has the soul implanted. The soul also carries the element of *longing*, which can be a higher or lower longing. As lower longing it carries the element of desire and passion, leading to death. With the first estrangement from the spiritual, from its origin in the light, the element of longing is also given. And every sigh tells us how much this element of longing is again connected with the air-breath.

3. The Two Elements in the Music from Bach to Beethoven and Chopin

Air — soul — longing — death as a significant line of development forms the background of Genesis 2:7. What does all this signify for the musical object of our contemplation? The breath of air, that we at the same time recognized as the earthly element of music — already according to the words of the Bible — is essentially united to the soul. In this connection it bears in itself an element of *the longing for death.* In the element of air, which at the same time is the earthly element of music, there is the inherent relationship of music to the soul-element that today is so obvious. And in this relationship to the soul, the musical element carries in itself an element of longing and of death. For the longing, this is again immediately apparent. In what a sublime sense, opening up wide vistas, one can speak of a relationship to death will become clear in the observations that follow.

The earthly element — dust

But this element of air that is significantly related to the soul, to longing and to death, is, as we have said, but the *secondary element* of music belonging to *earth* — its primary element lies deeper in the spirit, in the sound-ether.

In the sound-ether lives the cosmic element of music. Where it is experienced without an earthly medium it is also called spheric music, the harmony of the spheres. We have already mentioned here the billowing sea of the cosmic musical element, and if we want to remain with this picture we can compare the earthly element of music, the air and longing element, the glowing breath *with the wind. Wind and waves*, in the sense of a sublime picture, would be the two elements of music. Thereby we will remain with the fact that above and behind the earthly blowing of the wind stands the *cosmic wind* — also mentioned in John's Gospel [cf. John 3:8] — whereas for the cosmic realm, the 'sea of the ether', the *earthly sea* is given as a picture.

All earthly music — that means, music which is earthily experienced, earthily performed — in earthily presented music, the earthly is somehow bound to the secondary musical element of the breath of air (as it takes effect in the musical voice and musical instrument). No earthly music would be independent of this musical element. Besides and behind it there exists the relationship of everything musical to the primary cosmic, sound-etheric element of music. This primary cosmic element of music, we can also say, never appears in earthly music in its pure and primal nature, but always through the medium of the earthly musical elements, through the earthly condition in general, as broken, altered, modified and tempered. This breaking and tempering is simply conditioned through the earthly situations, given by necessity.

Consequently, it is hardly worth remarking how in the striving of music, everything corresponding to the mathematical relationships of oscillations of musical sounds and tuning simply breaks down, facing the [fact of the musical] keys, [of tonality, which is a spiritual phenomenon, not explained through acoustics]. At a certain point one meets the simple necessity of the 'tempered system', as least with the keys, which in themselves strive to close the circle, return to the starting point. This they can only do if one continues in the exact circle of fifths, with the appropriate tuning. Only today one is inclined to view this tempered system as a deviation from the 'reality of the notes', which is right as regards the cosmic perspective but not the earthly. Especially in that 'irrational' element, also arising in music, that is, that which in the counting, the mathematical numerical relationship does not fit.[31] This speaks to me of an element of a higher reality. Wherever something cosmic appears in an earthly inconsistency there arises this irrational situation. Through this secondary and earthly element that belongs to it, any earthly music stands separate and removed from the cosmic music. No earthly musical system exists that behaves differently and could make an exception. But there also exists not only *one* specific earthly element, *one* specific earthly way of being inconsistent, and consequently not *one* specific earthly system, which as such would be the only possibility.

One may look at 'cosmic music' – in the variety of all 'planetary tones'[32] – in a certain sense as something unified. In the earthly realm music experiences all kinds of differentiation, also regarding the timing, historical, and spatial elements. One recalls the tremendous differences between Oriental and Indian music and Western music. There is not only *one* music system: the music of the Ancient Greeks was built on completely different basic elements from the one given to us today in the West. How the primary cosmic musical elements are individually subdued through the earthly, secondary elements depends on different principles according to space and time.

We found with the earthly musical element, the breath of air, an element of the soul and of longing are connected; air, soul, longing and death—these motifs place themselves before us like a *line* of development of earthly music. Perhaps a secret of modern, the most modern, music today, and the future music striven for by many, could be found in the way it somehow tries to break through this secondary element of the soul in order to approach the primary element, towards the *spiritual* in music, towards its starry element, as we can also say. Many things may not be clear in the consciousness today—though in the subconscious, in the deeper levels of consciousness, such a striving can exist. If one cannot simply eliminate the secondary, the earthly element, one can yet hope, especially in the overcoming of the element of soul favoured today, to make it more permeable to the primary, the spiritual, the star-element of music. Many of the attempts today have initially become stuck in the pure chaos of the earthly level. But have we not also experienced in other contexts that where earthly chaos exists the star-forces want to enter? Some modern music may appear one-sided, coming from the composer's brain—and yet with attentive listening one can forcefully gain the impression that behind all this search in the musical realm there is hidden a certain development, a meaning, a future.

The Recent Epoch of Music

In order to gain more knowledge in this direction it will be good to glance at the music of today, at the music in a certain sense completed today. Even though as a musician today, one has a strong will towards the future, it is possible to do justice to this music that is completed today. Rudolf Steiner, who as the creator of the Mystery Drama of the future, with everything that he wrote on music or had performed, clearly had a will for the future and wanted to stage a music for the future. He looked critically towards music of the past, yet recognized that the musical element today 'has nevertheless reached a world-historic height'.[33]

How is this music, especially in its present completion, to be met right now—this music which without doubt has reached such 'a world-historic height'? Probably most importantly—if the great names may sum it up—in the music from Bach [1685–1750] to Bruckner [1824–1896]. Not as if there did not exist very important music, in its way remarkable music, before Bach. But this indeed belongs to another epoch, another phase of development; it contains, for example, in its treatment of intervals, certain things, especially for contemporary music, which become interesting again from new aspects. It is here, as often the case, that the newest thing meets with the distant past. Neither the significance of the most recent nor what is long past is disputed, but it can be stated—*as Bach is a beginning, Bruckner is an ending*—if between Bach and Bruckner there lies a phase and epoch of music, the epoch to which Steiner's words relate, that music today 'has nevertheless reached a certain world-historic height'.

[And this] with all the differences of space and time, in soul-feelings for time and soul-feelings of the folk—how different is the feeling of Bach's time from the soul of the eighteenth century, which reached its climax in Mozart [1756–91], and 'sang itself out' (Nietzsche) with Beethoven [1770–1827] in all emphatic soul-experience standing on the threshold of the nineteenth century! How different is this soul of the eighteenth century from the character of the nineteenth century, as it is finally expressed in Wagner [1813–83] and Bruckner! How different is Chopin's [1810–49] music from the German Romantics, or the Italian opera from Wagner's music drama! How different, when all is said and done, are all great musicians as individuals—despite all these differences we experience, with regard to this epoch as a whole, this completeness. That which in itself is so variously differentiated according to space (folk-soul), time, and separate individualities comes together to this unified, completed, miraculous building. (Just as we limit this completion in time at both ends, we have to limit it in space: for the musical epoch meant here in no way embraces the whole Earth, but essentially only Europe—hardly that we can say, just the West—and also within Europe we see certain areas strikingly standing before other developments).

Indeed, a completed building, a miraculous building in its way stands before us in this music of the eighteenth and nineteenth centuries from *Bach to Bruckner*, mainly from specific regions of Europe. Now, in the Bible different things flow together out of the most varying streams of times and cultures, yet the whole thing in its monumental, rounded unity—already rightly recognized by Novalis—stands before us in its great historical context and great artistic structure. So too the music from *Bach to Bruckner*, with all the different times, folk influences, individual contributions, can be felt as a rounded, unified work of art of monumental greatness, of inconceivable richness in the particulars.

Over very few sections of all human culture, of the entire creation of the human spirit in whatever area, is such a richness of revealing beauty, such a unified abundance of content poured out. Precisely the situation that one can today correctly judge this musical epoch in a certain sense as already rounded off, belonging to the past, gives us the possibility to gain that 'point outside' — Archimedes' fulcrum[34] — from which unbiased judgement is possible. The point of view that everything should be a 'development, in which we still find ourselves' is no longer tenable today. And it can be meaningful precisely here, when one turns the gaze towards the future, to review this past of music now ended — yet nevertheless so great, so full of content, rich in lasting moments — initially to examine the whole question. This is so eminently important for the future, to test on this completed, monumental building of music *from Bach to Bruckner* the question of the primary and secondary, the cosmic and the earthly elements of music, and so on.

The element of soul connected to the secondary, the earthly element of music seems to have achieved a certain high point in its expression in that musical epoch, today concluded. Especially in this fact, we saw, there could be an element that the most modern, future-orientated music today wants to overcome, to free itself. This soul-element, we said, carries in itself an element of longing — that longing that in Beethoven's music found such a mighty expression reaching towards the super-earthly realm — but this also contains in itself the possibility of passion, greed, sensuality and sentimentality. Some contemporary musicians will feel inclined to reject this soul-element in music as 'sentimental', especially in the forms of expression it took in the epoch from Beethoven to Wagner. But the soul-element cannot simply be equated to what is 'sentimental', although it might carry in itself this potential as a danger. This soul-element in the sense of Genesis 2:7 has entered into man with the imprint of the earthly element and the breathing-in of the air-breath; it has not yet realized the 'Fall of man', but carries it as a potential and a danger. And so it is also in music, in relation to the possibility of passion, sensuality, sentimentality, which for the modern musician may mean something like a 'Fall of music'. (More correct would be the view that observes in the line of development of music a real meaningful parallel to the line or curve of human development that contains the 'Fall' as a world-historic necessity.)

The Dual Soul

The whole problem of the element of soul in human development as well as in music is tremendously serious. The motif of air-breath — soul — longing — death points to this seriousness, to this tremendous background of human development. Precisely in the soul, as we see, lies the actual critical point of development, in the way it is placed between the spirit, the undying element, and the earthly as that which carries death in itself, in that way in which the two powers of life and of death struggle around the soul with all its possibilities and dangers of sin, waste, death and decay. At the same time, of course, it also carries the most courageous, the loveliest qualities and conditions to their highest unfolding. *''s mag was Liebes, ich gesteh' es ein, doch auch was Schreckliches um eine Seele sein* — It might be lovely, I confess, but also terrible about having a soul,' says Lortzing's Undine [first performed 1845]. (Such an opera text, today easily undervalued, has some background that we recognize again in the light of anthroposophy, especially with its important differentiation of body, soul and spirit.) The words of Undine meet the sentence of such a deep thinker as Novalis: *'Die Seele ist unter allen Giften das stärkste* — Amongst all poisons the soul is the strongest' (*Fragmente*, No. 1080). Of course, Novalis also speaks on the soul from completely different viewpoints. A musician of the past, like Mozart, Schubert or Chopin (with Beethoven and Wagner the voice is already more split) sees more the lovely side of the soul, a modern musician more the terrible side. This view of the soul can lead us further to review the separate phases of music in its recently concluded epoch.

4. The Two Elements of Music as 'Wind and Wave'

Bach

We felt with Bach we were actually still in the cosmic light and in the murmur of the cosmic ocean. Already small pieces, like the 'Little Prelude' in C-minor (for piano), allow us characteristically to hear this murmur of the ocean, then properly in that of the *Well-tempered Clavier* (typically, Part 1 in D-minor, Part 2 G#-minor) and the great organ preludes. In the fugue the 'air-architecture' predominates, as discussed above. In the G#-piece just mentioned, there lives in the fugue something of the regular, monotonous beat of the cosmic ocean, in Bach an otherwise foreign element of the unredeemed, recalling Strindberg's feeling for the sea.

One otherwise finds the soul-element in Bach as a higher and pure, genial, good-natured, balanced disposition of *Gemütsinnigkeit*. Even from the otherwise so lightly sensual key of G-major, smacking of the sentimental, he knows how to gain a pure good-natured 'shepherd-like' quality in the '*Sinfonie*' of his *Christmas Oratorio*. The soul-element of longing steps back completely in Bach. The air-element, in which he fashions architecturally and sculpturally, is still much more cosmic air than the light glittering in the earthly air. The billowing sea of his musical sounds still murmurs in the cosmic element, the cosmic wind, rather than from the wind's lament of earthly passion and longing. Bach's music hardly knows the *sigh* as revelation of the air-breath filled with longing, though it may be as a fugue theme (*WTC* I, C#-minor Fugue — which also in Beethoven is the key most related to longing); as weeping, when it does arise, still retains the biblical astringent expression (as with '*bitterlichen Weinen* — wept bitterly' of Peter after his denial in the *Matthew Passion*). Everything lives still more in the cosmic musical element than in the earthly element of music, in the earth-air. With Bach music is still transparent for the cosmic element; it is still music before the Fall of man (cf. what Dr Schwebsch says in his book on Bruckner).[35] *After* the Fall of man, and after the progress through the depths of the earthly-'I', with Bruckner music paves a way for itself to another level. Then with new, different expressive means — for Bruckner uses essentially those of the past — music of the future will aspire again (even if this aspiring is not yet living *consciously* in everything modern).

Mozart

The soul-element in the air-breath, the element of longing of music, the sigh, we find first in Mozart. The utter charm and appeal of his music is that everything is still alive in childlike innocence and tenderness. Think of the sigh-motif — in the voice and orchestral accompaniment — in Tamino's Portrait-Aria in *The Magic Flute*, in the C-minor Quartets and the G-minor Quintets (of all the keys, G-minor is the actual Mozart-key), from which a particular line of development leads right to the motif of longing in *Tristan and Isolde*. Earthly longing appears mostly in Mozart's music. In it the element of air already clearly appears, the sighing of the wind — here still a delicate breeze; the element of the sea — the 'billowing' steps back completely. The longing element, as we said, includes an element of death in itself. How singularly for music generally this significant element of death is revealed in Mozart's music precisely in its light, playful charm, cannot be more beautifully expressed than in Friedrich Doldinger's little book, *Alter, Krankheit, Tod*,[36] where he speaks of Mozart's butterfly-experiences and butterfly death-experience. Over his short life, breathing in the sunshine of childhood as in an element of immortality, we see how significant this shadow of death lies over this darling of musical sounds.

Mozart's music lives in an element woven entirely out of light and air. It is the element of the butterfly living and playing in the element of light. The butterfly is the sublime symbol of resurrection, of life having gone right through death. In pieces in the minor mood, in C-minor, G-minor, A-minor and so on (e.g. in the delicate A-minor *Rondo for piano* [KV 511]) this is most immediately evident. But also the effervescent lightness of a *Figaro*-Overture is only possible, in that Mozart's childlike soul leaves the all-too-human frivolity of this dramatic, finely-woven piece far behind and beneath him; he dances and hovers away in easy grace. In return, the seriousness of the mystery touching the threshold of death draws him in *The Magic Flute*. Death here leads to a higher life, to Initiation; it lives in the notes of this music, especially in Act II. And with all the seriousness of its spiritual backgrounds the music always retains the light, playful, fluttering grace of the butterfly.

Beethoven

On quite a different level the longing motif, the soul-element in music, appears with Beethoven. Here for the first time the breakthrough of the 'I' takes place. The air-element of music, the oscillating breathing, with Mozart still a tender breath, becomes here a powerful storm-wind, a wind of passion and longing. This Beethovenian moment is revealed most directly in the passion storming along in the *Piano Sonata*, op. 57, 'Appassionata' ('the passionate one'): in dark F-minor, the key of darkness without any light, into which no ray of hope breaks, the night of passion, out of which the soul finds no redemption (see the author's *The Essence of Tonality*, p. 53f.). The dark, dramatic tension at the opening of the first movement is abruptly interrupted by many stormy phrases. Between which sounding like fearful prayer . . . the prayer 'out of the depths' [cf. Psalm 130] as over the abyss, a second movement struggles through (Db-major), but it cannot reach the distant heavens, the tension between heaven and earth is already too great. The prayer finds no resolution, is not heard. It suddenly breaks off in a long sigh that becomes a cry and passes over to stormy, billowing passion. Now the storms blow endlessly without respite, again in dark F-minor, like a steady, monotonous blowing of the wind, for a fleeting moment hardly interrupted through tiredness. For the first time there sounds here with Beethoven the 'lament of the winds', for which Strindberg [1849–1912] found such a moving, poetic expression in *The Dream Play* [written 1901]. And when finally in the darkness of F-minor, in the night of passion, everything sinks down, one still feels that the storms are continuing endlessly, that they nowhere find rest or peace, as Byron expresses it:

> But where of ye, O tempests! is the goal?
> Are ye like those within the human breast,
> Or do ye find at length, like eagles, some high nest?
>   (Lord Byron, *Childe Harold's Pilgrimage*. Canto III, XCVI)

It is not our aim to categorize the unfathomably varied richness of Beethoven's music, yet the soul-element in his music should be pointed out in connection with the element of longing, the element of air and wind. And for this element of the wind, the element of the storm of passion, the F-minor *Piano Sonata* ('Appassionata') is directly characteristic.

The tender, longing element Beethoven developed especially in another piano sonata, the already-mentioned C#-minor, op. 27, no. 2 [1801], not without inner justification is called the *'Moonlight' Sonata*. This is completely the mood of longing of the eighteenth century, musically raised to its purest greatness by the composer, as we experience it poetically in the writings of Goethe's youth, cf. the poem 'To the Moon' (*'Füllest wieder Busch und Tal* . . . — You fill again bush and valley....') and the feeling of love in *The Sufferings of Werther*. Beethoven's C#-minor *Piano Sonata* arose from similar feelings and experiences. With Mozart everything still lives in the childlike sunlight of the butterfly; with Beethoven there appears impressively the lunar element of passion and longing, fully-awakened to the human condition. The last movement of the C#-minor *Sonata* brings again in a different way the restless storming of the last movement of the 'Appassionata' . . .

Chopin

If we speak of the soul-element, of longing in music, connected to the element of air and wind of the musical element, then we cannot by-pass Chopin [1810–1849], where this element of longing reaches its purest, amiable climax. The amiable, loving element, with Bach still completely derived from the love of Christ, towards which it strives again in Bruckner, is raised to its highest height of human love in Wagner's *Tristan and Isolde*. Prior to this it appears in childlike purity in Mozart and in the fully-awakened element of longing perhaps most impressively with Chopin. Chopin, too, knows the sudden might of the storm-wind of fate; one thinks of the transition passage in the F-major *Ballade* [No. 2, op. 38], or most correctly, F-major–A-minor, for the piece is written in double tonality. The poetic F-major section joins like a tender loving flower, only softly touched by a breath of wind. After the lengthy battle of the two motifs, it lies at the end broken by the storm-wind (the A-minor ending). As in this one, it is a similar wrestling of two motifs in Schubert's [1797–1928] immortal *String Quartet* 'Death and the Maiden' that also belongs to the most loving works in music. With Schubert the contrast lies between D-minor and F-major, with Chopin between F-major and A-minor. We can also think of Goethe's poem *'Heideröslein'* ['Rose on the heath']. This is a viewpoint—also that storm-wind and flower—to which Anton Rubinstein first drew attention.

But for the most part—apart from this storm-wind motif—the airy element, the element of wind and longing in Chopin is a soft blowing, but in which the highest degrees of soul-feeling are revealed. The childlike sighing of Mozart becomes here a bright stream of tears, for which there is no more moving expression in music than the E-minor *Prelude*. What is 'soul in music' can perhaps be more clearly recognized nowhere better than in this simple, yet otherwise so expressive, piece. In it the air-element of music (which is always meant here), the air-breath pulses at the same time like a soft, regular rhythmic breathing. The musical expression in this piece almost goes into the physiological realm ...

Chopin's *Prelude* in A-minor stands inwardly close to this piece (apart from the ending, settling into A-minor, it has as little to do with A-minor),[37] that it could appear to us as a premonition of atonal music in the time of tonality, consequently of special interest for our observations. With regard to the intervals it also belongs to the most strange in all music. It makes us think of the words that Nietzsche [1844–1900] wrote in a letter to Irwin Rohde, concerning the opening bars of the Prelude to Act III of Wagner's *Tristan and Isolde*. About the first five notes, they appear to him, he says, 'as a long-drawn, deep sounding bell, that is ringing all happiness and all the comforting light of the Earth to the night and the grave; it is terribly sad!' The whole of Chopin's *Prelude* in A-minor bears this character. Through the dull sound of the mourning bells at the Fall of Warsaw, Chopin supposedly received this inspiration (consequently also the strange and painful major and minor sevenths in the accompaniment marking the sound of the bells, in place of the usual octaves). We could also think of Byron's words:

> the far roll
> Of your departing voices, is the knoll
> Of what in me is sleepless, — if I rest ...

These words precede the earlier quotation of the description of the thunderstorm on the Lake of Geneva in *Childe Harold*, 'But where of ye, O tempests! is the goal? ...' (Lord Byron, *Childe Harold's Pilgrimage*. Canto III, XCVI).

Tristan and Isolde

That which in Wagner's *The Flying Dutchman* is there as a beginning in the early storm of youth appears in a perfect completion in Wagner's ripest work of art, in *Tristan and Isolde*. The connection of wind and waves that exists in Act I also in the staging, penetrates the whole music of *Tristan and Isolde*. This will have to be investigated in detail. With Bach we found the sea, the wave, as the decisive thing. With later composers we found the element of the wind — with Mozart it was still a 'tender soughing'; with Beethoven it became a storm, though here the sea does not join the storm-wind. With the 'Appassionata', for example, as with the thunderstorm in the 'Pastoral Symphony', everything takes place in the air. So also with the Romantics: with Schumann we hear the wind sighing and whispering mysteriously, like a fairy-tale, in the treetops of the German forest. Nobody has the 'billowing sea' of the cosmic music like Bach. But with Wagner, especially in *Tristan and Isolde*, the surging sea of the cosmic music appears again and with it the storm-wind, the blowing wind of passion and longing. The staging, as usual with Wagner, shows only that which is really present in the music.

One can understand the difficulties that some modern musicians have with Wagner in general, and with *Tristan and Isolde* in particular — even Wagner friends, who claim not to understand this work — when we become aware how the soul-element in the music, its element of longing is most strongly expressed, not so much with Wagner generally, but precisely with the music of *Tristan and Isolde*. In absolute music one may find this highest intensity of the soul with Chopin. In dramatic music we certainly find it in Wagner's greatest work, one with the strongest Wagnerian character, in *Tristan and Isolde*. Even if the dramatic style in his music may appear the most developed in *The Ring*, and *The Mastersingers*, the heights of the actual musical element are reached in *Tristan and Isolde*. For our present purposes, for the longing motif and its elements, amongst all other works of Wagner, this is most noticeable.

In a quite unique and splendid manner we see the connection between, on the one hand, the motif of longing with the air-breath as the carrier of the soul-element, and, on the other hand, the motif of death, containing the significant connection of the air-breath to Genesis 2:7. Here is to be felt the whole quintessence of viewpoints summarizing Genesis 2:7, equally for Wagner's *Tristan and Isolde* as a poetic work as well as for the music.

5. The *Tristan*-Chord and the Motif of Longing

As a starting point, we proceed from the musical element of longing with its characteristic chord of universal longing, the famous *Tristan*-chord — [reading from below] F-B-D#-G# in the Prelude, bar 3 — that opens the whole work. Furthermore, this chord governs the whole work right into the final ending, the last bars of the *Liebestod* (Act III), where it is concealed as a soft sighing, like a last gentle breath, in the middle voices.

For the structure and context of this whole contemplation, it is not without meaning that we could already find subtle traces of this motif of longing with Mozart. The chromatic dominant suspension in the sounding-out of the *Tristan*-motif is characteristically Mozartean. And Chopin, too, who was important for us with his rich expression of the feelings for the line of development of the soul-element, of the motif of longing in music — actually already uses this *Tristan*-motif of longing with all its components. In his [final] 49th *Mazurka* [op. 68, no. 4, in F-minor, bb. 13 & 14, leading to a passage in A-major], one only needs to leave out two transition chords and the chord-sequence stands there directly, so characteristic for the *Tristan*-motif, and in the same range. Even the mood of these bars in Chopin's *Mazurka* corresponds to the mood of *Tristan and Isolde*, the mood of Wagner's motif of longing.[38]

In this motif, with its grandiose expression of cosmic longing, we are dealing with one of the great waymarks in the development of music, and in soul-expression within the musical element. One can show how from an early beginning this motif of longing is gradually worked out ever more clearly in the historical development of music until it stands before us in Wagner's *Tristan and Isolde* where it speaks to us as out of deepest cosmic backgrounds, from the depths of eternity in its actual completion and world-historical heights of development.

In Wagner's motif of longing, in particular the characteristic 'Tristan-chord' (reading from below: F-B-D#-G#, also written F-C♭ -E♭ -A♭, for example, in Act III), there is really a super-tonal element, although theoretically it can be brought into tonal connections.[39] From this aspect one can look at the *Tristan*-Prelude that is entirely governed by this motif. The Prelude to Act I does not even contain a single A-minor chord, which would point to the key of A-minor according to its key signature, or the lack of it. One has to explain the chord in bar 3 as the 'dominant of A', though a really clear A-minor is never reached in the whole Prelude. The exuberant, joyful transition section, the counter-piece to the longing motif, is clearly A-major. The minor mood, in itself less tonal than the major, in the chromaticism in the *Tristan*-Prelude, of the *Tristan*-music in general, increasingly approaches the super-tonal mode, or style. With all its tendencies towards the element of sighing air, 'the wind', this *Tristan*-music, already the *Tristan*-Prelude, very strongly contains in itself the element of the sea, the billowing sea of the cosmic music, the element of cosmic longing. This cosmic, universal element, urges towards the super-tonal mode.

In the Prelude, there lives something that reminds us of Rudolf Steiner's Mystery-Drama *The Probation of the Soul* [Scene 10],[40] of the words of Capesius awakening out of his vision that looks back on his previous lives.

> I have emerged as if awaking from this yearning
> out of the wide-spread ocean of the spirit
> . . .
> I felt myself expanded to the universe,
> bereft of my own being . . .

This cosmic ocean of longing, which Steiner refers to here (he also coined the word *Geistesmeereswesen*, literally 'spirit-ocean-being' [in *Theosophy* [GA 9], III, iii, Steiner mentions *'ein Meere von Tönen'*, an 'ocean of musical sounds' in a passage devoted to 'cosmic music'] also billows and surges in the Prelude to *Tristan and Isolde*, and in the music of *Tristan* generally. The 'secondary' element of music strongly unites with the primary element.

The super-tonal element of the longing motif of *Tristan and Isolde* and its characteristic chord becomes especially clear in the episode in Act III that precedes Tristan's vision of Isolde walking over the waves of the sea. There we hear this chord, through many bars, through whole pages of the score, always in the same harmonic register, rhythmically pulsing, sounding forth until in the vision of the 'walking on the sea' the light blue E-major as the clearly tonal element is wrestled out of it. Not one of the 'ancient' or 'early keys' can one feel, but the super-tonal element lying in the longing chord in *Tristan* governs as 'musical key' of the whole. The supra-tonal character of the Prelude to *Tristan and Isolde,* which according to its outer notation stands in A-minor, can also remind us of the already-mentioned A-minor *Prelude* of Chopin with its dull sound of mourning bells, which also has a super-tonal—or may one say 'atonal'?—character. (Already in bar 1 an A# repeated in the following bars negates the key of A-minor. Only at the end does the recasting of E-major chords become the dominant of A-minor.) The Prelude to *Tristan and Isolde* that has no tonal ending at all is without this cadence in A-minor. To the end it retains a supra-tonal character.

This supra-tonal, or the new atonal quality, has a certain inner turning towards the primary, sound-etheric, cosmic-musical element of music, whereas in tonality its secondary earthly element, of the soul and the air, is expressed. These are the two elements in music, which in pictorial language we could also call here *wind and waves*.

- The 'wave' points towards the primary, cosmic element of musicality.
- The 'wind' shows the relationship to the element of air, the soul-element of music.

The element of longing possibly does not belong only to the earthly soul-element. In particular, in *Tristan and Isolde*, we can perceive that there also exists something like 'cosmic longing'. This element of cosmic longing also appears in Steiner's Mystery Dramas.

We did not yet find the connection of 'wind and wave' in such a way with Bach—with him the 'billowing sea of the cosmic musicality' predominates, in connection with the element of air that actually carries the soul—to which the 'light-ether' is the etheric correspondence. Nor did we find it with Mozart, Beethoven and Chopin. With these composers the soul-air element predominates or governs alone, from the soft breeze (Mozart), to the storm-wind [Beethoven], from the childlike sigh of longing (Mozart) to the wildest raging of passion [Beethoven and Chopin].

In Wagner's *The Flying Dutchman* [1843], the two elements of 'wind and wave' are initially announced—for with Wagner all this does not only exist in the staging—but truly very strongly in the music. And it appears in its greatest heights in *Tristan and Isolde* [completed 1859, performed 1865].

Tristan and Isolde

Before we come to the music, we shall look at Wagner's poetic text. We still hear the Prelude to *Tristan* dying away, with its tired repetitions of the longing, sighing motif with which it began, without finding actual harmonic resolution — because it belongs to that cosmic infinity in which there is no resolution, and then we hear at the beginning of Act 2, and already see the ship in full sail while the orchestra is silent (out of the cosmic, we are suddenly placed into the earthly realm), the voice of the young Sailor. A certain connection also exists to the world of *The Flying Dutchman* through this seaman's song at the beginning of *Tristan and Isolde*. The *Dutchman* and *Tristan* are the two Wagnerian operas to include the sea. Straightaway, the first words of the Sailor's song speak of the blowing of the wind and the longing.

Frisch weht der Wind	Fresh western wind
der Heimat zu	O blow us home —
mein irisch Kind,	My Irish child,
wo weilest du?	Where do you roam?
Sind's deiner Seufzer Wehen,	Is this your tearful sighing,
dir mir die Segel blähen?	Keeping the vessel flying?
Wehe! Wehe, du Wind!	Waft us, waft us O wind!
Weh'! Ach wehe, mein Kind!	Woe, ah woe to my child!

An Egyptian hieroglyph exists that means 'wind, air-breath, whisper, breathing, soul' and which portrays a sail swelling in the wind: ⛵. This Egyptian 'breath-hieroglyph' can be seen as a symbol of Wagner's whole poetic and musical creation *Tristan and Isolde*. The Hibernian Mysteries out of which the Tristan-and-Isolde motif has been created stand, as Rudolf Steiner has often pointed out, in a deep inner, as it were subterranean, connection with the early Egyptian Mysteries of Isis. The name 'Isolde' itself (as shown in the book *From the World of the Mysteries*, Temple Lodge, forthcoming) in the essay '*Der Lebensbaum* — The Tree of Life', Germ. ed. pp. 111–139) is inwardly connected to the early Egyptian name Isis. For Isolde (*Isot*, cf. the Egyptian *Iset*, *I-s-t*, *H-S-T* as the name of *Isis*) derives from *Is-Hild*, *Eis-Holde*, which indicates certain Mysteries of the sound-ether and of the cold light, which find their expression in the fairy-tale of the Ice Maiden as well as the Mystery-figure of the Egyptian Isis.

Isis (*Isit*) = Isolde (*Isot*), the carrier of the 'higher life-element', in the Bible called the 'Tree of Life', is woven out of the cold light of life-ether, sound-ether (further details in Günther Wachsmuth's book and the author's essays, mentioned above). The Tree of Life has been lost for the human being through the sin in Paradise, the estrangement from the divine primal life. The wish to regain it was expressed through trials and the life of initiation in the Mysteries. For a time it was possible to do this. In the Introduction we saw how much all this has its correspondence in the musical element.

Tristan is the initiate who is wrestling for Isolde, the carrier of the higher-life element, yet he repeatedly loses it. He should woo this higher life element out of the 'I' — instead of this he is wooing Isolde for King Marke, the carrier of the old, 'paternal powers'. The connection is not made through the forces of the awake 'I', or ego, but through the forces of the sub-consciousness of the soul [released] through the love-potion. The connection won in this way is tragically severed again through Marke, carrier of the paternal powers. When finally Marke, having become aware of the deep connection, in deepest resignation wants to give the inheritance to Tristan, the 'son', and wants to relinquish Isolde, he finds the 'son' dead. Tristan has sunk, dying, into the arms of Isolde, who had hastened over the sea to him. In Goethe's *Fairytale* the Youth finds death in the premature touch of Lily (she too is the carrier of the higher-life), and falls dying into her arms; Tristan, too, sinks dying into Isolde's arms.

Only the power of the 'I' — which is the 'power of Christ' — would have been able to unite them in life and awake consciousness. This is the case with Parsifal; in a higher consciousness, after passing the trials of purification, Parsifal combines both elements in himself. This is the Christian Mystery, as *The Ring of the Nibelung* and *Tristan and Isolde* — the pre-Christian, Teutonic and Hibernian Mysteries — whereby both pass over to the Christian Mysteries, the latter closely related to the same. Consequently, we find many echoes of the Christian gospel and Mysteries in Wagner's *Tristan and Isolde*.

The matter between Tristan and Isolde in the Hibernian Mysteries is like that between Siegfried and Brünhilde in the Teutonic Mysteries (Wagner's *Ring*-cycle). In both, the connection severed in life and made in dying exists in the Parsifal-consciousness on a higher level. From here a light is also shed on the ending of *The Flying Dutchman*, as well as on Wagner's youthful opera *Die Feen* [1834].

Like Brünhilde, Isolde in Wagner's music drama is the carrier of the 'higher life-element', to which Tristan, the initiate — like Siegfried in *The Ring* — is unable to connect himself permanently. This is weighty human destiny. We [living in a later age] have to keep far from us the thought 'we would have managed it better'. The will bequeathed to us from *Parsifal*, from the Christian element, is grace. From here we understand better the profound cosmic meaning of the longing of *Tristan and Isolde*, of the longing motif wonderfully penetrating Wagner's music. It is cosmic longing, Mystery longing, not only earthly-human longing for love. *Tristan and Isolde*, it has to be said, is not merely a usual earthly love-story, which many versions make of it. The 'love-story' is but a picture of profound cosmic contexts. This was recognized by Wagner out of the Mystery-depths of his own being, with his inborn accuracy. Wagner returns the poetry and the music of the incomparable saga of *Tristan and Isolde* to the purity and sublimity of its Mystery origin.

From here we understand even better what was said about the relationship of *Tristan and Isolde*, of the name 'Isolde' in particular, to the Egyptian Mysteries of Isis—the relationship of Wagner's poetic creation and music to the Egyptian air-breath hieroglyph, the picture of the sail filled by the wind that immediately meets us in the words of the Seaman's song at the beginning of the music drama.

Sind's deiner Seufzer Wehen,	Is this your tearful sighing,
Die mir die Segel blähen?	Keeping the vessel flying?

This reminds us directly of a place in *Tristan and Isolde*, Act III, of the great monologue of the mortally wounded Tristan.

Muss ich dich so verstehen,	Is that your song to me,
du alte ernste Weise,	O ancient, mournful piping,
mit deiner Klage Klang?	Is that your song of woe?
Durch Abendwehen	Through evening silence
Drang sie bang	Once it rang,
usw.	*etc.*

where, recalling his previous healing through Isolde, when in the lonely boat the winds of the sea came to him:

Sehnsucht klagend	Ah, I heard
klang die Weise;	That mournful piping,
den Segel blähte	My sails were blown
der Wind hin	By the wind
zu Irlands Kind.	There to Ireland's maid.

Right into the musical key, G-major [further details in the author's *The Essence of Tonality* and *The Language of Tonality*, both Anastasi; new edition Temple Lodge, forthcoming] the music speaks here of 'Isolde's healing power of love' (already in Act I, at

die Wunde, die ihn plagte,	the wound that caused his torment,
getreulich pflag sie da	with tender care she cured).

Like Isis in the Egyptian Mysteries, Isolde is the 'healing power of love' through Wagner's poetic and musically enlivened Hibernian Mystery.

We repeatedly meet in the poetic and musical element of *Tristan and Isolde* the wind-filled sail, corresponding to the Egyptian hieroglyph for breath.

Tristan:
Sie weht, sie weht,	It waves! It waves,
die Flagge am Mast.	The flag on the mast.

(He means the ship that should bring Isolde over the sea.) Thus speaks Tristan's joyful hope in Act III, immediately anxiously disappointed through the mournful shepherd's piping—

Noch ist kein Schiff zu sehen	There's still no ship in sight.

And over the whole of Act I there lies this '*wehende Flagge*—flying flag'; we find ourselves on the ship flying with a good wind speeding towards Cornwall. Think of the place where Kurvenal announces the imminent landing:

vom Mast der Freude Flagge,	Up there the joyful flag,
sie wehe lustig in's Land;	gaily waves toward the land

where the fluttering of the '*wehender Wimpel*—flying flag' in the rhythm of the music with its characteristic flute trills, becomes so eloquently expressive.

The very first words of Wagner's poetic work of the libretto of *Tristan and Isolde* already reveal much.

Wehe! Wehe, du Wind!	Waft us, waft us O wind!
Weh'! Ach wehe, mein Kind!	Woe, ah woe to my child!

One should note how here the word '*Wehe*' means at one time the blowing of the wind and then the longing, painful labour pains, a double meaning out of the depths of language. For in reality these two, seemingly so different meanings of the same word, are mutually connected through subterranean depths. We only need to think about the wonderfully revealing verse in Genesis 2:7, from where our observations commenced:

And Yahveh (I-H-W-H, also this Divine Name contains in H-W-H quite clearly the primal breath, the primal breath-motif in itself) formed man of dust from the ground, and breathed into his nostrils the breath of life; and man became a living being [RSV, adjusted A. S.].

We are reminded of what the connections pointed to here also mean for music, how the motif, 'air-breath — soul — longing — death' is expressed in it.

6. *Tristan and Isolde*: The Motif of Longing

The human being was originally created by God in the divine-spiritual world. The human being, whose creation is narrated in Genesis 1:27, is still this spiritual primordial man. And his physical, or as it were physical body [spatial, though not yet filled with earthly material], is still in etheric form. He still combines in himself the two poles of the cosmic creation of female-masculine — as the higher and lower ethers, or the Tree of Life and the Tree of Knowledge. This, then, is also the profound cosmic problem that resounds again in the Mystery-motif of *Tristan and Isolde*, finding in the Parsifal-consciousness its first literary-Johannine resolution. In the way language is used in the Bible, one can also call this spiritual, primordial human being the 'Elohim human being'. As we saw earlier, the human being who was previously [Genesis 1] created in the divine-spiritual world, is now in Genesis 2 created by Yahveh (Y-H-W-H) with the dust of the Earth. The earthly element is imprinted into him — which on this level we should not imagine in a coarse earthly manner. And we know from the often-quoted verse, 2:7, how the Bible accompanies this incorporation of the earthly element by a breathing-in of the earthly air-breath; the in-breathing of this air-breath is connected with the becoming of the soul. In his book *Esoteric/Occult Science* [GA 13], Rudolf Steiner presents these things in concrete details from an exact spiritual vision.

With the incorporation of the earthly element the possibility of dying, of the element of death, is also implanted into the human being. Of this element we also know how it is connected to the breathing of the air. The air-breath, which is the carrier of the soul-element, also becomes the bringer of death. This element of death, by carrying in itself the possibility of passion, of longing, of pain and suffering, is connected with the soul-element itself. As long as creation was still within the realm of the pure spiritual etheric (the Indian calls this element *brahman*), it was also still without pain, suffering or cares (this 'carefree' existence is much spoken about by the Indians). With the entering of the original, still purely etheric element into the element of air, with the wafting of the air-breath, there also begin the waves of pain.

All creation goes through pain. When the world-creation descends from the spiritual-etheric into the earthly-physical realm, it also descends into pain and suffering, taking these into itself. This is something extraordinarily important, revealing cosmic backgrounds, when we believe we hear in the blowing of the wind a note of mourning, when we speak of the 'howling of the storm', and so on. This is a profound cosmic intuition of the genius of language when '*Windeswehen* — blowing of the wind' and '*Schmerzenswehen, Sehnsuchswehen* — labour-pains, pains of longing' all meet in the word '*wehen* — blowing' (Wagner, *Tristan and Isolde*. Act I, 1):

Sind's deiner Seufzer Wehen,	Is this your tearful sighing,
Die mir die Segel blähen? —	Keeping the vessel flying?
Wehe! Wehe, du Wind!	Waft us, waft us O wind!
Weh'! Ach wehe, mein Kind!	Woe, ah woe to my child!

This intuition of the spirit of language is not at all limited to the German language; we also find it especially in the Indian language that stands close to the archetypal language. There the root '√*vā*' also means '*Windeswehen*' the 'blowing of the wind' (it is the same word as the German '*wehen*') as well as the call of pain '*wehe*'. In the lecture-cycle *Egyptian Myths and Mysteries* [GA 106, Lect. 4], Rudolf Steiner speaks about 'the primordial word √*vha*' (this is the same root). And the name Yahveh (I-H-W-H), so significant for the Mysteries of Genesis 2:7, contains this root and all the air-breath mysteries of the soul and of suffering.

If one looks at all these secrets of the Indian archetypal root √*vā* — '*wehen*', one can find enclosed in it the primal motif of Wagner's *Tristan and Isolde*, that primal motif that finds its mantric, musical expression, in the longing motif that directly opens the Prelude. In so far as this motif of the air-element contains the 'wafting breath', with all its connections to pains of longing and painful woes, therein we feel what we have called the *secondary* element of music. That the *primary* element is not missing was emphasized earlier. And in this direction the mystery of the Indian primal root √*vā* can lead us a step further.

This root signifies not only '*wehen*' and '*wehe*', the *Windeswehen* and *Schmerzenswehen* ('the blowing of the wind' and 'labour pains, pains of longing'), but there is *yet another* root √*vā* (also from the grammatical viewpoint, presented as *ve*) meaning '*weben* — weaving'. In other words, in the primal root √*vā* the German '*wehen*' with its overtone '*wehe*' (woe) and '*weben*' (weave) coincide. Already in the Indian *Rigveda* this '*Weben*' is a picture of the creative cosmic weaving.

Where does this creative cosmic weaving commence?
In the etheric realm, in the sound-ether.
Where does *Weben* become *Wehen*, with its overtone of pain?

Where the creation is led down from the etheric spirit into the material and earthly, where the earthly element of dust and with it the earthly air-breath is imprinted into the creature, where the air-ether becomes physically breathed air—where earthly air is breathed, suffering and death also begin. Our observations are to show how all this is not only a general truth, but also true in music and for the musical element.

The Motif of Longing

We will now attempt to show how the motif of longing in *Tristan and Isolde*, the motif of the wafting breath, at the same time relates to the primal, sound-etheric element of music, as expressed in Indian links to the meaning of $\sqrt{v\bar{a}}$[41] (*wehen*, and *wehe* with *weben* from $\sqrt{v\bar{a}}$ ('creatively weaving').

The music of *Tristan* in an inexhaustible manner, if not in all, but repeatedly in many of its breaths and pulse-beats, expresses the motif of the wafting breath connected to the soul and longing. It is completely aligned to the element of air, even when it does not have to do with it in a narrow sense. One recalls Isolde's outburst in Act I:

Luft! Luft!	Air! Air!
Mir erstickt das Herz!	My heart is stifled!
Öffne! Öffne doch weit!	Open up! Open wide there!

a passage, which in the descending scale of its harmony seems to express something of the eurythmical *H*. (The eurythmical *H* is absolutely related to what lies in the above-cited words of Isolde, as well as to Wagner's poetic and musical creation *Tristan and Isolde* in general.)[42]

The air-breath and with it the wishing, hoping and longing accompany human life from the first to the last breath, from birth to death; likewise the longing motif of the wafting-breath accompanies the whole music of *Tristan and Isolde*. This becomes most clear in Act III. The mortally wounded Tristan lies without hope in the arms of the faithful Kurvenal after the night of unconsciousness surrounds his [day-]consciousness that is wandering in far spiritual regions at the threshold of the spiritual world, erring, dreaming and fantasizing. Waking out of the swoon, he speaks of these experiences, disinterested in his immediate earthly surroundings; the boundless longing for Isolde, still on the ship that is to bring her over the sea to him, completely rules him. The mournful melody of the Shepherd's pipe:

(*Noch ist kein Schiff zu seh'n*)   (There's still no ship in sight!)

enters as the first mourning music into his whole life,

Muss ich dich so verstehn,	Must I understand you thus,
du alte ernste Weise, ... ?	you ancient, solemn tune ... ?

until he finally curses the love potion for the sake of the longing which leads him in and through life. And after this terrible outburst new unconsciousness lays hold of him. Tristan lies as if dead in the arms of Kurvenal:

Hier liegt er nun,	Here he lies,
der wonnige Mann,	the splendid man,
der wie keiner geliebt und geweint ...	loved and adored as no other ...
Bist du nun tot?	Are you dead?
Lebst du noch?	Are you still alive?
Hat dich der Fluch entführt? ...	Has the curse borne you away?

This is the already-mentioned passage following the breath (longing)-motif, or rather only the one characteristic *Tristan*-chord ([reading from below:] F-C♭-E♭-A♭) of this motif, marking this breath-rhythm is pulsing triplets, traversing several bars:

O Wonne! Nein!	O joy! No!
Er regt sich! Er lebt!	He is moving, he is alive!
Wie sanft er die Lippen rührt!	How gently he moves his lips!

Once more Tristan awakens to life, once more the softly pulsing, breathing rhythm proclaims that the life has not fled. In a dream-vision, Tristan sees Isolde walking on the blue, flowery waves through the fields of the sea, coming to him, to the land; this is the actual climax of the *Tristan*-music—besides Isolde's *Totenklage* and *Liebestod*—because he wrests himself away from the super-tonal element of the *Tristan*-harmony, to the light blue E-major. Then Isolde, announced through the shrill sound of the 'happy shepherd's tune'—the climax of the *Tristan*-tragedy lies precisely here, the ever flaring-up illusion of life— when she appears in reality, Tristan, rising from his death-bed, and tearing off his bandages, throws himself, dying, into the arms of his beloved. Here the 'wafting breath' of the 'motif of longing' becomes really the 'last sigh'. This breathing-motif accompanies the entire music of *Tristan and Isolde* in the same way as the breath of life accompanies the human being from the first to the last breath. It is the same motif with which the Prelude to Act 1 began; here it accompanies the outpouring of a true sigh, Tristan's last breath, his death. This belongs to the most expressive moments in the entire musical repertoire in the way death is expressed. Some things in the preceding rhythmic and harmonic development remind one of the dying scene at the beginning of Mozart's *Don Giovanni*. This passage in the *Tristan*-music helps us to experience how the breathing-motif, the motif of the wafting breath, is the longing that also encompasses death in itself.

Already at the beginning of Act I (Scene 2) we see the longing-motif passing over into the motif of death. Isolde:

Mir erkoren,	Chosen for me
Mir verloren	Lost to me
. . .	. . .
Todgeweihtes Haupt!	Head destined for death!
Todgeweihtes Herz!	Heart destined for death!

This death motif finds its climax in Act III, 2, after Tristan's death in Isolde's death lament.

Gebrochen der Blick!	Dimmed your eyes!
Still das Herz!	Silent your heart!
Nicht eines Atems	Not a breath's
flücht'ges Wehn! . . .	gentle wafting!

The ending of *Tristan and Isolde* (Isolde's transfiguration, the *Liebestod*) belongs to the supreme portrayals of the overcoming of death that exists in music.

At this climax of human sorrow, where the suffering, the pain, the longing is wrestled through to its last and highest point, indeed where it snaps its own sting, Wagner moves in the same key, G-minor, in which Mozart already expressed passionate pain — one recalls Mozart's *Symphony in G-minor* [No. 40, KV 550], and Pamina's Aria of lament in *The Magic Flute*. Wagner moves in the relative minor key, the 'starry key' of Bb-major, in which he begins Act II of *Tristan*, the Mystery of the *Liebesnacht*, the night of love. It is the same key of Bb-major that accompanies the rising of the shining Evening Star in Act III of *Tannhäuser*. Here, too, the music goes over into the serious G-minor, when Wolfram speaks about *Venus-Urania*, who, accompanying the soul through the fear of death, shows the soul the 'path out of death'.

With the 'wafting breath', with the longing motif, the death motif in a unique manner interweaves the music of *Tristan and Isolde*. This work, always on the threshold of consciousness, shows a completely different level of consciousness than other dramatic, other musical works, even among Wagner's other music dramas, not excluding *Parsifal*. That which the mystery of death signifies for music — we shall return to this question in detail — is revealed in a quite special manner in *Tristan and Isolde*. This goes right into the instrumentation; we can think of the unique step of a diminished seventh frequently emphasized by the bass tuba with the motif of the poisoned drink, the 'draught of death', recalling thereby what Rudolf Steiner says[43] about the significance of the interval of the seventh in Atlantean times. What was normal for plants during a specific epoch, placed into a later epoch becomes poisonous — which again can contain healing forces.

And so *death* lives in the music of *Tristan and Isolde*, as in a tremendous cosmic ocean, which can contain all pain and all rapture — we think of the 'ocean of milk' of Indian cosmogony, in which all deadly and healing juices, all ingredients of the whole becoming of the world are interspersed with their most deadly of all poisons. The strengthening forces of death, the refreshing element deriving from the subterranean sources of all life-forces, can be experienced in the music of *Tristan and Isolde*.

Friedrich Nietzsche, for a while deeply connected with Wagner's *Tristan and Isolde*, and who experienced this death motif in *Tristan and Isolde* especially strongly, writes about it to his friend, Erwin Rohde:

> Certainly there is no other music in the world of such *necessity*: my soul directly joined in singing in this sounding of the sea of streaming feeling. Here there is nothing of artificial, artistic whim, which facing such daemonic compulsion must appear to one as almost happy. The effect of the whole, however, was *too* passionate for me: this tremendous cultivation of the feelings tears the sympathizer completely out of the human world, a true death-wish carries him down into that twilight world, where *love* without end lives and starves; with a true struggle he has to find his way back into the human light of day ... I still hear, before all other memories, the beginning of the Prelude to Act III (the first five notes) always echoing in my heart: it appears to me as a long-drawn, deep-sounding bell, that is ringing all happiness and all the comforting light of the Earth to the night and the grave; it is terribly sad! ...

Precisely in this introduction to Act III of *Tristan and Isolde*, full of suffering, carrying all earthly pain, above all in those first five notes, it becomes clear that the pain, the longing of the music drama *Tristan and Isolde* does not at all lie *only* in the human soul. It is actually the pain of the whole Earth, from profound, cosmic depths as if of a primordial humanity, a cosmic pain bound with primal Mysteries of the becoming of the world. All Wagner's stage-sets are of direct Imaginative significance, uniquely harmonizing with the Inspiring element of the orchestral music, and not least the stage-sets in *Tristan and Isolde*. And once again in Act III the sea that we already met in Act I appears significantly, the wide horizon of the sea, the 'emptiness of the sea', as a counter picture of human soul-pain and human soul-loneliness, but precisely in a cosmic counter picture. For the sea in *Tristan and Isolde* is always at the same time the 'etheric sea', that cosmic element that we also recognize as the primal, the sound-etheric element of music — whereas the soul as such corresponds to the secondary element, the air.

The 'motif of longing', too, in Wagner's *Tristan and Isolde*, as we already saw earlier, contains not *only* the wafting breath, the sigh of longing — to which especially the dominant ending of this motif points, recalling Mozart's sighing motif — but, in its first characteristic harmony in the *Tristan*-chord, it also contains that super-tonal element, already discussed, that 'wafting of the spirit-sea', about which Rudolf Steiner spoke. Applied to music, this is precisely the world of the sound-ether, in which the primal element of music is contained. Not for nothing does this *Tristan*-chord play such a decisive role in its rhythmical forward-pulsing in that visionary episode of the 'walking on the sea' in Act III of *Tristan and Isolde*.

7. The primordial root √vā — 'blowing', and the experience of pain. The Hibernian Mysteries. The magic of the Mother. The Christian Mystery and *Parsifal*

We return ever again to this primal motif of the music of *Tristan and Isolde*, which, as we are trying to show, seems to be so strangely interwoven with a cosmic, primordial word, a linguistic primal motif. The Indian primordial root √vā, which on the one hand means *wehen* 'blowing' ('*Windeswehen*', the blowing of the wind) at the same time also means *wehe*, 'alas!' as an exclamation of pain [including inner pain]. But it has another, earlier meaning, corresponding to the German *weben*, 'to weave', especially in the sense of cosmic weaving. We pictorially summarized the two elements of the music as *Wind und Woge*, 'wind and wave'. We were able to connect with the 'wind' the secondary element of soul and air, and with the 'wave' the primary element of the sound-ether, the 'etheric sea' and 'sea of cosmic music'. This meets us in such a revealing manner initially in the music of Bach; it receded in later music with Beethoven and the romantics, appearing again strongly with Wagner, that is, already with *The Flying Dutchman* and then mainly in *Tristan and Isolde*.

√vā in its first meaning (*wehen*, 'to blow') would be the element of soul and air, the etheric *Weben*, 'weaving', this, wherein we see the etheric in the picture of the sea, becomes *Wogen*, a 'surging, waving', *Woge*, a 'wave'. Both secondary and primary elements, the air-element and the ether-element, the wind and the wave, are contained in the music of *Tristan and Isolde*, especially in the motif of longing, fundamental for this music.

Indeed, one can go so far that in the first harmonization of this motif, in the characteristic '*Tristan*-chord' that touches on the super-tonal, one finds more the etheric element, the 'wave', and in the following passage more in the dominant tonality, in the sighing motif reminiscent of Mozart, more the element of air, the 'wind'. Each glance into the libretto and score of *Tristan* shows how much all this also lived in Wagner's imagination.

The uniting of *wind* and *wave*, can it find a more powerful expression than at the beginning of Act I in Isolde's outbreak of rage, in her evocation to the wind?

Entartet Geschlecht!	Degenerate race!
Unwert der Ahnen!	Unworthy of your ancestors!
Wohin, Mutter,	How, O Mother,
vergabst du die Macht,	did you dispose of the power
über Meer und Sturm zu gebieten?	of ruling sea and tempest?
O zahme Kunst	O feeble art
der Zauberin,	of the sorceress,
die nur Balsamtränke noch braut!	still cooking up balsamic potions!
Erwache mir wieder,	Be stirred in me once again,
kühne Gewalt;	bold power;
herauf aus dem Busen,	rise up from my breast
wo du dich bargst!	where you have lain concealed!
Hört meinen Willen,	Give ear to my will,
zagende Winde!	half-hearted winds!
Heran zu Kampf	Off to battle
und Wettergetös'!	and turbulent elements!
Zu tobender Stürme	To the furious vortex
wütendem Wirbel!	of raging tempests!
Treibt aus dem Schlaf	Shake from her slumber
dies träumende Meer,	this somnolent sea,
weckt aus dem Grund	awaken from her depths
seine grollende Gier!	her malevolent greed!
Zeigt ihm die Beute,	Show her the prize
die ich ihm biete!	that I have to offer!
Zerschlag es dies trotzige Schiff,	Smash this insolent ship
des zerschellten Trümmer verschling's!	and gorge on her shattered wreckage!
Und was auf ihm lebt,	And whatever has life on her,
den wehenden Atem,	that faint breath
den lass' ich euch Winden zum Lohn!	I leave as reward for you winds!

All this is truly not only words of an 'opera libretto', but it lives with the power of the storm in the music of *Tristan and Isolde*. The longing motif of the blowing breath plays again a main role in a certain chromatic development with shortened rhythmic motifs. Especially at the place: 'O feeble art of the sorceress, . . .' and a little later with the words, 'Shake from her slumber this somnolent sea', the sound-etheric element in the longing motif becomes a motif of magic, in the same way as the sound-ether is indeed also the *magic* ether (more on this in the author's *John's Gospel: The Cosmic Rhythm* [p. 207ff., 220, in connection with the Marriage in Cana, John 2; also p. 244, and under the Cross, p. 404ff. etc.]). The *magical element*, the cosmic primal magic, is a main element in

Wagner's poetic *Tristan*-libretto, and especially in the music of *Tristan and Isolde*. This magical element is completely interwoven with the essence of the sound-ether, which with the life-ether can be taken as the *female* ether. This is the element of Isolde and of the *Mother*, the *magical* power of the Mother, which expresses cosmic primal magic, the divine-magical power revealed in the primal becoming of the world.

This is the meaning of the root √vā in its second meaning expressing the *creative world-becoming*. From here we also understand the motif of love in *Tristan and Isolde* as the motif of *magic love*, as Novalis meant: 'Love is the foundation for the possibility of magic. Love works magically.' And we can link this to Isolde's words in Act II of *Tristan and Isolde*:

Frau Minne kenntest du nicht?	Do you not know the Love Spirit,
Nicht ihres Zaubers Macht?	not know her magic's power?
Des kühnsten Mutes	The Queen
Königin?	of boldest courage,
des Weltenwerdens	Regent of the
Wälterin?	world's course?
Leben und Told	Love and Death
sind untertan ihr,	are subject to her,
die sie webt aus Lust und Leid,	she weaves them out of bliss and sorrow,
in Liebe wandelnd den Neid.	transmuting envy into love.

The passage is completely woven through and carried by the wafting of the motif of longing. As in Act I, it clearly appears here as the *magical motif*, corresponding in significance with √vā in Act II.

The development of human consciousness, understood in anthroposophy as leading to the awake 'I', ultimately finds in itself the creative power — which is the power of Christ. The magical power in the higher life-element appears as the essential thing in pre-Christian times and in their Mysteries. In his Fall from Paradise, the life-element, which as the 'Tree of Life' was wrenched from man, he sought to regain through the trial of the Mysteries; he was unable to regain it completely. We experience it indeed with Tristan, too, the initiate of the Hibernian Mysteries. He is not quite able fully and permanently to win for himself the higher life, Isolde; he sinks dying into Isolde's arms, who came over the sea in order to marry him. Isolde herself is the bearer of this higher, this magical life-element, and alongside her the Mother. This *magical motif* of the *Mother* we see traversing the early

Mysteries, up to the moment when Christ on the Cross unites the Disciple with the Mother (John 19:27), finding the connection to the Christian Mystery. In the Christian Mystery the *magical power* of the *Mother* is taken up into the Disciple's own 'I'. At the Marriage in Cana (John 2) at the beginning of Christ's ministry, we see the Christ still turning outwardly to the power of the Mother, strengthening His own power with it (John 2:40).[44] Here the pre-Christian, magical forces of the Mother extend into the Christian realm. And Tristan, the initiate of the Hibernian Mysteries, is not yet able to take up the forces of the Mother, or the forces of Isolde, into his 'I', into the forces of the Son (for this reason he [qua 'Son'] is wooing her for Marke, the bearer of the forces of the Father).[45] He still remains in the pre-Christian realm, not yet able to take the step into the Christian Mystery. This connection only takes place in the Parsifal-consciousness that lies completely within the Christian Mystery.

From here we suddenly understand the profound cosmic connection of the reference in the *Tristan*-libretto to the motif of the Christian gospel. Act I, 1, Isolde:

Wohin, Mutter,	How, O Mother,
vergabst du die Macht,	did you dispose of the power
über Meer und Sturm zu gebieten?	of ruling sea and tempest?

The power with which Christ in the gospel commands the storm on the Lake (Mark 6:51), which on the level of Christian consciousness is the power of the 'I', the ego, which still lived in pre-Christian times with the 'Mother'; for the human soul this is still difficult to reach in the higher life-element. However, the accord with the Christian [consciousness] is already quite clear in the language of *Tristan and Isolde*. As with Isolde's outburst in Act I, here the 'stilling of the storm on the Lake', or the 'power to rebuke wind and sea' (Mark 4:39, 6:51; John 6:20; Matt. 14:32), we find in Act III in Tristan's vision of Isolde, the 'walking on the waves' [Act III, 1, Tristan]:

Wie sie selig,	as she sweetly
hehr und milde	bravely and gently
wandelt durch	wanders across
des Meers Gefilde?	the watery plains?
Auf wonniger Blumen	On soft waves
lichten Wogen	of blissful flowers
kommt sie sanft	she gently comes
ans Land gezogen.	into land.

Sie lächelt mir Trost	She smiles at me,
und süsse Ruh',	giving comfort and sweet peace,
sie führt mir letzte	she brings me
Labung zu.	my last refreshment.

Here, however, it is precisely still the dream-experience of distant Isolde; in the gospel (Matt. 14:25; Mark 6:48; John 6:14) the experience of the power awakening in the 'I', the awake experience of Christ. In the same passage in *Tristan and Isolde* we find in the 'last refreshment' the accord with the Last Anointing and the Eucharist. And in the manner Tristan and Isolde together drink the 'draught of reconciliation' — an allusion to this comes once more in Act III, 1:

Und drauf Isolde,	And on it Isolde,
wie sie winkt, —	how she is waving,
wie sie hold	how sweetly she is drinking
mir Sühne trinkt:	reconciliation to me.

In 'the draught of death' that becomes the 'draught of love', there positively lies a Mystery motif of 'communion'. Isolde's lament in Act III is full of Christian motifs, how she throws herself on the body of the dead man, who has sunk dying into her arms, the dramatic climax of the whole story and the musical climax of *Tristan and Isolde*. The pain of longing is no longer at all earthly pain; it itself reverses the sting by penetrating to the threshold of the spiritual world, passing over into the transfiguration in the light of the spirit-world. It is the most expressive G-minor of the entire musical repertoire, Act III, 2:

Auf, noch einmal	Up, just once more,
hör' meinen Ruf!	listen to my call!
Isolde ruft:	Isolde is calling:
Isolde kam,	Isolde has come
mit Tristan treu zu sterben!	faithfully to die with Tristan.
Bleibst du mir stumm?	Will you not answer me?
Nur eine Stunde,	Just for one hour,
nur eine Stunde	just for one hour
bleibe mir wach!	stay awake for me!
So bange Tage	For so many anxious days
wachte sie sehnend,	she kept watch, longing
um eine Stunde,	to watch with you
mit dir noch zu wachen ...	for an hour.

This is the language of the gospels, a conscious reference to the words of Jesus to the sleeping Peter in Gethsemane: 'So could you not watch with me one hour?' (Matt. 26:40); Mark 14:37 reads: 'Simon, are you asleep? Could you not watch one hour?' The whole picture of Isolde bending over the body of the beloved is inwardly related to the picture of the Pietà, of the Mother, who holds the body of her Son in her arms; or even more directly to how this picture lives in the *Parzival* saga, with Sigune, who carries the body of her beloved in her arms. Wagner was completely aware of the objective connection between the Tristan Mystery and the Parzifal Mystery ('Parsifal' is Wagner's spelling). In the letters to Mathilde Wesendonck he speaks about this: how to him the ailing Tristan of Act III appears as a preliminary stage of the ailing Amfortas, and how he for a while had the intention to make the young Parsifal himself appear at Tristan's sick-bed.

All this, partly seeming subsidiary, had nevertheless to be mentioned in order to characterize the 'magical motif'. We have seen how it also bears on the musical element, especially the musical element of *Tristan and Isolde*. It is already woven into the archetypal longing motif of *Tristan and Isolde*, into that motif in which *'Wehen und Weben'*, 'blowing and weaving', the blowing breath of the soul-element with the creative-magical weaving of the spiritual element of the sound-ether, are so strangely woven together. And this 'magical element' again is of eminent significance for the unique Christian element, in the overarching sense as the future-bearing impulse of world-development springing from the Mystery of Golgotha. The magic of primal times, fallen into decadence, the 'magic of the Mother', finds here its transition into the magic in the 'I' that has its sublime archetypal pattern in the Mystery [of Golgotha] itself. From here spring the new magical forces, magically transforming and bearing the future of the Earth.

The 'magic of the Mother' is indeed always spoken of in *Tristan and Isolde*; it is expressly mentioned in that passage which is found twice in Act I — once in the mouth of Brangäne, and the second time in the mouth of Isolde herself — which at the same time is one of the principal passages for the main motif of *Tristan and Isolde*. It is recognized from the beginning of the Prelude, missing only the upbeat, so that the remaining harmonic sequence by itself alone expresses the 'magic' of this motif [Act I, 3]:

Brangäne:

Kennst du der Mutter	Do you not know our
Künste nicht?	mother's craft?
Wähnst du, die alles	Do you imagine that she,

klug erwägt,	who considers everything,
ohne Rat in fremdes Land	would have sent me away with you
hätt' sie mit dir mich entsandt?	without means of help into foreign land?
. . .	. . .
Für Weh und Wunden	For pain and wounds
Balsam hier;	here is ointment;
für böse Gifte	for evil poisons
Gegengift.	antidote.

Nowhere so clear as here do we recognize the primal motif of longing of *Tristan and Isolde* as the 'magical motif'.

This is the one magic, the magic of the primal age, the 'magic of the Mother', which extends only as a declining, decadent phenomenon in later times, in the age of the developing 'I'. The other, the new, the future-bearing, is found earlier only in weak, hardly visible beginnings. It is a magic that changes the Earth, that which develops in the 'I' itself, the magic of Christ. It is the magic incorporated in the events of the Earth, performed for the first time by Christ Himself in the Mystery of Golgotha. (The details are developed by the author, linking to Rudolf Steiner's anthroposophy, in the little book, *The Parsifal=Christ=Experience*.) This Christ-magic is presented by Wagner in his way in *Parsifal*, though we have tried to show that already *Tristan and Isolde* contains indications throughout. It takes place in the whole manner Wagner has everywhere conjured before us the Christian Mystery of the blood in the poetry and music of *Parsifal*, initially already in the Prelude. It finally finds its climax in the *Karfreitagszauber*, the 'Good Friday magic' in Act III, which is the poetic and musical climax of the whole. This is simply the name Wagner himself found for the magic of that changing and transfiguring the Earth, which in the vernal mood of Easter shines so gratefully out of all the flower-chalices and glitters in dew drops on the flower.

How Richard Wagner in his presentation of the Christian Mysteries of the blood in *Parsifal* touches on the deepest Mysteries of Christianity, Rudolf Steiner also expressed in an Easter lecture (Berlin 25 March 1907),[46] where, regarding the Mysteries of the Blood of Golgotha, he said:

Vielleicht hat keiner dieses Mysterium exoterisch so nahe gestreift wie Richard Wagner in dem Aufsatz über die Konzeption des 'Parsifal'. Es streift da ein Exoteriker an die tiefsten esoterischen Wahrheiten der Mysterien.

Perhaps no-one else has touched exoterically more closely on this mystery than Richard Wagner in his essay on the conception of *Parsifal*. Here an exotericist touches the deepest truth of the esoteric Mysteries of Christianity.

On the other hand, Rudolf Steiner always strongly emphasized how Wagner, through the manner he made the music serve the drama, had estranged the musical element, though not exclusively, for this musical element still very strongly lived in Wagner. For example, in many passages of *Tristan and Isolde*, especially in Act II, and then again in the *Karfreitagszauber* in *Parsifal*, the musical element struggles through to the purely musical, symphonic element. Indeed, the whole of *Tristan and Isolde*, if one has the inner feeling for it, can be experienced as a 'symphony'. In the final lecture of *True and False Paths of Spiritual Investigation* (Torquay, 22 August 1924. GA 243),[47] Steiner spoke about how in Wagner's *Parsifal*, on the one side lives the urgency to enchant the Christ-Impulse into the physical-sensory world, but how all this may not yet be completely achieved in the music of *Parsifal*.

What is meant has to be closely considered. What, then, does it mean, the Earth-transforming power of Christ's magic? This is not an abstract generality; it relates in a completely concrete manner to everything earthly, leastways not to expressions of the human soul and revelations of the same, to the whole manner the human soul experiences the spiritual, lives it out, and how it reveals it in art. This relates, for example, to the development of music itself, which is the subject of these observations, to the whole question of modern and most recent creations, to the whole manner how the conscious, or also still unconscious, striving to overcome the soul-element in music (which concerns us here so much) emerges, the striving to penetrate right through this 'secondary' element of music, to the primal, the pure-spiritual, sound-ether. Especially when this element in its starry significance as the 'starry element' of music is recognized, then will the highest Mystery-contents of music be revealed musically in a completely new manner, not yet achieved today and hardly imagined. This will be the time when the Christ-Impulse—as this word is always understood in anthroposophy—becomes fully effective and also musically presented in the music of the future. That this has not yet been achieved in Wagner's *Parsifal*—still largely relying on the musical style of the past, drawing on elements of the past—this Rudolf Steiner wanted to say in the above-cited passage. What he went on to say concerning the corresponding musical incorporation of the motif of the Incarnation of Christ in his presentation of the musical intervals is, however, interesting for us here. They correspond quite closely, these intervals and degrees of the scale, to the construction of the Last Supper theme,[48] which begins the Prelude to *Parsifal*—also Act III, that is, the whole music drama ends with the same theme, here coming to a significant motif, an 'experience of the octave' in this exalted theme.

8. *Parsifal*. The starry quality. *Karfreitagszauber* and the *Liebestod*. A 'super-tonal' style. Bruckner's *Ninth Symphony*. Planets, stars and the musical keys

Despite dependence in many ways still on music's past, especially at the end of Act III, the 'Grail communion', also touched on by Rudolf Steiner in *True and False Paths* (cited above); despite this 'content of the past' of the music of *Parsifal* (whereas the 'content of eternity' predominates in the music of *Tristan and Isolde*), Wagner's *Parsifal* does musically also contains several things that strongly point to the future. This can be felt mostly in Act III (even if, apart from the 'octave experience', not yet in its final ending), partly also already in Act II, and in individual passages already in Act I. It should be noted above all in Act III, quite apart from the *Karfreitagszauber*, already in the initial beginning the delicate mood of the 'resurrection morning' is expressed in a musical manner as has never before existed, till today also hardly approached, one would like to say [something] musically esoteric. This *is* the Christian-esoteric experience incorporated in music. This does not exclude the fact that in the Mystery-music of the future these things one day will be presented with completely other musical means.

How, for example, the 'starry quality' in music begins to shine already in Wagner's *Parsifal*, is shown especially in the motif of the pure fool: '*Durch Mitleid wissend, der reine Tor*[49] — Enlightened through compassion, the innocent fool.'

To analyze this well-known motif in its separate harmonies according to its key, as taught by the usual music theory, is of course possible, but does not lead us far. The decisive thing is only found when one turns to the spiritual viewpoint as described in the author's little book, *The Essence of Tonality* [and as later developed in *The Language of Tonality*], whereby a star-rhythm becomes a part of the twelve — or twice twelve [counting both the major and minor] — keys of the tempered system. This star-rhythm is reflected on Earth in the rhythm of the events of the year and its twelve monthly stages. Its nature is starry, that yet is expressed, revealed again, in the purely earthly realm. Here

Ex. 13: The Prophecy Motif: "Await him whom I have chosen, the simpleton without guile, made wise through compassion."

one can straight away think of both musical elements we characterized as the primary, starry, cosmic sound-ether; and as the secondary, earthly, bound to the air-element of the earth and the earthly construction of musical instruments that can be constructed differently according to the various earthly tonal systems. To find how the earthly is woven with the starry element in the most varying realms, in a completely concrete manner, will be a knowledge of the future of humanity, to be worked out on an anthroposophical basis.[50]

The 'motif of the innocent fool' permits itself so to be seen, that the 'starry circle of keys' somehow forms its basis. One relates the different harmonies of the motif not artificially to *one* key, but takes each harmony as representative of its own key. Then we will be led in this motif by the actual solar and starry heights of the circle of keys, A-major, through the earthly depths, E♭-major, and up again to the heights striving to reach D-major, to the initial high-point; the circle of keys is complete in the starry heights, in the super-earthly realm. As noted, the necessary details can be found in the author's writings. Someone who cannot follow this can let this episode meet him for the present as 'future wisdom'. We may recall how, also according to Rudolf Steiner's lecture-cycle *Christ and the Spiritual World* [Leipzig 1913. GA 149], the starry motifs link the paths of Parsifal riding through the starry nights seeking the Grail.

It does *not* mean that, if the 'starry quality in music' is one day sought in the musical style of the future, this will be undertaken in Wagner's musical style. On the contrary, the musical style of the future will certainly be something else. It should be recognized that Wagner's musical style is a unique event in the history of music — this is also what Rudolf Steiner meant when he once used the expression 'dead end' in respect of Wagner — that basically it doesn't lend itself to be repeated, continued or led further. Where this is nevertheless attempted, it was either still decadent, or, when it took place out of genial forces, it led to decadent phenomena of music. Wagner's musical style is not to be repeated and not to be continued. For this reason, though, it is important not to deny it, but rather to gain knowledge and insights from this unique, this perhaps so far most interesting phenomenon of music history. These insights can be made fruitful for the musical developments of the future also without any imitation.

In this way, if at all the starry, cosmic understanding of the rhythm of the musical keys is once more widely known one day, much can be learnt out of the manner Wagner uses the keys[51] without one thereby taking over the 'tonality' [classical harmony] of the earlier music. Wagner himself stands, relatively speaking, quite free in relation to the keys. He uses tonality as a means of expression where out of the spiritual element it is appropriate, whether in longer passages (as in the Prelude to *Lohengrin*, the Prelude to *The Rhinegold*, and in the F-major Introduction of the Rhinedaughters in Act III of *Twilight of the Gods*), or whether it is in transitional passages (even a single chord with Wagner frequently has the meaning of the corresponding key). But he often increasingly approaches a super-tonal style. This can be felt especially in the music of *Tristan and Isolde* and in the Prelude to Act III of *Parsifal*.[52]

There simply exists with Wagner — and other composers — degrees, or shades of tonality, not only the contrast of tonal and super-tonal, or atonal, music. Through this the key loses its character of compulsion, which it can easily assume in earlier music. The composer here confronts musical composition, freely governing, freely creating. In a certain sense this is still more than when tonality, as one of the possible means of musical expression, from the outset is excluded [i.e. atonality abolishes the seven-note system]. But only out of the cosmic, starry quality of music can this higher understanding of the keys be won.[53]

Then, if one has more closely approached the starry element of music, if, for example, one learns especially from Wagner's use of the keys, one will be able to express this starry element also in another, a more super-tonal, or atonal manner. The Scherzo [second] movement in Bruckner's *Ninth Symphony*, with its still tonal transitional themes and passages — the super-tonal element in this is very much related to the super-tonal element of the primal motif of *Tristan and Isolde* — opens many perspectives in this direction.

Let us look from here once more at the 'transformation motif' in the *Karfreitagszauber*, how Wagner expresses this magic transformation motif right into the tonality. In the author's little book, *Alchymy: The Mystery of the Material World*, it is shown how in the 'earthly sign of Virgo, the Virgin' the mystery of the transformation of the Earth, of the penetration of the earthly with the spiritual-etheric element, is expressed in a special manner. It also appears in the gospel as the sign of the 'starry Feeding [of the Five Thousand]' and of the Last Supper (see the author's *Mark's Gospel: The Cosmic Rhythm* and *John's Gospel: The Cosmic Rhythm*). In harmony with the earlier, primeval wisdom, confirmed by new experiences, one can also combine this earthly 'sign' (in which the unity of twelve of the heavenly zodiac, the starry zodiac, is reflected) with the planets.[54] Then the earthly sign of the Virgin appears as the sign of Mercury. This Mercury viewpoint also leads to the 'transformation of the physical', to transubstantiation, to Last-Supper Mysteries, and so on. The essential motif announcing the beginning of the *Karfreitagszauber* in Wagner's *Parsifal* is completely woven out of this B-major of the Virgin, in which the 'mystery of the Virgin' seems to behold us through nature transfigured and purified from sin through Christ's sacrificial blood:

> Parsifal:
> *Wie dünkt mich doch die Aue heut so schön!*
> *Wohl traf ich Wunderblumen an,*
> *die bis zum Haupte süchtig mich umrankten;*
> *doch sah ich nie so mild und zart*
> *die Halme, Blüten und Blumen,*
> *noch duftet' all' so kindisch hold*
> *und sprach so lieblich traut zu mir.*

> How fair seem the meadows today!
> Once I came upon magic flowers
> which twined their tainted tendrils about my head;
> but never did I see so fresh and charming

the grass, the blossoms and flowers,
nor did they smell so sweet of youth
or speak with such tender love to me.

Only in the answer of Gurnemanz to Parsifal's question do the motifs similarly return; they stand in the etherically clear thought-quality of D-major:

Gurnemanz:
Nun freut sich alle Kreatur
auf des Erlösers holder Spur,
will sein Gebet ihm weihen.
Ihn selbst am Kreuze kann sie nicht erschauen:
da blickt sie zum erlösten Menschen auf;
der fühlt sich frei von Sündenlast und Grauen,
durch Gottes Liebesopfer rein und heil ...

Now all creation rejoices
at the Saviour's sign of love
and dedicates to Him its prayer.
No more can it see Him Himself on the Cross;
it looks up to man redeemed,
who feels freed from the burden of sin and terror,
made clean and whole through God's loving sacrifice.

All these matters will one day be understood when the starry mysteries of the musical keys, so eloquent with Wagner, are more generally accessed. Then it will be understood how and why B-major, the key of the Virgin, the main key of the *Karfreitagszauber*, has really to do with the miracle of Good Friday, of the transformed and transfigured nature of the Earth.

This leads us back again to *Tristan and Isolde*, to the tremendous work that portrays [aspects of] the eternal world in dramatic music. (*Parsifal* is an initial, still fragmentary beginning, pointing towards something that only in the future will find its completion; *Tristan and Isolde* is an ending, complete in itself, something that in its form cannot be surpassed.) Like the Christ-magic of the *Karfreitagszauber* in *Parsifal*, the final ending of *Tristan and Isolde*, Isolde's transfiguration and *Liebestod*, stands in B-major. It will simply have to be acknowledged that this is the greatest and most expressive B-major of all music. If the connections of the *Karfreitagszauber* have been understood, then from this one realizes that for Wagner Isolde's *Liebestod* was not a mere floating off from the Earth—as might easily be believed. This transfiguration has never been expressed in music in such an unbelievably pure and sublime manner, communicating itself to everyone involved, similar to how in his day Buddha (see the publication, *The Passing and Nirvaṇa of the Perfected One*, Temple Lodge, forthcoming),[55] proclaiming to the whole of earthly existence, as it were, prepared this earthly existence for the Christ-magic of the future, in which the earthly tragedy of *Tristan and Isolde* finds its completion and fulfilment. *Tristan and Isolde* and *Parsifal*, these two poetical works belonging to the sphere of the Hibernian Mysteries, cannot be understood unless it is recognized how they both relate to each other. The cosmic magic speaks, namely in the musical element, much more directly and powerfully in *Tristan and Isolde* than in *Parsifal*.

Isolde's *Liebestod*, as the cosmic-magical completion of the whole work, brings to an end in the highest intensification that which is already present in Act II. Only with the appearance of Marke is it movingly interrupted through a sudden earthly tragedy. (In this turning of the ecstasy into the tragedy and the catastrophe of death lies the necessity; here is revealed the authenticity in Wagner's proclamation.) Here we also have to cast a final glance at the tremendous symphonic writing, from the purely musical viewpoint perhaps the most significant of the three Acts of *Tristan and Isolde*. Act III brings the climax of the final ending, the climax of the pain (the Introduction and later Isolde's *Totenklage* ['death lament']), the climax also in the visionary aspect, in the poetry of the sea ('she who walks on the waves'). In the mystery of the *Liebesnacht*, which surges in an unheard of magical flood and which rises to the stars — the key, as with the Grail Mystery in *Parsifal*, is the profoundly dark, ceremonial Ab-major — Act II brings forth the actual 'starry climax', the climax of the starry, the 'Uranian' element in Wagner's *Tristan and Isolde*. Here we shall not concentrate on its overall construction, but only on some intimate details — which one can regard as the intimate, unrevealed climaxes of the music of *Tristan and Isolde*.

Act II of *Tristan and Isolde* leads us into the starry, Uranian element. And truly, it does this already in the key in which it begins, in Bb-major, which we have already learnt to recognize as the key of the starry quality (♒ ☉) (see footnote 54). In this respect there is nothing in Wagner that is contrived. In a letter he writes about how far removed all theorizing lies with respect to choice of keys, but at the same time there is no coincidence, but only the certain accuracy rising out of the depths of his own geniality. Already in *Tannhäuser* Wagner helps us to experience B♭-major as the characteristic starry key, as the passage where he introduces the bright Evening Star, Venus, shining in the evening sky. And Wolfram's subsequent G-minor still stands, as we have seen, in the realm of this starry, Uranian element of 'Venus Urania'.

In Act II of *Tristan and Isolde* the opening, starry key of B♭-major reveals the whole magic of the weaving love in nature, the whole transfiguration of the summer night. *Tristan and Isolde* and the summer night belong together. Friedrich Nietzsche once called Wagner — actually in a late work, *Nietzsche kontra Wagner* [1888] — the 'greatest miniaturist of music, who in the shortest space draws together an infinity of meaning and sweetness'. Such ultimate intimate things are found especially in Act II; here actually are the most intimate climaxes of the music of *Tristan and Isolde*. Here human feeling, the human soul-element, no longer sounds alone, but the whole weaving of nature here becomes sounding life, begins to sound in human souls. This is no 'programme music' committing the artistic error of harnessing the unmusical outer side of the world into the musical form of expression, of violating the musical element through such external elements that are inwardly foreign to it.

But *musical* life hidden in the innermost part of the world, the inner *harmony* of the stars, penetrates to the surface, to the open heart, the starry life that can only be laid hold of by an Inspired consciousness. *Musical* secrets of the world are revealed; human feeling merges with the inner pulse-beat of the weaving of nature and the weaving of the stars, towards the sound-etheric element in the heart of the world, towards a sounding, musical experience.

Nicht Hörnerschall	No hunting call
tönt so hold;	sounds so fair;
des Quelles sanft	I hear the soft
rieselnde Welle	murmuring streamlet
rauscht so wonnig daher	gently flow on its way.

Note in this passage, and already in an earlier one (where the violins, violas and cellos playing near the bridge enchant forth peculiar sounds) where distant horn-calls from Marke's hunting party really merge into the nocturnal noises of the rustling of the leaves and murmuring of the brook, above all this, sounds the soft sweetness of the soprano voice, the whole magic of Isolde ...

'The notes are not the music. The music lies between the notes,'

Steiner declares in *Eurythmy as Visible Singing*. 'What is the musical element? That which one does *not* hear.'[56] The musical element that is not heard by the outer ear, which lies between the notes, has to be listened for with the inner ear in such a passage as in Act II of *Tristan and Isolde*. Such passages are touchstones for being musical not just with the ear but the whole human nature ... And this musical element lying between the notes is precisely the sound-etheric element, the 'primary element' of music that is also its 'starry element'. Thus, especially with the music for *Tristan and Isolde* in a revealing manner, we have seen growing out of the secondary element of music, out of the wafting breath of the soul-element, the primary, the sound-ether element; we have experienced in 'wind and wave' the connection of the two elements; until finally we were able to follow the primary, the sound-etheric musical element lying between the notes of music, up to its purest, most sublime starry heights.

9. The trinity of instruments: strings, woodwind and brass in Wagner and in Bruckner

Barg im Busen
uns sich die Sonne,
leuchten lachend
Sterne der Wonne.

The sun concealed
itself in our bosom,
the stars of bliss
gleam with laughter.

This passage is [sung by Isolde] in the *Liebesnacht* duet [*Tristan and Isolde*, Act II, 2], where the profound, nocturnally dark, mysterious A♭-major is then followed expressively by the bright and light, elevated key of A-major; it then passes through modulation to the starry key of B♭-major. The harmony of the two voices, which in the opera of all times has always been the aim, is raised in this whole duet of *Tristan and Isolde* to the heights of Mystery-life and Mystery-consciousness. It speaks of a union of the two poles of the soul, which in the *Parsifal*-consciousness exists in inner unity. The transition from A♭-major to A-major reminds us of a similar transition in the 'Benedictus' in Bruckner's *Mass in F-minor* (before the transition into the Allegro), which transports us into a completely different cosmic atmosphere, conjuring before our [inner] eyes the splendour of the clouds and the angelic grace of Raphael's Sistine Madonna.

*

The whole section dedicated to the development of the soul-element in the music finally leads us with inner necessity to Bruckner [1824–1896], with whom the epoch of musical creation that began with Bach comes to its actual tremendous finale. Music, which was made available by Wagner for the music drama, is returned by Bruckner to the pure ['absolute'] musical element from which it derived from Bach; with Beethoven it had partly begun in a certain way to move away from it — Steiner also once emphasized this. In Bruckner's music we find everything that Wagner had achieved in expressive means — not only in the harmonic realm but also in instrumentation. Without Wagner [d. 1883] — whom he mourns in the consecrated C#-minor Adagio of his *Eighth Symphony* [1887, rev. 1890] with its ceremonial tuba sounds — Bruckner's music would be inconceivable. Those brazen sounds of the tenor and bass tubas were indeed freshly created by Wagner for *The Ring of the Nibelung* — only there did he use the tenor tubas, otherwise only the bass or contra-bass tuba — adding to the orchestral sound a ceremonial means of expression. The question of instrumentation, too, is not unimportant for the theme of these considerations; it could and should be looked at in much more detail. It could be shown how especially the changes in instrumentation correspond to the situation of changing consciousness of various times.

With Bach the organ still dominated as the instrument of the *original* element, the cosmic musical element of the 'cosmic sounding of the sea'. In the various epochs, the primary, cosmic element of music translates into the secondary earthly element; in partly ever-new ways the 'cosmic Imaginations' become musical instruments on the Earth. The orchestra, still secondary with Bach, is actually only with Wagner raised to its full means of expression. Only with Wagner, especially in *Tristan and Isolde*, is something of the 'cosmic sounding of the sea' taken up, which with Bach was entrusted to the organ. More clearly than with Mozart, or even with Beethoven, we experience with the Wagnerian orchestra how in the instrumental realm, too, the mystery of the 'threefold human being', as it is termed in anthroposophy, is expressed.[57]

Trinity of instruments[58]

This can be shown in the [mutual] relationship of the string instruments, woodwind and brass, to which the percussion are added as expression of the actual earthly element, the depths of the Earth. 'Music is the human being' is a phrase of Steiner's.[59] In the trinity of melody, harmony and rhythm, lives the human soul-trinity of thinking, the feelings and the will, of:

- the upper human being (thinking consciousness in the nerve-sense system);
- the middle human being (rhythmic system, breathing and heart-beat);

- the lower human being (the human being of will, the system of the digestion and the limbs).

Similarly, the trinity lives in the musical instruments. It is not only that in the string instruments the upper human being lives, in the wood-wind the middle human being, and in the brass the lower will-element, the earthly element—in a certain context, also for *Tristan and Isolde* the strings, too, express the rhythmic system very strongly in the orchestra—one cannot always take these things schematically.[60] People also speak of a trinity of starry forces, elemental forces, and earthly forces—but also within the individual instrumentations this triune arrangement can be found again.

To the [...?] string instruments, on the other hand, harps are added from above, by Wagner—and others—variously used as the expression of the super-earthly, heavenly, the pure etheric, as in the dissolving out of the physical with the 'magic fire' in *The Valkyrie*, with Brünhild's awakening in *Siegfried*, with Siegfried's death in *Twilight of the Gods*, with the endings of *Parsifal* and *Tristan and Isolde*, and with Brangäne's awakening call in Act II.

Already Schopenhauer [1788–1860] intuited how, between the various registers of the string instruments (violin, viola, cello and double bass), between the four voices: soprano, alto, tenor and bass in general, a relationship exists between the human, animal, vegetable and mineral realms. This exactly corresponds, translated into anthroposophical terms, to the human membering of 'I', astral body, etheric body and physical body, for:

- the physical body the human being shares with the minerals,
- the etheric (life) body with the plants,
- the astral (the feeling soul) with the animals, whereas
- the 'I', or ego (the self-consciousness in the soul) belongs to him alone.

This same division exists also with the woodwind (flutes, oboes, clarinets, and bassoon). Further differentiations exist. One thinks of the piccolo; the cor anglais (in *Tristan and Isolde* Wagner entrusts it with the 'mournful shepherd's tune', the *Urklage*, the primal lament of the human soul), that appears already in Beethoven's *Ninth Symphony* curiously connected with the contrabassoon; the bass clarinet, important with Wagner everywhere (think especially of the 'Prayer of Elisabeth' in *Tannhäuser*, and King Marke in Act II of *Tristan and Isolde*).

Wagner uses the contrabassoon for the first time in *Parsifal*, as the expressive means for the deepest challenges of the soul and Christ-challenges, for the 'subconscious', for the deeply moving experience of Christ in the depths of the human soul.[61]

Also with the *brass* instruments an important division governs, which once again leads to the threefold human being. In the heights we have the bright trumpets, the 'shining lights' of the Wagnerian orchestra, to which Wagner added the bass trumpet in *The Ring*, expressing in particular the Valkyrie element; the ceremonial trombones. As Mystery instruments they were already used by Mozart in *The Magic Flute*, similar to Beethoven in his *Ninth Symphony*, then by Wagner above all in *Tristan and Isolde* to express the 'Mystery of the cosmic night', the 'cosmic festival'. In the *The Ring of the Nibelung*, apart from the usual divisions of tenor and bass trombones, it is still a bass trombone (in *The Valkyrie*) with Siegfried in Act I, 3, in one passage that expresses deepest nocturnal darkness:

da bleicht die Blüte,	Then the blossom faded,
das Licht verlischt;	the light went out.

The same trumpets, the instrument of the 'call of the army' ... as outwardly, for example, in *Lohengrin*, he uses with spiritual purity, quite gently (pp), in *Tristan and Isolde* at the passage [II, 3]:

das bietet dir Tristan,	That is what Tristan offers you,
dahin geht er voran:	thither he will precede you.

In *The Ring* Wagner has entrusted the same trumpets especially with the Sword Motif; afterwards in the 'I' Motif, that already in the ending of *The Rhinegold*, as Wotan's thoughts, for the first time they blaze forth, then in *Twilight of the Gods* bursting forth in the Funeral Music at Siegfried's death in shining splendour.

The woodwind instruments (one may think of their characteristic use in the Prayer of Elisabeth [*Tannhäuser*] where they alone accompany the singing voice), are strongly related on the one hand to human inwardness, to that which in anthroposophy is called the middle, the rhythmic system (here the word 'rhythmic' does not mean rhythm in the musical element, but the life-rhythm), on the other hand to the 'elemental realm', to that which lives in the elements. Certainly, it can quite obviously be felt that:

- the flute corresponds to the element of fire,
- the oboe to the element of air (one may think of the '*wehender*

Seufzerodem, the wafting, sighing breath' of the cor anglais
related to the oboe at the 'mournful shepherd's tune' in *Tristan
and Isolde,*

- the clarinets to the element of water (this can be especially felt in
  the 'damp' sound of the bass clarinet, which in Wagner's *The
  Ring of the Nibelung* marks the depths of the waters of the Rhine),
- the bassoon would correspond to the element of earth.

Those possessing the 'fairytale consciousness' can take as a basis the
fourfold concept of fire beings [salamanders], sylphs, undines and then
gnomes to which the bassoon fits well. The whole membering corresponds to what was ascribed to the string instruments, yet the 'elemental' level as such is perceptible with the woodwind. The woodwind
instruments also coincide in a certain way with the fourfold concept:
'I' — soul-body — etheric body — physical body.

Brass

The brass instruments correspond in general, yet with many individual
differentiations, more to the lower element, the human being of will,
the strong earthly element. Only the *horns* that belong here are
inwardly related to the woodwind, that is to the 'rhythmic system', to
inwardness, especially, too, the elemental and romantic sphere. Thus
Wagner characteristically uses them in the music for the Rhine-
daughters. In *Tristan and Isolde* they are especially characteristic
sounding from the distance as 'horn calls' of the hunt, and again in Act
III, 1, with the blue flowering paths of the sea in Tristan's vision:

Wie sie selig,	as she sweetly,
hehr und milde	bravely and gently
wandelt durch	wanders across
des Meers Gefilde?	the watery plains?

If one can align the *trombones* to the middle, the 'rhythmical' human
being (in *Tristan and Isolde* they are at the same time the 'cosmic' [voice],
in *The Ring* the 'governing destiny', cf. Schiller's phrase, 'in thy breast
are thy stars of destiny'), then the *tubas* are the actual instruments of the
lower, earthly nature. But at the same time with their esoteric-spiritual
nature they form first with Wagner in *The Ring* an actual instrumental
choir. As expressions of the earthly element, they are at the same time
the main expression of moments of destiny, the core of the deep cer-

emonial mood, also the sinister mood, of the Earth's depths, of death, of the blood and of fire. (Of the fire-signal instruments, Wagner originally made certain tubas that he also designed. The bass tuba with the motif of the draught of death in *Tristan and Isolde* was already discussed above.)

The 'first angelic hierarchy', one can say using anthroposophical terms, are eloquent in Wagner — and then with Bruckner — in the *tubas*. They appear first in *The Rhinegold*, in the scenes with Alberich:

Nur wer der Minne	Only the man who forswears
Macht verssagt,	love's sway,

then with the shimmering magnificence of Valhalla, for the tenor tubas especially characteristic, with Nibelheim's nocturnal depths. Then they are heard in *The Valkyrie* with the appearance of Hunding, who appears like the fate of death before Siegmund, with:

heiliger Minne höchster Not	the highest need of sacred love

(the same motif as '*nur war der Minne Macht* — it was only the power of love . . .'). They then sound over almost the whole of Act II. (For *Tristan and Isolde*, Wagner did not award a single [tenor] tuba.) In a most expressive manner they appear as a destiny motif in Brünhilde's proclamation of death, then amongst other places, with Sieglinde's fantasizing of the burning house — in order then to disappear in Act III that lifts itself from the earthly element towards the heights (similarly the second half of the Siegfried Act), only the bass tuba (playing still at the end of the fire-magic) still marks the depths of the Earth. In *Siegfried* the tubas are especially the black elvish nature, the fifth element of the Nibelung and the dragon. Similarly in *Twilight of the Gods*, they are characteristic at the destiny mood of the scene with the Norns, at the blood-brother oath-making, at Siegfried's death (chorus of trombones and chorus of tubas in the Funeral Music festively alternating, later sounding together), and finally at the conflagration of Valhalla (the fire-element is especially characteristic of the tubas). All this can be followed in the question of threefold man, as an introduction to the theme 'Music is the human being' (Rudolf Steiner [in GA 278; see footnote 55]).

Bruckner, from whom we took out departure here, took over from Wagner his use of the tenor tuba besides the bass tuba, and especially the bass tuba. These instruments embodying spiritual earnestness with the great masters, possess with Bruckner the mood of destiny, also pointing towards death, especially in the dream-Adagio of the *Seventh Symphony*, as well as his *Ninth*, which Bruckner called 'Farewell to life'. The tubas are especially characteristic here in the final E-major ending of the third movement, where they give their element of warmth, of fire, to the horns in the key of E-major.[62] In the final sounding-out of the E-major chords, in particular the third [of the chord], the interval of the 'I' (more on this in the Appendix on the intervals [apparently unwritten]) is taken hold of by the festive tenor tuba, within the dark sonorous tuba still strangely bright, concluding the whole [symphony] in a super-earthly radiance.[63] This can be felt like the experience of the 'I' resting from the inner fire, the inner warmth, or — to speak in a picture from Strindberg's *The Dream Play* [1902] — the higher life, freeing itself [... *two words illegible*] out of the 'growing castle' (the human body).

The soul-element of music lived with Bach first as inwardness of the soul, as religious feeling, with Mozart already as a child-like, tender sigh of longing, and with Beethoven, besides the deep, often super-earthly longing that he could express so well, growing into a storm of passion. The soul-element, as the 'element of longing', then reaches its actual climax in Wagner's *Tristan and Isolde*. For this reason, we had to remain longer with this work.

Bruckner still standing within the musical epoch beginning with Bach, working with its methods — that is, in no way a modernist in the most modern sense — seeks to overcome this element of longing, this soul-element, at least as earthly soul-element. That is, not, as some super-modern [people], to erase it, but to lead it back again to the purely spiritual and religious heights of Bach's music, the music before the alienation of the human 'I'. He does this not to restore music to sound like Bach, but for music to take into itself everything that lies between, not least what is contained in Wagner's dramatic music. It leads this through a certain process of purification, just as in the instrumental realm it is no longer based on Bach's organ, but on the contrary, on the Wagnerian orchestra with all its percussion and tubas.

The element of the sea in Bach is not found in Bruckner's music — this is much rather contained in the music of *Tristan and Isolde* — but certainly Bruckner contains the element of the air that is in Bach. We find in it air-architecture, air-painting — Bruckner's music is a kingdom of colour, of colour experiences, much more drenched in colour compared to the sound of a symphony orchestra for Haydn and Beethoven. The problems that nevertheless are present in Bruckner's music are free from the element of human passion, which has woven through music since Beethoven. Bruckner's music appears to us as though standing over the elements of earthly passion and longing, and for this reason it is of such strong blessing and healing power.

But does not this element of passion and longing, from the Fall of man onwards (cf. here again Genesis 2:17), live in everyone? Was Bruckner an exception? In his musical being he was perhaps indeed such, similar to Bach. Yet it is especially interesting how in Bruckner this element of passion and longing, that somehow lives in *every* fully developed human soul, even if lurking in the unconscious, has, as it were, been dragged out of its hiding-place by Bruckner and called to battle, and has been overcome. This is achieved in his famous *Eighth Symphony*, also called the 'Michaelic Symphony' because a Michaelic struggle against the 'Dragon element' of earthly-human passion and longing is here fought out, struggling on to a victorious conclusion. The beginning—already the C-minor key shows here the passionate element in Beethoven (cf. the early *Piano Sonata*, 'The Pathétique', op. 13)—has been compared[64] to the picture of the dragon's influence concealed in the heights (the whole first movement, the entire symphony, is very imaginative). Not only the rearing-up of passion and longing but also its most intimate secrecies and matters of the heart are called upon; there exists a tender woodwind passage in the first movement, reminding us of Nietzsche's 'Midnight Song' and 'Midnight Episode' in the last section of his *Zarathustra* [1883]:

> *Ach, was gräbt noch der Wurm? Es naht, es naht die Stunde —*
> *— es brummt die Glocke, es schnarrt noch das Herz, es gräbt noch der Holzwurm, der Herzenswurm.*
> Ah, why does the worm still burrow? It is near, the hour is nigh —
> —the bell now booms, the heart is still rasping, the woodworm, heart's work still burrowing.[65]

Bruckner himself is meant to have said after the music died away, 'This is the clock of death; it ticks relentlessly, without giving way until everything is finished ...!' Before his eyes there also stood the motif of rest—longing—death. He recognized the powers of passion as the powers of death. The Michaelic element, in the sense of Christ, to overcome death, stood before his soul. The second movement brings the picture of the youthful, pure hero, untouched by the powers of the dragon, of the youthful Parsifal-nature. The third movement, 'the prayer of consecration before the battle',[66] the third battle and victory, the overcoming—already striven for by Beethoven—of the C-minor *Path[étique]* into a pure, clear C-major. What is otherwise unconscious in the human soul, Bruckner here has called up into consciousness and has overcome in consciousness. How he does this is significant for the whole line of musical development.

Yet perhaps still more important is what follows, how this *longing* that is overcome in its earthly appearance then comes once more to life as if from above, out of a higher element. This is the case in Bruckner's last, his *Ninth Symphony*. But here the whole tremendous motif of longing is present again as in a new transfiguration from above.

- Already the first movement has repeatedly brought echoes of *Tristan and Isolde*, sounds of the longing of *Tristan and Isolde*.
- The last, the great Adagio movement, beginning with the interval of a ninth of super-earthly longing, so characteristic with Beethoven, in the fading of the main motifs reminds us completely of the longing motif of *Tristan and Isolde*, weaving like the latter, only here [in Bruckner] lifted into the super-earthly spheres of longing of *Tristan and Isolde*.
- The ghostly middle movement (Scherzo) is based overall on the *Tristan*-chord (one only needs to transpose the beginning of the Prelude from A ['minor'] into D ['minor'] and it will be immediately recognized), which only in a somewhat changed position already forms the beginning and then (similar to another passage in Act III of *Tristan and Isolde*), passing on through many bars, lies over the whole, until in the Trio the stars lighting up in F#-major (the 'key of the threshold') hail new motifs.

The whole middle movement experienced pictorially reminds us very much of Albert Steffen's poem in *Wegzehrung*[67] ('Provisions for the way'):

> *Die Geisterscharen, die den Leib gebaut,*
> *und sich zurück zu ihrem Ursprung schwingen ...*
> [The chorus of spirits who have built the body
> and rush back to their origin,]

ending with the words:

> *Und es geschieht auf wunderbare Weise,*
> *dass leuchten und ertönen alle Sterne:*
> *der Tod des Christus hat dich neu geboren*
> [And it happens in a marvellous way,
> all the stars are shining and resounding:
> through Christ's death you are born anew.][68]

10. The Mystery of death in *Tristan and Isolde* and Bruckner's *Ninth Symphony*. The key of D-minor

Like *Tristan and Isolde*, Bruckner's *Ninth Symphony* completely plunges into the experience of death, the element of death, only with a difference. With *Tristan and Isolde* we stand as it were on *this* side, in the earthly realm, but in the mysterious depths of the Earth we hear the rushing torrents of the 'waters of death'. Moreover, in death we again feel the source of life, sensing the mysterious threshold it contains, behind which, when earthly sunlight has sunk, the stars of the spiritual world shine ... The longing, which is ignited there and unceasingly yearns and pines is actually the longing for death. Already in Act I, where Tristan and Isolde drink the 'draught of death', which then for them becomes the 'draught of love', this longing for death is actually present, and in Act II hardly anything else is mentioned [Act II, 1]:

Die Leuchte,	This light,
und wär sie meines Lebens Licht, –	were it the light of my life,
lachend	laughing,
sie zu löschen zag' ich nicht!	I do not hesitate to extinguish it.

(with this, the 'death motif' in the orchestra). The bright torch, the *Zünde*, the kindling fire that shines before Isolde's chamber, as a warning sign for Tristan, as long as the sound of the hunt nearby still announces danger, is actually in *Tristan and Isolde* a picture for the glaring, deceptive element of the 'day' and for the consciousness of the day, for the whole 'viewpoint' of the day, of this side of life. Consequently, the glaring 'motif of the day' with which Act II immediately begins is at the same time the motif of suffering in *Tristan and Isolde*, the *Tristan*-form of the archetypal motif of suffering running through all Wagner's operas. The connection with the motif of Christ's suffering and the Spear motif in *Parsifal* was pointed out in the author's study *The Parsifal=Christ=Experience in Wagner's Music Drama* (Anastasi 2015; Temple Lodge, forthcoming). The day, life, in *Tristan and Isolde* is the deceiving semblance; the night, death, the world of the consecrated stars is truth, the truthful, loving realm, the aim of longing [Act II, 2]:

Wer des Todes Nacht	Before him who has seen with love death's night,
liebend erschaut,	before him to whom she confided
wem sie ihr tief	her dark secret,
Geheimnis vertraut:	are scattered
des Tages Lügen,	the lies, the renown
Ruhm und Ehr',	and honour of Day,
Macht und Gewinn,	power and advantage
so schimmernd hehr,	shining and glorious,
wie eitler Staub der Sonnen	as the paltry dust
sind sie vor dem zersponnen!	caught in the sunbeam!
In des Tages eitlem Wähnen	Amid the vain fancy of Day
bleibt ihm ein einzig Sehnen –	he still harbours one desire –
das Sehnen hin	the yearning
zur heil'gen Nacht,	for sacred Night
wo urewig,	where, all-eternal,
einzig wahr	true alone,
Liebeswonne ihm lacht!	love's bliss smiles on him!
So stürben wir,	Thus would we die,
um ungetrennt,	that together –
ewig ewig,	ever one,
ohne End ...	without end

(with this in the orchestra, almost inaudibly softly, the deep whisper of the trombones and the tuba).

In Bruckner's *Ninth Symphony* the stage of consciousness is different. We stand already on the *other* side of death, looking not from the earthly element to death, to the threshold of death and its Mysteries, but from the beyond death back to the earthly, first to the corpse in the coffin, to the earthly element of death, to the rigid stony element of the grave itself, and the longing which is enkindled here in a certain way. But this has to be more closely explained. It has to be understood in a very sacred and sublime sense – the *longing* for the earthly element, the looking back on to the life that now lies completed in its holy significance before the spiritual gaze – the beholding of the future of the Earth, of the coming earthly lives ...

Initially, in the first D-minor, we stand in the world of the corpse, the world of decay, of the vault, before the rigid stony element of death and the grave. Already in Mozart's *Don Giovanni* the 'stony' key of D-minor expresses this. The 'stony visitor' in D-minor is actually nothing other than Death itself who calls away the soul given to passions, who now stands before the soul as the reverse side of the devouring fire of greed and passion. Also in Beethoven's *Ninth Symphony* there appears to us as the dark emptiness of a Saturnian realm, in which the Sun-filled life is not yet born, like the dark beholding of death of a budding world-becoming ... Something akin to a rigid primal rock — the mineral realm is indeed the exterior of death — lies in the key of D-minor. Chopin has probably encapsulated this in the most expressive manner in his D-minor *Prelude* that sounds as if brought up from depths of the primordial rock. Only once, in the middle, in D♭-major, does Chopin's poetic soul want to breathe life and soul into the primordial rock, until in the most wonderful augmented triad in the whole of music, here held for many bars, the soul dies ... This augmented triad can be felt as a primordial harmony magically honed into the depths of the rock, showing us here, as often in Wagner, that it is not only a transitional chord, but can also be fundamental harmony. The augmented triad may accordingly be related to the descending whole-tone scale. One will find a new access to 'atonal music', perhaps to cosmic atonal music.

The most tremendous D-minor, the actual climax of D-minor in musical composition, Bruckner achieved in his *Ninth Symphony*; in particular the astonishing, tremendous, towering D-minor ending of the first movement reveals the whole 'Father Majesty of Death' (the thought, 'death is the Father', Rudolf Steiner spoke[69] of at the end of *John's Gospel*, concerning the Farewell Discourses of Jesus). Here, too, there is a relationship to *Tristan and Isolde*, where in Act II the consecrated experience of the *Liebesnacht* is suddenly interrupted through the catastrophe, through the breaking in of the pursuers. In Marke and his followers actually death stands before Tristan — who indeed soon after receives from Melot the mortal wound — the key of D-minor appears, too, in the music with the death motif. It remains till the end of the Act, with short interruptions, where Tristan, not attending to the presence of 'day', once again calls up A♭-major, the consecration of the night, in his consciousness:

Dem Land das Tristan meint,	To that land of which Tristan spoke,
der Sonne Licht nicht scheint ...	where the sun's light does not shine ...

Earlier we met King Marke as bearer of the forces of the Father, and the motif that the *Father* is actually *death*, or *death* is the Father, is also not foreign to Wagner's poetic work *Tristan and Isolde*. In Act I [5], Isolde offering what she thinks is the poisonous drink — that they both stand before death — says with a bitter ironic twist:

Wir sind am Ziel,	We have arrived,
in kurzer Frist	in a short while
stehen wir vor König Marke.	we'll stand before King Marke.

(where, at the same time, in the music the death-motif sounds). Thus there also appears with the catastrophe in Act II the Marke motif in the rigid death-key of D-minor, the key which, after Tristan receives his wound, once more suddenly flares up bringing the Act to an end. With Wagner the dramatic element still dominates, which Bruckner in the tremendous ending of the first movement of his *Ninth Symphony*, then raises into the purely musical, symphonic element.

One can clearly feel how from the moment in Act II when Marke enters, a completely different element reigns in the music. One can say, hitherto everything was in the etheric element of the Son, and now suddenly everything is ruled by the Father-death element of the D-minor of Marke's motif. Right into the key the contrast of the beginning and ending of Act II is manifest: the beginning, the love magic of the summer night, in the loving starry key of Bb-major; the end in the rigid, stony D-minor of death. Act II is as if framed by two tremendous pillars, life and death. In relation to this Act, Wagner himself in his letters to Mathilda Wesendonck, uses a similar picture (original edition, p. 189).

Right into the libretto and music of *Tristan and Isolde* we could follow the motif of development: earthly desire—soul—longing—death. Death and what lies behind it, the 'realm of wonder of the night' with its starry mysteries, is here like an ending, a goal. With Bruckner, or rather especially only with Bruckner's *Ninth Symphony*, so related to the world of *Tristan and Isolde*, the matter is actually reversed. With the former we already stand in the world where everything appears reversed. Death is here the starting point, and the motif of development is now called: death—longing—life in the light—rebirth. This is the striking, tremendous thing about Bruckner, who in his earthly life and work, at least in the realm of music, can appear to us free from earthly passion and longing, as can only appear at the moment of death, looking back from death to the earthly life, seeing the greatest longings and conveying them in musical expression in *Tristan*-sounds and harmonies. Through Bruckner we experience something quite new about the sacred mystery of longing, something whereby *Tristan and Isolde* is not extinguished for us, but only becomes more meaningful and precious.

Rudolf Steiner speaks about this (especially the lecture-cycle, *The Inner Life of Man and Life between Death and Rebirth*. Vienna 9–14 April 1914. GA 153). In the world beyond the portal of death, in life between death and a new birth, a force of longing exists that shines over our now completed past, in such a way that only out of this longing a light shines into the future that creates in us the strength for a new life, a new earthly life in which we can continue what has remained incomplete in the previous earthly life. As longing in earthly life is the most passive strength, so, says Steiner (GA 153),[70] longing on the other side becomes an active, creative power. The most sublime, holy longing, the one in the sense of the plan of the divine creator spirits, now comes to the fore. Steiner also speaks how here on earth 'to be religious is a striving towards divinity, a looking towards divinity'. On the other side there exists, as it were, a religion of the gods, a looking towards the completion of the human being. A looking towards the sacredness of the human future can be felt with the same devotion as man on Earth towards the sacredness of what is divine. A turning point exists in the development of consciousness. Human consciousness and human existence in the moment of descent is able to take up in itself this vision of the future after the ascent. One of these turning points is connected to the Christ-events of the 'turning point of time'. To show this to humanity was Steiner's deed; to take it up into the recognizing, feeling and willing consciousness, to take it up into the will itself, remains the task of present and future humanity.

Something of this knowledge lives in the consciousness of great personalities such as Richard Wagner and Anton Bruckner and their artistic creations. Wagner's last music drama speaks most clearly of this, the 'sacred stage festival play' *Parsifal* and Bruckner's last symphonic work, his *Ninth Symphony*. But this is prepared in all the earlier works of the two masters, with Wagner especially in *Tristan and Isolde*, and with Bruckner in his *Eighth Symphony*. The impulse awakening in the soul, looking towards Christ's Deed of overcoming death, which in the sense of Genesis 2:7, changes the viewpoint given to man. The motif 'earthly desire – soul – longing – death' that changes into the viewpoint 'death – longing – life in the light – reincarnation' is called in anthroposophy the Christ-Impulse. An exhaustive explanation of this word is not imagined, for it cannot be exhausted through concepts. In Wagner's artistic output, this impulse was prepared; in that of Bruckner's output, especially in his last symphony, its existence can be felt.

It remains moving and significant how hereby in Bruckner's *Ninth*

Symphony something of the mood of longing of *Tristan and Isolde* — which Oswald Spengler[71] calls the great work of art of the nineteenth century — comes to life once more. But now the viewpoint is changed. The quintessence of that which in the soul-expression of music has been reached, is to end in the highest impulses of the human soul, in the Christ-Impulse. Human longing is not only that element that paralyzes and pulls down, and consequently has to be overcome. It is indeed also a high and sublime, a sacred longing. Without it the human being in the truest sense could not be human. This longing gives wings to the soul, towards all the ideals of a human future. They are 'the wings of the great Eagle' which were given to the Woman ['clothed with the Sun . . .'], in Chapter 12 of the Apocalypse; certain Isis-motifs appear in this, worked on by John the seer.

It remains to be seen how all this in the music of the future — or in the present that today partly still wants to exclude everything of the nature of soul — can be fashioned and will be fashioned. Much that exists today can be felt as earthly chaos and earthly darkness. But this passing through the darkness and the chaos of the present may be necessary for that which will come, for the gaining, or re-gaining, of the higher, starry element in music with new means of expression. Especially where chaos reigns in the earthly element is the ground for the working-in of the starry forces being created. This was known to the early alchemists and is shown afresh through anthroposophy (cf. the author's work on alchemy, *Alchemy: The Mystery of the Material World*, Chapter 3). That the Christ-Impulse, mentioned above, can be expressed in music, and can be expressed ever more clearly in the future, Rudolf Steiner mentions in *True and False Paths of Spiritual Investigation* (Torquay, 22 Aug. 1924. GA 243; see footnote 44) a matter to which we shall return [see Chapter 15].

11. Earthly and Cosmic Music. Strindberg's *The Dream Play*

After we have reached a certain ending in overviewing an important period of musical creation of the past, we recall how at the beginning of this summary two principles of music presented themselves.

- One is bound to the element of air, to the breath of air that communicates to the ear, as an *earthly* element, an earthly-sensory element of music;
- another lies between the musical sounds which can be laid hold of by the sense of hearing. This is a higher, supersensory, *cosmic* element of music that can only be laid hold of by the *total* human being who, more than merely a sensory being, is himself of cosmic, supersensory origin and being.

This cosmic, supersensory element of music we could also call in the anthroposophical sense the *sound-ether element of music*. And because everything etheric is basically a star-element, it can be called the *star-element*. This at the same time is the *spiritual* element in music. On the other hand, recalling Genesis 2:7, we found how the earthly, sensory element of music, is, at the same time, connected with the air-element, the *soul* element of music. This also carries the element of *longing*, the element of pain and suffering of music, the passionate element, the element of death. The *sigh* in music appeared to us as the observable connection between the breath of air and longing. Just this element of soul and longing of music, thus it appeared to us, could be that which a modern, contemporary music tries consciously or unconsciously to overcome. One day a true future music, today still lying in the future, will have found the means and the path to penetrate through this soul-element to the actual spiritual, to the cosmic, to the *star-element* of music.

Of this cosmic element of music, we also spoke of the billowing, surging sea of cosmic music — the etheric, too, is pictured in the 'etheric sea'. The other, the soul-element of music, connected to the breath of the air, could appear to us in the picture of the wind, of the sighing breath of longing, the storm-wind of passion, and so on. *Wind* and *wave* became discernible pictures for us to lay hold of the two elements of music, the earthly and the cosmic.

In *Bach's* music we found the *wave* dominating throughout the surging sea of cosmic music. The wind-element, the longing, beginning with *Mozart* as a gentle wafting air, as a tender child-like sigh, we then found already with *Beethoven* growing towards a *storm of passion*. A grandiose connection of the two elements of music, of wind *and* wave we experienced in *Wagner's Tristan and Isolde*.

The knowledge of the two elements of the musical element, discussed in anthroposophical writings and lectures, we saw, is already contained in *Novalis' Fragmente*. It has also found a wonderful poetic expression in a dramatist whose works are marked throughout with a richness of spiritual insights, better said, the soul-feelings of the world-secrets, with *August Strindberg* [1849–1912], in *The Dream Play* [1902].[72] In this whole exposition we seek to connect the musical element with the world-secrets. This connection cannot be expressed more splendidly, and at the same time artistically and poetically, than it appears in Act 3 of Strindberg's play, in the scene where the daughter of Indra and the poet meet on the beach in Fingal's Cave. Already the introductory remarks to the stage-set, 'music of the wind, music of the waves' refer pictorially to that motif in our observations which we recognized as the secret of the musical element — the relationship of earthly to cosmic music as the essential matter.

In the sea-cave itself we find secrets of the sound-ether and of the [shape of the] musical ear indicated. To the question of the poet:

> *The poet.* Where are you leading me?
> *The daughter.* Far away from the noise and lament of the children of man, to the utmost end of the ocean, to the cave that we name Indra's Ear because it is the place where the king of the heavens is said to listen to the complaints of the mortals.

And to the question of the poet, she answers again,

> *The daughter.* Do you see how this cave is built like a shell? Yes, you can see it. Do you know that *your ear, too, is built in the form of a shell?* You know it, but have not thought of it.

At first it may be pointed out from Indology, that *Indra* appears here in the name of the daughter as well as in the name of the sea-grotto — 'Indra's ear'. This again is thought of as a picture of the human ear. In the Indian language *Indra* is the lord of the etheric element, and in the first instance the sound-ether (as the sound-ether, *akasha*, for the Indian is the primary essential ether). The elements fire, earth, water and air are the carriers of the visible, the scent, the taste, the touch; the 'element ether', the 'fifth element' [quintessence], is the carrier of sound.

Indra's daughter, the being of the cosmic sound-ether, speaks to the poet of the sound-ether secrets in that grotto of the sea presented to us as the macrocosmic picture of the human ear and of its sound-etheric mysteries. She picks up a [spirally formed] shell from the beach:

> 'Have you not as a child held such a shell to your ear and listened – and heard the ripple of your heart-blood, the humming of your thoughts in the brain, the snapping of a thousand little worn-out threads in the tissues of your body? All that you hear in this small shell. Imagine then what may be heard in this larger one! ...'

The modern theorist of knowledge may be satisfied with how Strindberg remains here at the physiological phenomena at first. But this physiological view becomes a picture here for that etheric, sound-etheric element which we are exploring in that we hear in the shell held to our ear – however the sound may be physiologically explained – something like the sound of the sea. It is as if the sea, from which the sea-shell or sea-snail has been taken, itself sounds forth and echoes on.

An Indian *Upanishad* (Chandogya 3, 13, 7, 8) mentions how the etheric in the human being is experienced as a phenomenon of light, a phenomenon of warmth and of sound. It is that etheric [element] which, when it contains the highest secret of life, is called *brahman*. This means the hidden nature, the hidden word in which 'we live and weave and have our being', more exactly translated, 'become, pass away and breathe' (*tajjalān*, sounding 'taddshalan'):

> What shines as lights beyond the heavens, on the background of the universe, what at the same time is the light within the human being; what is his perception, that one is here in the body and feels in touching warmth and that one, *if one closes one's ears, one hears a sound, a noise like flaming fire.*[73]

This Indian description of what is heard, the noise in the external ear, or ear conch, points very much in the direction of Strindberg's description of the sound in the sea-shell, interesting to us in the way it is here connected to the secret of the etheric. For the early Indian, as well as the poet Strindberg, the sound in the outer ear is the direct picture of the essence of the sound-ether ...

The sounding of the sea-shell, which in its construction is compared to the shape of the outer ear, reminds us of the *music of the waves*, as Strindberg calls it, of the music of the sound of the sea. And in the sea-grotto 'Indra's ear', which in its construction again is like the sea-shell (sea-snail), likened to the outer ear ('snail' of the ear), there resounds with the music of the waves the *music of the wind,* which we took as the picture of the secondary, the air-element of music, as the music of the waves could appear to us as the picture of the primary sound-etheric element of music. And we recall how we found connected with this secondary, air-element of music, the element of the soul, of longing, of pain, or mourning. This again is expressed magnificently in Strindberg's *The Dream Play* where he allows to sound the *moaning and wailing of the winds* within this great sea-grotto, sea-snail, sea-shell (the second verse is quoted here).

> We, winds that wander,
> We, the air's offspring,
> Bear with us men's lament.
> Heard us you have
> During gloom-filled autumn nights,
> In chimneys and pipes,
> In key-holes and door cracks,
> When the rain wept on the roof:
> Heard us you have
> In the snow-clad pine woods
> Midst wintry gloom:
> Heard us you have,
> Crooning and moaning
> In ropes and rigging
> On the high-heaving sea.
> It was we, the winds,
> Offspring of the air,
> Who learned how to grieve
> Within human breasts
> Through which we passed —
> In sick-rooms, on battle-fields,
> But mostly where the new-born
> Whimpered and wailed
> At the pain of living.
> We, we, the winds,
> We are whining and whistling:
> Woe! Woe! Woe!

Strindberg allows the storm-wind to tell so expressively of the suffering of the earthly state, the pains and woes of the Earth. He lets us feel how in what exists in the element of air—and this also concerns everything musical — pain is expressed, an ingredient mixed into everything earthly.

[Following the above-quoted complaint of the winds in *The Dream Play*, the 'music of the waves', not quoted by Beckh:

The poet. It seems to me that I have already —
The daughter. Hush! Now the waves are singing.
Recites to subdued music:
It is we, we the waves,
that rock the winds
to rest.
Green cradling waves,
wet are we and salt.
Like flames of fire,
wet flames we are.
Quenching, burning,
cleansing, bathing,
generating, multiplying.
We, we the waves,
that rock the winds
to rest.][74]

Indra's daughter, who out of pure spheres of existence has descended into this earthly human realm, takes part in all these pains of the earthly-human realm. She takes part in it so much that she feels she is pulled away from her origin, that she can no longer find the inner connection. She feels completely pulled down to the earthly, and fettered to the elements of earth:

'My thoughts have lost their power of flight; there is clay on their wings — mire on their feet — and I myself — [*raising her arms*] I sink, I sink — Help me, father, Lord of the Heavens! [*Silence*] I can no longer hear his answer. *The ether no longer carries the sound from his lips to my ear's shell, the silvery thread has snapped — Woe is me, I am earthbound!*'

In these words a secret of the musical element is quite directly expressed, *the secret of the two elements of music*. The 'silver thread' is the secret, etheric connection which leads from the sensory, the earth-element of music towards the supersensory, to the cosmic, to the element of the stars in music. Already in the ancient Indian esotericism of the *Atharvaveda* we find similar pictures. To find again this 'silver thread', is the task of the spiritual path of knowledge. The musician today, too, will need this thread if he or she wants to find access into the higher, the cosmic realms, into the starry realms of music, the actual realm of musical creation ...

Many things are secretly woven into Strindberg's *The Dream Play* that speak especially about the musical element: the buoy that one sees floating on the ever stormy sea carries the form of lung and larynx ... the picture of the storm on the waters that we know from the gospel, which in music we know from Wagner's *Tristan and Isolde* that rises before us and with it the picture of Christ walking on the waves. This brings the people to whom this 'silver thread is ripped' once again into a screaming fear ... 'Wind' and 'wave' whose symbolic meaning we also tried to recognize for the problems of music, find in this picture of the One walking over the waves a higher synthesis that allows us to divine in what direction the great issues of the future of musical creation can one day be found ...

The 'complaint of the winds' in Strindberg's *The Dream Play* can remind us of many things we have met in the musical realm ... the 'groaning and whimpering in the sails and ropes on the wild billowing sea' can to us sound like the music of Wagner's *The Flying Dutchman*. For *The Dream Play* itself there exists a melodramatic accompanying music by [Emil Nikolaus] *Reznicek*,[75] often happily used for stage productions. Especially the musical accompaniment of the complaint of the winds is very expressive, hitting the right note to which the whole is inwardly attuned. But it seems to us as if we have already met this 'mood' in that *Prelude* by *Chopin*, which according its key-signature (or absence of key-signature) is in A-minor, in reality that unique almost atonal character, especially at the place where major thirds and minor thirds alternate characteristically. And this is also the place that reminds us mostly of Reznicek's music to the complaint of the winds. It has been suggested how Chopin's *Prelude* that is so revealing for all sorts of musical issues is historically connected with the dull sound of funeral bells carried on the winds ... The sounding together of human soul pain with that which lives and weaves in the element of air we can especially experience in Chopin's music. And Strindberg's *The Dream Play* shows us in expressively clear poetic pictures, in the 'music of the winds' in the 'complaint of the winds' the earthly element of music as its element of pain, of longing, of passion:

- in the 'music of the waves', especially where it mysteriously resounds out of the sea-shell, its super-earthly, cosmic element, its creative weaving in the sound-ether ...

12. Novalis. Nature and the Musical Element. *The Mastersingers.* Beethoven's *Pastoral Symphony*

At this point we have to interrupt our observations through an apparently reasonable, transitional question. Coming across this 'music of the wind', this 'music of the waves', we have to ask, does something like this really exist? May a music of the wind, a music of the waves really be spoken about, as it is expressed in *Tristan and Isolde*, concerning the connection of music at the beginning of Act II with the secret of the sunrise, with that which murmurs in all springs, rustles in all the leaves? Is it justified by a theory of knowledge? Does it correspond to the true essence of music?

Once again we link thereby, as already at the beginning of these observations, to the *Fragmente* of Novalis, which here in essential points—this can be shown in detail—most closely touches on that which Rudolf Steiner discusses in anthroposophical lectures on the essence of the musical element. One important *Fragmente* of Novalis (No. 1786 in ed. Kamnitzer. 571) runs:

> *Nirgends aber ist es auf-affallender, daß es nur der Geist ist, der die Gegenstände, die Veränderungen des Stoffes poetisiert, und daß das Schöne, der Gegenstand der Kunst, uns nicht gegeben wird oder in den Erscheinungen schon fertig liegt – als in der Musik. Alle Töne, die die Natur hervorbringt, sind rauh und geistlos – nur der musikalischen Seele dünkt oft das Rauschen des Waldes, der Gesang der Nachtigall, das Plätschern des Baches melodisch und bedeutsam. Der Musiker nimmt das Wesen seiner Kunst aus sich – auch nicht der leiseste Verdacht einer Nachahmung kann ihn treffen.*

> Nowhere, however, is it more noticeable that it is only the spirit that poetises objects, the changes of material, and that the most beautiful things, the objects of art, would not be given to us or would lie to all appearances already finished—otherwise than in music. All musical sounds that nature produces are raw and spiritless—only to the musical soul does the rustling of the forest, the song of the nightingale, the gurgling of the brook appear melodic and meaningful. The musician takes the essence of his art out of himself—he cannot be accused even on the slightest suspicion that he imitates.

Especially the last sentence, to which we shall return, is significant here, whereas the previous sentences, especially the one, 'all musical sounds that nature produces are rough and spiritless', can appear somewhat one-sided. Furthermore, the whistling of the wind, indeed the song of the nightingale, are denied as objectively musical. Have we not ourselves already experienced all this differently? However, here with such words of Novalis it is not different from the later anthroposophy: we may never remain one-sidedly fixed with the words of a single, lone sentence, but we have to connect it with others, supplement it with others, in order finally to come to that which is really intended. For all true anthroposophical work this active application of thinking is already a necessity — in the highest sense — for the correct understanding of the *Fragmente* of Novalis.

In another place Novalis himself has softened what appears to us in these sentences as one-sided (*Fragmente*, op. cit., p. 528, p. 209), where he says:

> The brook and un-ensouled nature speaks *for the greater part* prose, *only the wind is sometimes musical.*

This means, Novalis' cosmically deep, musical soul was not completely insensitive to the 'music of the winds', even if we simply want one-sidedly to tie him down to the words of his *Fragmente*. And concerning the 'song of the nightingale', he says in another place (p. 571), when he wants to show that painting, 'as it were, may be a stage nearer the sanctuary of the spirit than music': 'already the animals know and have music; but of painting they have no idea'. This sentence would be meaningless if the nightingale, and songsters in general — which must be meant here in the first instance — should be purely and simply denied possessing objective musicality. This means we have to make a more intimate effort to understand the meaning of those other sentences of his, here first quoted.

What they tell us is nothing other than the indisputable truth, also repeatedly emphasized by Dr Steiner in his lectures on music, that the object of the musical piece of art is in no way taken by the musician from the outer world. It is completely drawn out of the human inner world, that all the outer sounds only serve to reveal this inner content; these musical sounds do not want nor are able to imitate something given by nature. Indeed, the latter is valid for *any* true art. The painter, too, as a true artist does not only want to copy an outer nature picture, but in his art wants to reveal that which lies above and behind the mere sense-impression. He wants to let speak to us the spiritual, the supersensory element of things and beings, that which is more than the mere natural exterior. But in order to let it speak to us, he uses colours of which one could say that they exist in a certain way, are there for us in the outer world.

The same cannot be said of the musician and the musical piece of art, although musical sounds exist here and there in nature — we have frequently mentioned, for example, the wind, the wave, birdsong — which here and there seem to approach the musical element. This has still very little to do with earthly human music, with the essence of the musical piece of art, that one has to ask: if a musical piece of art had to listen for its object and content from those natural sounds, a musical revelation of the human being would never have come about. If the human being did not have song, singing, from the inner source of his own inner life, no birdsong would have taught him singing, would have taught him any musicality. But for the soul that carries in itself this musical element, feeling it is connected to the cosmic musical element, birdsong in spring can become the most wonderful inspiration. This is also what Walter Stolzing means in Act I, 3, of *The Mastersingers*, when he calls the songsters his teachers:

> *Wenn dann die Flur vom Frost befreit*
> *und wiederkehrt die Sommerszeit;*
> *was einst in langer Wintersnacht*
> *das alte Buch mir kundgemacht,*
> *das schallte laut in Waldes Pracht,*
> *das hört' ich hell erklingen:*
> *im Wald dort auf der Vogelweid'*
> *da lernt' ich auch das Singen.*

> When the meadow was free from frost
> and summertime returned,
> what previously in long winter nights
> the old book had told me
> now resounded loudly in the forests' splendour,
> I heard it ring out brightly:
> in the forest at Vogelweide
> I also learnt how to sing.

Then Beckmesser comes and takes this all externally.

> *Oho! Von Finken und Meisen*
> *lerntet ihr Meisterweisen?*
> *Das wird denn wohl auch darnach sein!*

Oho! from finches and titmice
you learnt the Master's melodies?
So your song will be in this vein?

And in his way he is also right: if the human being did not have the soul
of the song, the soul of the musical element in himself, then no birdsong
would teach him singing, just as little would any bubbling book, wind
soughing in the treetops, or howling storm.

> Only to the musical soul does the rustling of the forest, the whistling of
> the wind, the singing of the nightingale, the babbling of the brook often
> appear melodious and meaningful (Novalis).

> *Der Musiker nimmt das Wesen seiner Kunst aus sich — auch nicht der leiseste
> Verdacht von Nachahmung kann ihn treffen —* The musician takes the essence
> of his art out of himself — he cannot be accused even on the slightest
> suspicion that he imitates.

We will now no longer have a problem to accept this saying of Novalis
as an exact knowledge of the essence of the musical element. In this
sense Dr Steiner also emphasizes [lecture, Stuttgart, 7 March 1923. *The
Inner Nature of Music and the Nature of Tone*. GA 283. Spring Valley, New
York: Anthroposophic Press. 1983. p. 46. Tr. rev. A. S.] that:

> *das Musikalische eigentlich in der uns gegebenen physischen Welt nicht vor-
> handen ist. Es muß erst in diese gegebene physische Welt hineingeschaffen
> werden. —* The musical element is actually not to be found given to us in
> the physical world. It has first has to be created into this given physical
> world.

The classical example for this, how also the deep and true musician can
at least feel stimulated through the sounding in nature, through the
bubbling of the brook, the song of the birds, and so on, is Beethoven's
Pastoral Symphony in F-major. Not without meaning does he choose this
natural key, of which it is said that the natural sounds are somewhat in
tune with it (or with the connection of F with the chord of C). Perhaps
the accompanying words in their somewhat old-fashioned, clumsy
style recall a certain kind of 'programme music',[76] from which a
spiritual view of music, especially an anthroposophical view, with
justification always distances itself. In reality Beethoven's *Pastoral
Symphony* does *not* constitute such 'programme music' or 'tone painting', that is, not with music that somehow wants musically to express
the outer, sensory side of things.[77] It is concerned with listening into the
inner sound of the life of nature, the whole world that precisely har-

monizes so singularly only with the musical element in the human soul. Only in certain natural sounds — in the gurgling brook, in the sighing of the storm-wind, in the roar of the tempest, in the melodic song of the birds — it appears to distance the borders of the outer world, but always only so that the soul carrying the musical element in itself recreates in feeling these natural sounds. And for the musical soul it is not really a matter of becoming fixed on certain details of the programme of Beethoven's *Pastoral Symphony*, such as the peasants' dance interrupted by a storm. But the musical soul will in this storm be able to feel the moving musical expression of primal forces of existence and cosmic catastrophes.

The whole music of the beginning of Act II of Wagner's *Tristan and Isolde* in its singular captivating charm likewise does not have much to do with 'tone painting'. It, too, is an immediate listening into the sounding life of the whole of nature, which in the summer night, in the rustling of the leaves and gurgling of the brook, is audible to the musical soul. It is wonderful, right into the instrumentation, the way Wagner has expressed how and where the outer sound passes over into that which begins to sound within the human soul.

[*The next two paragraphs are the author's additions in the Ms.*]

Novalis expresses what is meant here with the following words from his *Fragmente*: '*Die Natur ist eine Äolsharfe, sie ist ein musikalisches Instrument, dessen Töne wieder Tasten höherer Saiten in uns sind* — Nature is an Æolian harp;[78] she is a musical instrument whose musical sounds are the keyboard keys of higher strings in us.'

In the lecture-course held in Penmaenmawr, Wales [*The Evolution of Consciousness.* 19–31 August 1923. GA 227], Rudolf Steiner explains how the early Mystery teaching of nocturnal experience, drawn out of the soul of the pupil, points out to him, 'in the night you live with your soul in the spiritual world, which lives in every spring, in every nightingale, in every flower'. This is also the world in which Wagner's *Tristan and Isolde*, especially the beginning of Act II, gains life in sound.

Beethoven's *Pastoral Symphony* is of interest to us where it turns to the governing mystery in the song of the birds. Even when what Novalis says is true, that only to the musical soul is the song of the nightingale really significant, the other [counter side] is nevertheless also true, that already an objective musical fact, a cosmic musical fact of the musical soul, meets us in it. Why does the song of the birds inspire, move us so mightily, why does it touch us so deeply? Because it really appears to us to emerge from the innermost heart of the world; because the otherwise hidden sounding life of the cosmos appears to have found access to our senses, to our souls.

Anthroposophy and other esoteric views on the world calls this sounding life of the world, which is carried on the waves of the sound-ether to our feeling souls, the *astral element* of the world. We know that the word 'astral' actually means 'starry'; the hidden life within the world and its feelings, is a starry life, because the cosmic indeed is precisely the starry world. This, though, is not the world of the stars calculated by astronomers according to the laws of physical reckoning, but the starry world experienced in its reality by the ether-body, the point when the astral of the world goes over into sounding life for the awakened organs of the soul. Access is opened for us to the musical mystery of the world, as to the cosmic mystery of the musical element. And nowhere amongst all the phenomena of the outer world are we so close to this musical mystery of the world, than when in spring, in the love-life of nature the singing-birds allow their melodic songs to sound. What sounds to us directly in the song of the birds is not earthly-human music, but *cosmic music*.

Novalis knew the experience of the etheric-astral world as the *roaring sea of cosmic music* — about which we spoke at the beginning. He knew that in sleep, in deep sleep, we unconsciously or half-consciously contact this sounding world, and he speaks about it in the poetic prose-work *The Novices of Sais*:

> Even sleep is nothing other than the high tide of that invisible ocean, and awakening but the commencement of its ebb. How many a human being stands on the brink of the heady flow and hears not the lullaby of these maternal waters; and enjoys not the enchanting play of their infinite undulations!

We know that with '*Wassern* — waters' he means the 'etheric primal waters'. Also the earlier characterized relationships of the watery element to the sound-ether seems to us to mean the same.

This ocean of cosmic music that murmurs around us during sleep is properly the world that, of course in varying degrees of consciousness, we enter through death, in the transition through the portal of death. We recognized this cosmic music, the sound-etheric, and the starry (astral) element which is revealed in it as the primary element of music, whereas that which is revealed in earthly sounds and through the earthly breath of air is the secondary, the earthly element of music.

We differentiated these two elements of music as spirit and soul, the cosmic starry element and the earthly element. Thereby we stand before the correct insight, that *the threshold to the spiritual world,* which we cross either in the transition through the portal of death, or while still here on the Earth in initiation, *is fundamentally also the threshold, which differentiates between the primary and the secondary element of the music.* And we understand now more clearly the relationship of music to the experience of death, concerning which we discussed at the beginning, especially with Mozart. We understand better those words that enlightened spirits have expressed in this direction concerning the essence of music that has engaged their own being.

And so we have the saying from the philosopher Schopenhauer (in the *Neue Paralipomena*), who in his innermost being was completely aligned to the sounding element of the world:

> My imagination plays (especially in music) with the thought that all human life and my own would only be dreams of an Eternal Spirit, bad and good dreams, and each death an awakening.

What interests us here is not so much the thought as such, but the fact that it was engendered in Schopenhauer through listening to music. Similar trains of thought directed Schopenhauer's mind to Mozart's *The Magic Flute* (*Neue Paralipomena*, p. 286):

> *The Magic Flute* is a symbolic piece, death will soon call me. It is the unknown guide who brought me into this life; I do not hesitate at his call: nothing calls me to hesitate; he is unknown to me, yet I follow with trust: he appears in *The Magic Flute* as the priest who brings the blindfold, which he places on the hero and the ones who hold out, before he leads them further. *The Magic Flute* is a symbolic piece.

Many things of the relationship of the musical element to the mystery-element, to the experience of initiation, to the mystery of the threshold, are in these words of Schopenhauer, or are divined between these words.

How much music connects us with the world of our origins, the world of our homeland, nobody has divined, known more deeply, than Novalis, who was so deeply touched by cosmic music. He consequently finds in music that which lies above all earthly differentiation, as it is inherent in speech:

> Concerning the general language of music. The spirit becomes free, indistinctly stimulated; this does the spirit good, whatever seems to it so familiar, so much to do with the homeland, it is for these short moments

in its Indian homeland, everything of love and goodness, future and past stirs in it, hope and longing. Our language in its beginnings was much more musical and gradually over time became prosaic and de-tonalized.

In the expression Novalis uses, 'Indian homeland' lives the imagination of the Indian primordial culture, in which the human being in post-Atlantean times still possessed the purest, the most inward connection of consciousness to the Paradisal world of his origin. When Novalis was dying, he asked his brother to play on the piano and fell asleep to the sound of music. Dr Steiner spoke impressively about this once [Dornach, 9 April 1921, in GA 271]; there he coined the phrase 'the entering of the poetic spirit of Novalis into his musical homeland', in the same way as Novalis himself speaks of the 'Indian homeland' in direct relationship to the musical element. Also the following are Rudolf Steiner's words, from an earlier lecture (Berlin, 12 Nov 1906, in GA 283. *The Inner Nature of Music* ... p. 21):

> Consequently, the intimate effect of music on the soul. Out of the most primordial kinship, in the most inwardly deep sense, sounds from the homeland sing into the soul. Out of its primal, real homeland, out of the spiritual world, the world of the homeland, sounds of music reach us, speaking to us comfortingly and encouragingly out of the surging melodies and harmonies.

Here, too, Steiner speaks of Schopenhauer's conception of the private [aspect] of music, because 'it stands higher to the heart of the world than any other art', whereas in anthroposophy, the other point of view is emphasized that the sense of sight is the foremost sense, and consequently painting is the foremost art.[79]

Still more clearly and more concretely Rudolf Steiner spoke in later lectures of the time after the [Great] War of the relationship of the musical relationship to the experience of death and to the experience of initiation. Thus we find in the lecture 'The Supersensible Origin of the Arts' [Dornach, 12 Sept. 1920. GA 271] the following, about the experience of music in passing through the portal of death:

> And it is the astral body, which already now lives in the world of musical sound that forms the world of musical sound in melody and harmony that we find in life in the outer, physical world, because what it experiences after death is already in our astral body ... This astral body contains the actual musical element ... When we now reach the stage after death when we lay aside our astral body, then we also put aside all that which reminds us of earthly life from the musical [aspect]. *But at this cosmic*

moment, *the musical element transforms*[80] *into the music of the spheres.* We become independent of what we experience as music in the air, and ascend into a musical element, which is the music of the spheres. For that which is here experienced as music in the air, this above is the music of the spheres, so that in music and poetry we have a foretaste of that which after death is our world.

If there exists for all this a sufficient clarity, or let us say, a divining imagination at least of the experience of initiation as that which carries into earthly experience in a certain way what otherwise is experienced — in various degrees of consciousness — in the passing through the portal of death, then we may gradually understand Rudolf Steiner's words [lecture, Dornach, 30 Dec. 1914, *Art as seen in the Light of Mystery Wisdom.* GA 275. London: Rudolf Steiner Press 1996, p. 60, rev. A. S.]:

> In the final analysis genuine music is essentially a developing drama of life taking its course in musical sounds, which are an external picture of what the soul consciously experiences in the life of initiation.

13. The Life of Initiation. Opera and the musical future. Novalis and the musical 'homeland'. Wagner and 'not music'. Opera and absolute music. Mystery backgrounds. *Tannhäuser*

With these words [quoted above] of Rudolf Steiner, especially interesting is the *element of soul*, the indication to what the *soul* experiences during initiation — which as such is indeed a *spiritual* event. The previous consideration has shown us how important the involvement of the soul-element is everywhere in music; also in passing the threshold towards the spirit, or in approaching this threshold, where the more earthly soul-element is overcome, that means, the soul is not consciously felt, for it is metamorphosed to a higher spiritual level. This was already shown to us in an impressive way in Bruckner's music, in the chapter dedicated to the music of the past. And also for the music of the future it could be that it does not find its actual climax where, as is the case in some music of the present day, it altogether excludes the element of soul, but where in achieving the truly higher element, the starry element of music, it also raises the soul-element on to a spiritual level divined by Rudolf Steiner and divined by Bruckner in his musical works.

Someone who wants to know, or to form a divining imagination how to think of 'what the soul consciously experiences during the life of initiation' should read Novalis. Already in the first chapter of the *Ofterdingen* novel, Novalis' poetic-musical soul develops these things in a wonderful picture, in Heinrich's dream of the blue flower. These pictures harmonize with later pictures, especially with the fascinating pictures in the chapter with the miners, and with the ending of the fragmentary novel the meeting with Cyane, the 'fulfilment' of the 'blue flower'.

In the same direction lies the narration of 'Rosebud and Hyacinth' in the prose-poem *The Novices of Sais*, which in all seeming graceful simplicity contains such Mystery-depths. Towards the end it is significant how the experience of a dreamlike, pictorial experience goes over into an experience of sound, until finally the connection is there with the presence of the divine, of Isis, who then merges so gracefully with

Rosebud. Here in splendid, colourful pictures Novalis has described nothing other than what in sober anthroposophical language is called the three stages of [higher cognitive] consciousness, of Imagination (picture experience), Inspiration and Intuition. What is here said of inner sound-experience, of experienced sounding harmonies, corresponds to the stage of Inspiration. The experience of the sounding cosmic harmony is in a higher sense *Inspiration*. The connection of this musical element with Inspiration is revealed here, although one has to be clear that earthly music can ever only be something of a substitute, a vehicle for the higher musical element.

It would be a noble task for the musician of the future to transform into music the pictorial world of Novalis, corresponding so gracefully to the soul-element of the life of initiation, to which we have pointed. Much has to be learned before this can be achieved; music will have to go through much chaos. It will be important for the musician of the future that one has gained at least some sort of provisional relationship to the life of initiation, to the path of initiation. The anthroposophical impulse for knowledge, as described by Rudolf Steiner in his book *Knowledge of the Higher Worlds: How is it Attained?* [GA 10] and elsewhere, will become fundamentally significant for musicians, for their whole musical creating. The musician, and precisely him- or herself, will have to come to terms with the stages of consciousness of Imagination, Inspiration and Intuition developed there. The life of dreams, the enlivening of the life of dreams, as Rudolf Steiner presents it in his book, will thereby gain for them a quite practical significance. The point where the picture-world of dreams [goes over] into the experience of inner sounding, the becoming conscious of that which in deep sleep is precisely slept through, the experience of the sounding cosmic harmony, will thereby be of particular importance. Musicians of the past have gently touched on this point, especially the 'romantics'; one thinks of Schumann's '*Traumes Wirren* — Dream Visions' [op. 12, no. 7, in F-major].

Musicians of the future will have to learn with much stronger forces of consciousness to approach these things. If at the same time they perceive in their own inner life, and in this perception can also understand the mysterious world that murmurs in the sea-shell, which Indra's daughter in Strindberg's *The Dream Play* wants to reveal to the poet; when one has a correct concept of the sound-etheric of music, of that which lies between the notes, then one will carry the music *over the threshold of the spiritual world*, and will then approach the actual future task of music. One will be able to convey the Mystery-experience, for which the consciousness of humanity today awaits with longing, to the consciousness of those people through music.

In the way he talks about these things in his lectures on music, Rudolf Steiner intends to point directly to a future development of music. But how very much music in its innermost nature really is aligned to this Mystery-experience is already shown from a glance at music of the past. One recalls the music of the Indians, the ancient Greeks, the church music of Bach and before Bach. The birth of opera is also absolutely to be brought into relationship here. It has been said, and Dr Steiner rightly emphasizes, that opera is precisely no longer 'pure music', because it makes music subservient to the drama. This pre-eminently applies to the music of Wagner, who in his music dramas (from *The Ring of the Nibelung* onwards) in this area pursued it to its final consequences. If any music is 'not music' in this sense it is Wagner's.[81] In a much more far-reaching manner Mozart, who in his manner did have a sense for dramatic music, for the nature of opera, still preserved the pure musical element within the dramatic style.

In more recent times we see something similar in Italian opera, with Verdi. And nevertheless one can feel that the experiment that Wagner took on with music had to come at one time, that in its innermost being, in the whole line of operatic development, indeed [such] music itself was logically founded, its course prepared. One would thereby not do Richard Wagner justice by not seeing how much he carried in himself that pure and profound musical element that becomes completely musical. In a certain sense he sacrifices it to the dramatic element, yet carried it in his inner being.

This [pure, 'absolute' music], even if it could not be known generally, we also see everywhere shining through his music-drama style. How much he himself envied Bach, that he was 'permitted' to write pure music! What climaxes in the sense of pure music are especially contained in the music of *Tristan and Isolde*! Wagner's 'not music', also taken purely musically, is often more interesting than the music of many other, even significant composers, who, remaining in the realm of pure, 'absolute music', yet have not avoided falling into the danger of appearing boring or without expression. Especially through deviating from 'pure music', through the tendency towards drama, certainly new realms have been opened up for music. One may also think especially what the music of Wagner means, for example, for the experience of the musical keys. Much more directly and convincing, the keys can speak of their innermost being, where this connection of the musical element exists with the drama, with the outer dramatic situation and the stage scenery. (This one can find here and there with Mozart, Weber, indeed with Verdi. One recalls the ending of *Aida* in G♭-major, the key of the Scales, the key of Venus-Urania.) When the starry mystery of the circle of keys will one day win recognition with musicians, the music of Wagner will be the first to render examples.[82]

Thereby, the Mystery-element, the starry element of the keys, can appear quite differently. How much the Mystery-element of music, especially through opera — whether one calls it 'not music' or whatever — is revealed through the element of dramatic music, shown — not mentioning Greek tragedy here — already by glancing at the earliest opera music, to Gluck and Mozart. The first great example, how the musical element expresses Mystery-content, of initiation mysteries, is Mozart's *The Magic Flute*, which was already mentioned, the opera to which Schopenhauer felt especially drawn. Also the deeply musical, and at the same time philosophical, Novalis often speaks in his *Fragmente*, as well as the beginning of the *Ofterdingen* novel, of opera in an exalted sense of the far future, which seems to contain much of what today we conceive as Mystery Drama.

Nevertheless, opera has not always escaped the danger, out of its own element of the fantastic and romantic, of falling into inartistic impropriety, indeed into the banal and showy. Already Mozart brought the purity of his light-filled musical sounds towards many coquettish operatic libretti. With this he shows on the one side how much in itself his music belongs to a higher element that hovers above the lower earthly, human element and can never really be drawn down into it. On the other hand, it intensifies in him the urge to connect music nevertheless with those contents which really belong to it. And so — even here making many compromises with the libretto — at the end of his life when Death himself already faced him as Initiator, as Priest of Initiation, he wrote *The Magic Flute*, the first truly highly significant mystery drama of the musical repertoire.[83]

In the ensuing development we see how the opera repeatedly wrestles itself from the lower fantastical, showy element, its constant danger, to approach the realm of the Mysteries. This is, for example, in a way today [1936] little known and valued, the case in Weber's *Freischütz*. Wagner knew and loved this opera, in which he found many seeds for his own creations, and worked them further both in music and drama.

The actual heights of the working-out of the Mystery-element in the musical element, are given us again in Wagner's music dramas. If anywhere, then here the music of the past helps us to recognize how it is inwardly directed towards this Mystery element; much according to its whole inner being music waits to become the expression of the Mystery of Initiation. This is already quite clearly shown in the early fairy-tale opera *Die Feen* [1834]. Musically still indebted to his fore-runners, Weber, Lortzing, indeed Mozart, yet it brings certain characteristic motifs of immortality, probations and crises, of the path of initiation. In *The Flying Dutchman*, especially the musical ending reminding us of *Tristan and Isolde*, is imbued with the Mystery element. The theme of redeeming love is beautifully worked out, the outer event can, to a strong degree, be felt as a picture of soul-destinies, for the storm of the human soul — similar to the later *Tristan and Isolde*, which is artistically far more significant — the sea-storm, the storm of the ocean, becomes a mighty picture. In the background stands the Indian picture of the suffering circle of births and the final redemption, Samsara and Nirvana.

Tannhäuser

Tannhäuser is already full of true Mystery motifs. In the centre stands the Mystery of Saint Elisabeth. Right into the musical element this is eloquently expressed. At the beginning of Act II Elisabeth is introduced in the key of May (G-major)[84] — even outwardly we are placed into this season. In Act III in the midst of the falling blossoms of the whole dying of nature, in the Michaelmas key of Gb-major, she passes over the threshold of the spiritual world, dies the sacrificial death — this is the spiritual fact hidden behind the Prayer of Elisabeth. There lies already in these two keys the Mystery of St Elizabeth as one Christened-through by Christ's love, which Mystery belongs to the key of the month of May, G-major, as well as the key of the Michaelmas season, F#-major — Gb-major.

Venus as the planet governing the sign of May (Bull ♉) as well as the Michaelmas-sign of the Scales (♎): in the one she is Venus, the May-Queen, the healing power of light; in the other *Venus-Urania*, the comforter and advocate in dying. Both are divine revelations, whereas Venus in the Venusberg is the daemonic counter-picture, the being of love entangled into the abysses of physical, sensual nature. The contrast, as Wagner presents it, is impressive. By appealing to the name of Elisabeth in Act III, the Venusberg rising once more before the spiritual eye of Tannhäuser disappears — as in Act I with the appeal to the name Mary. The Mystery of St Elisabeth is closely connected to that of Mary, as indeed in the New Testament, in Luke's Gospel, a close relationship exists between Mary, the mother of Jesus, and Elizabeth, the mother of John [the Baptist].

Thus in *Tannhäuser* Wagner gracefully and poetically links the motif of the Teutonic saga of Venus in the Venusberg (cf. the fairytale motif of Mother Holle)[85] with the Christian mystery of St Elisabeth. The whole matter is full of 'Mystery-motifs of transformation':

- initially the disappearance of the Venusberg, in place of which there appears the refreshing, healing influence of the spring landscape in the realm of the Wartburg;
- in Act II the love of Elisabeth, calming the moody storms, evoking grace;
- in Act III, through her sacrifice effecting complete transformation — the barren staff damned by the Pope bursts into fresh greenery.

Elisabeth's virginal-Christened, burgeoning power of love leads to the re-enlivening of the dying, dried up earthly existence. What poetically and musically lives in the 'Prayer of Elisabeth' is Imaginatively revealed in the picture of the greening, burgeoning staff. The miracle of the burgeoning staff in Wagner's *Tannhäuser* also stands inwardly connected to the 'miracle of the roses' of the legend of Elisabeth. Both touch closely on the 'Mystery of the Rosy Cross', for the first time in modern times placed before us by Goethe in his poetic fragment '*Die Geheimnisse*', then spiritually explained in modern terms by Rudolf Steiner in his book *Esoteric/Occult Science* [in Chapter 5].

Elisabeth's life itself falls during the time of the beginning of Rosicrucianism. By sacrificing her pure, burgeoning, virginal forces in an age of decadent, dried up human forces, also a dried-up Christianity, she creates the possibilities of a new, powerfully living Christianity, slowly prepared in the Mysteries of the Rosicrucians. Not the external, historic connections, but their Mystery backgrounds are reflected pictorially in Wagner's *Tannhäuser*; they find their corresponding expression in music, even into the choice of keys.

At the beginning of these considerations, what we called the *starry element* in music, its higher ether-element, which at the same time is a starry element, can be observed in Wagner for the first time in *Tann-häuser*, that is, also in the 'starry' use of the musical keys. The star of St Elisabeth is expressed, right into the choice of the corresponding key, right into the 'starry key' of B♭-major when the Evening Star becomes visible in the heavens.

The time will come when the organs will be created for this Mystery of the stars of music. The starry-mystery of music will open up for humanity especially in Wagner's music dramas.

14. Mystery contexts in Wagner. The Mystery of human life; prophecy, fulfilment and the future

In *Lohengrin* the Mystery hovers in the cosmic heights [Act III]:

> *In fernen Land, unnahbar euren Schritten*
> In the land beyond the realm of mortals

more in the background of the action, yet shining over everything, and from the first sound of the Prelude onwards this clearly imprints itself on the music. The strangely mysterious secret of the Grail motif in *Lohengrin* is found precisely through this characteristic of the cosmic heights, cosmic distances, through this background mood. This works right into the revelation of the key; nowhere in the whole music repertoire does A-major, the key of the highest, brightest heights, have this expression of the Mysteries, as in the Grail-motif of *Lohengrin*. In all its simplicity — 'too simple', some experts will say — we can call it the quintessence of A-major. In other places too, for example, also in the Prelude to *The Rhinegold*, we experience with Wagner how the basic qualities of the musical element express the mood of the Mysteries.

The Ring of the Nibelung

Thereby something characteristic is already said of *The Ring of the Nibelung*. More than anywhere else, also with Wagner himself, the musical element in its primal form is released, or as it were 'broken through', in this basic work of the new music drama. The contrary to 'pure music' appears here the strongest, still stronger than in *Tristan and Isolde*, *The Mastersingers*, and *Parsifal*. For this reason *The Ring of the Nibelung* is so interesting, so important for Wagner's actual musical style, not least in the realm of instrumentation. On the first of the four evenings we are taken through the elements of water, air, earth and fire (which in *The Valkyrie* is visible as the 'pulsing flames'),[86] which are gently incorporated. Each motif of the music is completely woven out of the individual element, from the first deep fundamental E♭ of the key of E♭-major that begins the Prelude, where in the depths of the River Rhine, the starry depths of the fundamental ground of things, the creative pulse of the primal waters comes musically to sound.

It is similar with the motifs of the 'earthly depths', of the flickering fire of the free beams of light, of the etheric ... The 'passing right through the elements' itself was among the primal motifs of the various paths of the Mysteries (compare, for the Egyptian Mysteries, the Temple Scene [Scene 8] in Dr Steiner's [fourth] Mystery Drama *The Soul's Awakening*). Connections with the pre-history of the Earth of mythical, primordial history ray forth into the still completely super-human Mystery events in *The Rhinegold*. In *The Valkyrie* for the first time we are taken to initial human concerns, but not yet to the historical human age, but the heroic epoch which, following the mythological age, precedes actual history. Mystery contexts of the pre-historical age of the gods still come into play here. The cosmic, primal guilt, that we saw begin in *The Rhinegold* in still super-human regions, begins to reach into the human region, finding its ending in *Twilight of the Gods*. In *The Valkyrie* we experience a deep impression of how the divine incarnates in Brünhilde, withdrawing from human consciousness. Through Wotan Brünhilde sinks into sleep, surrounded by the flaming wall of flickering flame only passable by the fearless initiate. This, in wonderful pictorial clarity, is the 'retreat of early clairvoyance', that is only to be attained again on the paths of initiation. It is the most beautiful of all fairytale pictures, in which Wagner here brings to life objective facts of the development of human history and human consciousness. Because this objective background of facts is there, the effect of the fairytale picture so strong, the border of the real spiritual Imagination can be touched. Through the manner in which the magic of the pictures is woven and enhanced by a strongly inspired music, eloquent right into the details, the impression of the Mystery quality is intensified to the magical level.

The initiate, who fearlessly passes through the fiery wall of flickering flame, the liminal area dividing the lower existence from the consciousness of the higher element of life, already pointed to in the ending of *The Valkyrie*, appears in Siegfried. *Siegfried*, the third evening of the *Ring*-Mystery, is throughout a Mystery drama, picturing Teutonic initiation to a higher degree than *The Valkyrie*.

Once again the Imaginative stage set, without any doubt points to the individual stages and transitional cases of the path of initiation, closely linked with the Inspirations of the music. On the last evening, in *Twilight of the Gods*, the actual tremendous Mystery mood still governs the Prelude, in order gradually to withdraw into the background in the face of the human drama. But also from this background it still governs the whole situation, until finally in the actual 'twilight of the gods' it forms the most tremendous climax. In the book, *Alchymy: The Mystery of the Material World* [Chapter II], we could speak, as it were, of a 'chymical motif' in the music of Act III of *Twilight of the Gods*. It could be shown, while already appearing at the beginning of *The Rhinegold* in the 'chymical motif' indicated in the gold of the Rhinegold glittering in the stream, it comes to life again in *Twilight of the Gods*, where 'the stormy uproar of chaotic darkness can appear to us as the musical expression of chymical processes. Finally, after the regaining of the Ring through the Rhine-daughters, in the motif of redemptive love the pure flow of gold wrests itself free' [cf. also the author's *The Language of Tonality*, p. 278. Anastasi 2015; Temple Lodge, forthcoming].

Tristan and Isolde

Much more than in *The Ring of the Nibelung* and in the earlier Wagner operas, the Mystery has entered directly into the music, has wedded itself to that work of Wagner's, which precisely because of its significance for the Mysteries of music we have frequently mentioned in these observations, that is, in *Tristan and Isolde*. We recall how we found here the two basic motifs of music, wind and wave: on the one side, the element of the soul and the air, on the other side, the spiritual sound-etheric, right into the poetic libretto. For the first time, we said, the music of *Tristan and Isolde* helps us experience in a tremendous manner the union of these two basic motifs.

Already with the first primal motif of longing, the actual 'Tristan-motif', can be taken as the union of these two elements. All the motifs of the becoming of the world and the passing of the world appear to be included as mysterious ingredients in this music of *Tristan and Isolde*:

- the wrath of the primordial depths,
- the magic of the Mother,
- the sea-storm of passion and longing,
- the deepest suffering,
- the highest desire,
- the wild poison,
- the healing balsam,
- the rigid death,
- the deepest love, which is the primal source of all cosmic magic — as has already been expressed by Novalis.

All the heights and depths which the soul lives through and suffers through in experiencing the Mysteries, awakens the soul to sounding life in this music.

Whereas in Act I, that which has to do with the sea, the waves, the storm at sea predominates; the music of Act II raises us into the starry heights. A starry dome of love arches over us; the expression of the music becomes completely starry, Uranian:

[Isolde:] *Barg im Busen*	The sun concealed
uns sich die Sonne,	itself in our bosom,
leuchten lachend	the stars of bliss
Sterne der Wonne.	gleam, laughing,

If the other Wagner music dramas can be allotted to the spiritual nature of the other planets,[87] *Tristan and Isolde* is aligned with the Uranian [influence]. Act II of *Tristan and Isolde*, moreover, in no way allows itself to be taken any more as 'dramatic non-music', but in the higher sense is absolutely symphonic. No longer some kind of specific individual Mystery, but here the cosmic Mystery itself begins to shine and sound. At the end of this Act, in the way everything is pulled down again into the depths of death, Wagner's ultimate truthfulness is revealed.

Wagner himself in his letters to Mathilde Wesendonck once spoke about how the love scene in Act II is held between two tremendous cosmic pillars or Mystery-pillars, in the same way that the feeling of the highest passion of love develops towards the deepest most trans-figured peace. One can also find both these 'Mystery pillars' in the construction of the whole Act:

- in the beginning the forces of love leading into existence poured out into the whole weaving of nature, into the whole magic of the summer night;
- at the end of the Act the whole horror, the rigidity of death.
- Love and death themselves in a tremendous way frame Act II of *Tristan and Isolde*;
- love at the beginning shines up aloft in the starry key of B♭-major, the same key in which the Evening Star shines in *Tann-häuser*;
- death at the end in the rigid, stony D-minor, which may be experienced so movingly also in Bruckner's *Ninth Symphony* as the key of the grave and of death. An inner connection exists between the fading out of Act II of *Tristan and Isolde*, and the fading of Bruckner's *Ninth Symphony*.

In Act III the sea takes us once again, now no longer as a picture of the cosmic surging sea, but the deepest earthly-human desolation, of the deepest pain of longing. After we experienced in Act II the ecstasy of the starry world, of the Mystery of the stars, and at the end are suddenly pulled down into the earthly element, we then experience in Act III the whole desolation and loneliness, the whole pain of this earthly element, which we find in the 'sad journey of hell' that finds its most complete expression in the Shepherd's tune played by the cor anglais, while the orchestra (which in *Tristan and Isolde* always expresses the cosmic harmony) is completely silent. All this take place in the earthly realm, whereas Tristan, wounded to death, lying on his sick-bed, lives spiritually in his fever still in the 'extensive realm of the cosmic night', into which Act II of *Tristan and Isolde* raised us.

In the friendly F-major, akin to nature, Kurvenal's homecoming motif sounds meanwhile gripping, reaching the heart. Then it breaks off in Eb-minor, the 'threshold key', meaning at the same time the 'threshold to the spiritual world', where Tristan's lonely consciousness, still hovering towards it, awakens. Act III of *Tristan and Isolde* also musically leads us through all the mysteries of pain and loneliness, and the passage:

Tristan: *Muss ich dich so verstehn,*   Tristan: Must I understand you thus,
du alte ernste Weise,   you ancient, solemn tune

is a climax also in the music — in the actual chromatic, atonal style of the music of *Tristan and Isolde* — until, in the 'walking on the waves' in the blue E-major new colours shine forth. The loneliness of the sea itself unites with the brightest of all visions, which as a Mystery-motif, can be taken as a premonition of the Christian element, of Christ walking on the waves (which also meets us in a scene in Strindberg's *The Dream Play* that is so revealing for many musical matters). The actual climax of the pain we saw in Isolde's death-lament, the highest, most painful revelation of the key of G-minor, with which already in *The Magic Flute* Mozart linked Pamina's lament.

The pain wrestled through to the last heights and depths then leads to the last transfiguration in Isolde's *Liebestod*, in which the transition [into it] still reveals a significant 'Mystery of transformation'. Once more, all the star-Mysteries live and shine out, up to which Act II of *Tristan and Isolde* has already led us. But now in Isolde's last transfiguration, this immediately connects with the earthly element, as something which takes part in this experience, indeed, communicating something of this experience of this shining to the Earth itself that also takes part in the experience. The key of B-major also speaks of this, in which the whole [music drama] finds its exalted close, the same key in which Wagner in *Parsifal* has achieved the Christian miracle of transformation of the *Karfreitagszauber*.

Parsifal

In *Parsifal*, Wagner's Mystery work finds its ending, in which he finally fashions the Christian Mystery, that is, the Mystery flowing from the Christ-Event into dramatic and musical form. Previously, apart from *The Ring of the Nibelung* (*Siegfried* and *Twilight of the Gods*), he completed *The Mastersingers*, in which the world of the Mysteries retreated from those of the purely human realm. But precisely still to work out this purely human and universally human realm, and still to struggle with the loneliness of *Tristan and Isolde*, full of human suffering, was a necessary preliminary stage for the great Mystery of humanity of *Parsifal*.

The Mastersingers

The Mastersingers does not have to do directly with the realm of the Mysteries, but with that of art, yet it draws its deeper inspiration from the background of the Mysteries. It appears most purely in the Quintet of Act III, which not without deep meaning is placed in the 'threshold key' of Gb-major. The 'threshold to the spirit-world' appears here as the threshold to the land of art, poetry, the homeland of everything which that transfigures and fills daily life with the shimmer of a higher life. The cosmic element is not missing here too, even if the human element stands in the foreground — the magic of the summer night, which in *Tristan and Isolde* frames the mystery of the stars of the cosmic night, shines and also sends its fragrance into the everyday world of *The Mastersingers of Nuremberg*: the musical element of this unique masterwork is penetrated and inspired by the scent of the lilac — or [should it be] jasmine? — of St John's Night [Midsummer Night]. And with the main characteristic passages, for example:

> *Der Flieder war's — Johannisnacht! —*   It was the lilac — Midsummer Eve!

we find again significantly the key of B-major, which speaks in *Tristan and Isolde* as well as in *Parsifal* of the transfiguration and transformation of the earthly element.

The Mystery of Human Life

The inner necessity and logical consequence with which, out of the presentation of pre-Christian Mysteries, the presentation of the Christian Mystery finally develops, makes the life's work of Richard Wagner particularly impressive. All the pre-Christian [Mysteries] carried in themselves the Christian [Mystery] like a seed, as their actual completion. If we follow Rudolf Steiner's presentation in this matter:

- [On the one hand] the Christ-Event was prophesied in the Hibernian Mysteries in the clearest manner. Despite the perceived spatial separation, later when the moment had arrived it was experienced as it happened precisely in its spiritual significance and effect. (And so, also with Wagner, with the inner relationship between *Tristan and Isolde* and *Parsifal*, about which he speaks in the Wesendonck letters.)
- On the other hand, through the Christ-Event, the Mystery-consciousness, which in the descent of humanity had gradually become lost, is freshly enlivened here, receiving a new direction. The descent, working from the past is followed by a new ascent, developing into the future.

Only in this way is the difference between the pre-Christian and the Christian Mystery basically to be understood: the Mystery and its history is something contained in itself, carrying the Christ-Event at its centre, out of its own inner dogma, its own teaching. The Mystery of Golgotha is also the actual central Event for the Mystery history of humanity.

The phenomenon, how this fact, completely independent of Wagner, is mirrored in Richard Wagner's life's work, can be felt as impressive. The Christian element in Wagner's *Parsifal* is not diminished because it had been preceded by the 'heathen', pre-Christian Mysteries, the Teutonic Mysteries in *The Ring,* and the Hibernian Mysteries in *Tristan and Isolde*. On the contrary, especially through these tremendous human and primal-Christian backgrounds embracing the primal Mysteries, the Christian element in *Parsifal* receives the esoteric

'Christianity of the Holy Spirit', that cosmically wide and cosmically embracing Mystery.

But things stand here in harmony. The Christian Mystery, because — as the future Mysteries — itself stands in its beginnings, and with Wagner possessing this character, appears as an indication towards a still greater distant future. Whereas especially *Tristan and Isolde* strongly awakens the impression of something closed and completed in itself, with *Parsifal* there exists far more the impression of something fragmentary, of a beginning pointing towards the future. Rudolf Steiner thought the same; in the last lecture of the Torquay lecture-cycle [Lecture 22 Aug. 1924, in *True and False Paths of Spiritual Investigation*, GA 243] he emphasizes that Wagner's *Parsifal*, regarding 'the conjuring in (*Hereinzaubern*) of the Christ-Impulse into the physical-sensory world [that] dissolves into a symbolistical [*sic*] indication — the Dove appears and such things'. This is based especially on examples in Act III, and for the final scenes of this Act it is especially shown in several aspects. Motifs exist in which Wagner clearly relies on his earlier fairytale music, rather like Goethe who at the end of his *Faust* draws on elements from church history. They, of course, face other motifs which already strongly possess a future character of music. Especially at the beginning of Act III, up to the *Karfreitagszauber*, this is clearly tangible. Never, not even by Bach, has this Christian esoteric element — and this is something other than church music — hitherto found such expression.

15. The Christian Mystery dramatized in music

[*The Ms of this chapter is the most difficult to decipher, rendering certain passages doubtful*—Tr. note.]

That the Christian Mystery has *really* finally emerged out of the presentation of the pre-Christian Mystery, is and remains the actual decisive element with Wagner's *Parsifal*. It shows how the history of the Mysteries possesses a significant parallel in the history of music.

The whole development of consciousness and the teaching of the consciousness of humanity is ultimately geared towards the Christian Mystery; the musical element, too, is geared towards expressing the Christian Mystery. Wagner as a single example is perhaps only to be seen as a precursor. If we did find in 'wind' and 'wave', as the two elemental principles, the polarity of the musical element, then the Christ-principle may be understood as that which produces the balance between the two. Certain pictures from the gospel, also referred to by [*page cut off*], pictures present themselves before the soul. *The musical element itself is geared towards presenting the Christ-Impulse*, even if in this regard the perfected presentation is still a concern of the future. In his lecture in *True and False Paths in Spiritual Investigation*[88] Rudolf Steiner said nothing otherwise, in the following sentences:

> The musical element is capable of placing before the world this Christ-Impulse in music, in formed, ensouled and spiritually permeated sounds. If music allows itself to be inspired by anthroposophical spiritual science, it will find the way in the purely artistic sphere to solve with feeling the riddle of how to bring to life symphonically in sound what lives as the Christ-Impulse in the universe and the Earth.

This passage is immediately preceded by another one, referring to Wagner's *Parsifal*, that here, in the element of music, that which actually constitutes the Christ-Impulse in the cosmos and in the Earth is not achieved. But in what follows it, there is expressed right into the tangible details of the musical intervals *how* consequently the Christ-Impulse will one day be expressed in music. As was already expressed in the earlier study *The Parsifal=Christ=Experience in Wagner's Music Drama*,[89] the sequence of intervals given by Dr Steiner is essentially none other than the one that can be found in the first main theme introducing *Parsifal*, in the Last-Supper theme. The Last-Supper theme in Wagner's *Parsifal*, the musical expression of the Christ-Impulse, of the divine love sacrificing itself into the earthly event, transforming the Earth, does clearly have something to do with what Dr Steiner imagined as the musical fashioning of this Impulse through the qualities of the intervals.

In 'the Holy Grail', in the Mystery of the earthly transformed Christ's blood which is again penetrated by the cosmic starry depths, all the Mystery-events of humanity are completed; every musical element can also be felt as the expression geared towards this motif. The beginnings can already be found in the music of Bach and pre-Bach — which Wagner did not merely take into his music, into his *Parsifal*. How much Wagner in the poetry and music of *Parsifal* approaches the expression of the mystery of the blood on Golgotha, Rudolf Steiner has recently mentioned in a lecture [?].[90] Already the Prelude to *Parsifal* helps us to recognize this expressively and clearly (more details in *The Parsifal=Christ=Experience*). And no longer as something arbitrary, but as something which is intensely connected with the being and the task of the musical element, we will now recognize of which already the notation ? and the ? purely musical element, when they have found their way towards 'music as expression', especially towards the Christ-Mystery, where Bach in his great Passion music, above all the *B-minor Mass* (similarly before him already Palestrina and others). Mozart, too, whose eternity we sought to honour in an earlier chapter, has created in his *Mass in C-minor* a work of highest significance with deep expressive power penetrating into the Christian Mystery. Nowhere perhaps is the purely musical element, that which follows the musical laws of expression, been brought into such a harmony with the depths of the Christian Mystery. Beethoven, too, the great symphonist, has expressed through powerful choruses in his great *Missa Solemnis*, in his way and his level of consciousness, the tremendous cosmic Mystery in the Christ-Mystery, as after him especially Bruckner in various Masses, especially the *Mass in F-minor* with the blessing-consecrated Benedictus.

We see how the great musicians of various epochs and directions of style all felt the pull towards the one great, main object of musical creation lying in the direction of the Christian Mystery: Bach, Mozart, Beethoven, and Bruckner — precisely those main names we met in our previous considerations we also find here. And examples could be found also in most recent times from musicians of most modern directions. Of the ones mentioned here, especially Beethoven's music helps us feel the strong pull towards the Mystery-element. How strongly it is expressed, for example, in the theme of the slow movement of the *'Kreutzer' Sonata* [for violin and piano, op. 47]! Especially in the late works, he is drawn towards this, in the last quartets, the last piano sonatas, especially op. 111, and in the last symphony. That even he, the symphonist, has felt inclined through the Mystery-aspect to leave the purely musical element is remarkable. Dr Steiner has also pointed to this aspect. It was not only Wagner who, for the sake of dramatizing the Mysteries, gives up the purely musical element, and yet we recognize that this musical element is geared again towards the dramatizing of these Mysteries. Thus the moment had to come when music as an expression of the Mystery drama had to be developed beyond the musical element. And the name Richard Wagner, without any doubt, means a landmark in these developments.

Amongst those works that express in the musical element the Mystery viewpoint, or yet certain aspects of it, symphonically in the almost-musical [category] there stands besides Beethoven's *Ninth Symphony* Bruckner's *Ninth Symphony*, which we have already discussed in these observations. Like Beethoven's, it stands in the key of D-minor, and is here worked out of the cosmic mysteries of this key, of the deepest depths of the Earth (besides these two works, Chopin's D-minor *Prelude* is a most genial example for the laying hold of the earthly Mystery of this key). With Bruckner this character of the key of D-minor comes still more to the fore than with Beethoven. Bruckner's *Ninth Symphony* stands before us as a ??-peaceful ending of a whole musical epoch. The previous eight symphonies can be felt, similar to the case of Beethoven, as a preparation for this closing Mystery-work.

It may be that all these presentations of the cosmic Mystery, the human Mystery, the Christ-Mystery, beginning with Bach's *Mass* and the *Passions*, up to Wagner's *Parsifal* and Bruckner's *Ninth Symphony*, are still future indications that one day quite a different musical style will be found, still far removed from the modern style today, in order to express the spiritual, cosmic Mystery in a new form that bears the future. Rudolf Steiner foretold many things in this direction. To give already concrete indications today concerning the *how* of this new musical style appears neither possible nor advisable. The reality of the future and the free creative initiation of the creating musician cannot be anticipated. The present observation that initially had to take its starting point from the earlier completed music of the past is of limited help, in the differentiation of the earthly element and the starry element of music, of the earthly and cosmic element, of the spiritual sound-etheric and the soul-element in the music to work out essential viewpoints of [?] the fashioning of the musical work of art of the future.

Appendix One

Hermann Beckh

The Mystery of The Night in Wagner and Novalis

(from Prof. Dr Hermann Beckh. *Indische Weisheit und Christentum*. Stuttgart: Urachhaus 1938. 132–140. Tr. A. S. 2014; Wagner's libretto for *Tristan and Isolde*, English singing version by Andrew Porter, and the tr. from www.wagner.net/libretti; Novalis quotations from *Hymns to the Night*, based on trs. by George MacDonald and Simon Elmer)

After the previous chapter on 'Nirvāṇa and the Mystery of the Night Sky in early India (Sāmavidhāna-Brāhmaṇa)', where this Indian consecration of the night was described like an Indian votive offering to the night, we suddenly find ourselves as if in the midst of that world Wagner (1813–83) portrays with unsurpassed eloquence in *Tristan and Isolde* [first performed 1865], not only poetically but at the same time in music. To the Eternal Feminine, as it spoke to the early Indian out of the depths of the night sky, besides the strange-sounding secrets of the life-ether in that Brahmaṇa text, there belongs the other secret of the sound-ether which is the carrier of cosmic music. And from the depths of this cosmic music, Wagner's *Tristan and Isolde* was received like no other work. In the music as in the poetry of this music drama, these Isis-like mysteries of the Eternal Feminine and the female Eternal Magic approach the feelings and experiences of the Nirvāṇa of Indian Buddhism.

We see this, for example, at the beginning of Act II where, despite all the warnings and pleas of the faithful Brangäne, Isolde extinguishes the torch. As a warning light, this is burning before the house in order to hold away from the lovers the danger of listeners and spies, as long as these are imminent.

Die Leuchte –	The torch here
Wär's meines Lebens Licht, –	Though it were my light of life,
Lachend	Laughing
Sie zu löschen zag' ich nicht.	I'll extinguish, come fair night!

This – in immediate pictures – is truly the exact meaning of the Indian word, Nirvāṇa, the picture of how the Indian has always beheld Nirvāṇa. In addition to this, in the woodwind in the orchestra is heard the strong accents of the motif of death into which there sounds the motif of the life of the night, the consecration of night, finding its climax in the previous passage:

Das Zeichen, Brangäne!	The signal, Brangäne!
O gieb das Zeichen!	Oh give the signal!
Lösche des Lichtes	Out with torch's
letzten Schein!	Final gleam!
Dass ganz sie sich neige,	Let night now enfold us;
winke der Nacht!	Call on the night.
Schon goss sie ihr Schweigen	For night pours her silence
durch Hain und Haus;	On grove and hall
schon füllt sie das Herz,	And night holds my heart
mit wonnigem Graus:	In rapturous thrall.
O lösche das Licht nun aus!	Extinguish the burning light,
Lösche den scheuchenden Schein!	End now the warning glare.
Lass' meinen Liebsten ein!	Ah bring my lover here!

An archetypal motif of Wagner's *Tristan and Isolde* can even remind us of the motif of the Indian Vedic Mitra-Varuṇa in the contrast of day and night. Both are completely taken in a spiritual sense; 'day' and 'night' become pictures of mysteries that can only be laid hold of in the depths of consciousness. There is, in the sense of the above-mentioned picture, the shrill, deceiving torch of the 'day'-consciousness. This harbours the source of all suffering, the deceiving torch that extinguishes a higher, stellar reality hidden in the depths of our consciousness, the mysterious 'realm of wonder of the night'. This we can divine if, with devotion, we sink spiritually into the depths of the nocturnal sky. Then the 'day' appears as that which is torturing, full of suffering and deceiving; the 'night' appears as deep, sublime, all-encompassing, healing, loving, comforting and redeeming. It appears as the higher and only true reality to which we belong with our deepest being, and already belonged before we entered through the portal of birth into earthly existence. The maternal, pre-birth world appears as a picture in *Tristan and Isolde*. That motherly, archetypal world, looking at us out of the depths of the night sky, beholds us and speaks to us out of the depths of the night sky.

In this sense at the end of Act II, Tristan tells Isolde how through Melot's betrayal the lover's destiny of death seems to be sealed:

Wohin nun Tristan scheidet,	To land where Tristan's bound for,
Willst du, Isold', ihm folgen?	Wilt thou Isolde follow?
Dem Land, das Tristan meint,	The land that Tristan means,
Der Sonne Licht nicht scheint:	Where sunlight casts no beams,

Es ist das dunkel	It is the sacred
Nächt'ge Land,	Realm of night
daraus die Mutter	From which my mother
mich entsandt',	Sent me forth.
als, den im Tode	I am conceived
sie empfange,	In death and darkness,
im Tod' sie liess	In death to languish,
an das Licht gelangen.	In light she left me.
Was, da sie mich gebar,	And the refuge on earth
Ihr Liebes-Berge war,	Of her who gave me birth,
das Wunderreich der Nacht,	The wondrous realm of night
aus der ich einst erwacht:	From which I came to light:
das bietet dir Tristan,	I offer now to thee
dahin geht er voran.	Yet I must go there first.
Ob sie ihm folge	So let Isolde
treu und hold,	Now declare
das sag' ihm nun Isold'.	If she will join me there.

Those conversant with Indian texts know how Nirvāṇa is frequently mentioned as a place where the Sun and Moon no longer shine, earthly light no longer illumines. Similarly in Act III, the words of Tristan, waking from his feverous fantasies, to Kurvenal:

Wo ich erwacht',	Where I awoke
Weilt' ich nicht;	Stayed I not:
doch wo ich weilte,	But where I wandered
das kann ich dir nicht sagen.	Ah, that I cannot tell you.
Die Sonne sah' ich nicht,	The sun I could not see
Noch sah' ich Land und Leute:	I saw no land nor people,
Doch was ich sah,	But what I saw,
Das kann ich dir nicht sagen.	That I can never tell you.
Ich war –	I was –
wo ich von je gewesen,	Where I have been forever
wohin auf je ich geh':	Where I must ever go:
im weiten Reich	The boundless realm
der Welten Nacht.	Of endless night,
Nur ein Wissen	And there we know
dort uns eigen:	One thing only:
göttlich ew'ges	Endless godlike
Ur-Vergessen!	All forgetting!

The significant Nirvāṇa motif of the stars, becoming visible only when the Sun of the day is extinguished, is experienced as an inner starry world. This sounds most beautifully in the love duet of Act II:

Barg im Busen	The Sun concealed
uns sich die Sonne,	concealed itself in our bosom,
leuchten lachend	the stars of bliss
Sterne der Wonne.	gleam, laughing.

The transition speaks especially eloquently from the deep, nightly dark in the key of A♭-major (the key of the *Liebesnacht*, the 'night of love', in *Tristan and Isolde*) to the bright, high A-major, then again from A-major to the starry key B♭-major (cf. H. Beckh, *The Language of Tonality*).

As the Sāmavidhāna-Brāhmaṇa, Wagner's *Tristan and Isolde* focuses on a 'consecration of the night', as in Act II:

O nun waren wir	Oh, were we but
Nachtgeweihte!	dedicated to Night!
Der tückische Tag,	The envious day,
der Neid bereite,	so keen and spiteful,
trennen konnt' uns sein Trug,	could part us with its tricks
doch nicht mehr täuschen sein Lug!	but no longer mislead us with guile.
Seine eitle Pracht,	its vain glory,
seinen prahlenden Schein	Its flaunting display
verlacht, wem die Nacht	are mocked by those to whom night
den Blick geweiht:	has granted sight.
seines flackernden Lichtes	The fleeting flashes
flüchtige Blitze	of its flickering light
blenden uns nicht mehr.	no longer dazzle us.
In des Tages eitlem Wähnen	Amid the vain fancy of Day
bleibt ihm ein einzig Sehnen,	he still harbours one desire—
das Sehnen hin	the yearning
zu heil'gen Nacht,	for sacred Night,
wo ur-ewig,	where, all eternal,
einzig wahr,	true alone,
Liebeswonne ihm lacht.	love's bliss smiles on him!

In the expression '*Nachtgeweihte*—dedicated to Night', that is, 'consecrated to the night', as well as in the whole mood flowing especially over Act II of *Tristan and Isolde* poetically and musically, Wagner touches closely and directly on one of the deepest examples of Christian poetry, with Novalis' *Hymns to the Night* [2]:

Heiliger Schlaf! Beglücke zu selten nicht der Nacht Geweihte
—Holy Sleep, gladden not too seldom in this earthly day-labour, the devoted servant of the Night.

What with Wagner has still a soft tinge towards Indian Buddhism appears with the early German Romantic poet Novalis (1772–1801)—

and this turning is highly significant — in the full light of Christianity. With Nirvāṇa we are dealing with more than a mere Indian Buddhist idea, or even 'speculation', as the scholar always suggests. Here we are dealing with real values and experiences of what is eternal and valid in Christianity, and especially there. This is something clearly recognized with Novalis. We also strongly perceive this breath of Eternity in *Tristan and Isolde*, especially in the music.

The *Hymns to the Night*, too, begins with the mystery of opposites, of the archetypal motif of day and night, with the *'Wundern des Lichtes* — the wonder of light'. Here we read:

> *Abwärts wend' ich mich zu der heiligen, unaussprechlichen, geheimnisvollen Nacht — fernab liegt die Welt*, etc.
> Aside I turn to the holy, unspeakable, mysterious Night. Afar lies the world, etc. [HN, 1]

We believe we perceive in the language itself — with Novalis all this already lies in his simple words, without the addition of an outer musical setting — we perceive the deep A♭-major of the music of *Tristan and Isolde*. Also the following [HN, 1] lies completely in this sphere:

> *Wie arm und kindisch dünkt mir das Licht mit seinen bunten Dingen, wie erfreulich und gesegnet des Tages Abschied!*
> How poor and childish a thing seems to me now the Light! how joyous and welcome the departure of the day!

This picture of the starry heavens, which is no longer an outer but an inner starry heaven, we also find in Novalis' nocturnal hymns [HN, 1].

> *Himmlischer als jene blitzenden Sterne in jenen Weiten dünken uns die unendlichen Augen, die Nacht in uns geöffnet. Weiter sehn sie als die blässesten jener zahllosen Heere, unbedürftig des Lichts, durchschauen sie die Tiefen eines liebenden Gemüts, was einen höhern Raum mit unsäglicher Wollust füllt.*
> More heavenly than those glittering stars we hold the eternal eyes which the Night hath opened within us. Farther they see than the palest of those countless hosts — needing no aid from the light, they penetrate the depths of a loving soul — that fills a loftier region with bliss ineffable.

The spatial world without, outer space, the starry spaces disappear, a spiritual, an 'inner space', appears at this point, about which Novalis also speaks elsewhere. A later passage of the same *Hymns* [5] is important, too; the picture of the starry heavens as seen today was not always seen like this. Human beings of far-earlier times with quite another, higher consciousness looked to the heavenly spaces in a pictorial and spiritual manner. The spiritual stars were still experienced ...

> *Unfreundlich blies ein kalter Nordwind über die erstarrte Flur, und die Wunderheimat verflog in den Äther, und des Himmels unendliche Fernen füllten mit leuchtenden Welten sich. Ins tiefere Heiligtum, in des Gemüts höhern Raum zog die Seele der Welt mit ihren Mächten, zu walten dort bis zum Anbruch des neuen Tags, der höhern Weltherrlichkeit.*
>
> A cold north wind blew unkindly over the rigid plain, and the rigid wonderland first froze, then evaporated into ether. The far depths of heaven filled with glowing worlds. Into the deeper sanctuary, into the more exalted region of feeling, the soul of the world retired with all its earthly powers, there to rule until the dawn should break of universal Glory.

In these last words, the actual Mystery of Christ is expressed most significantly, that is, in exactly the same sense in which Rudolf Steiner also explains it. Christ, who was beheld in earlier times still in the cosmos, and Whom Zarathustra still experienced in the Sun, has now connected Himself with the Earth in the Mystery of Golgotha, and from now on can be found deep in the soul. This experience is connected to the whole change of, and development in, the consciousness of humanity.

Let us return to the place where for the first time, in connection to 'the depths of a loving soul' the Mystery of the inner realm of the soul is mentioned as a 'higher realm': this is followed immediately by '*Preis der Weltkönigin, der hohen Verkünderin heiliger Welt, der Pflegerin seliger Liebe* — Glory to the Queen of the World, to the great prophet of the holier worlds, to the Guardian of blissful Love' [HN, 1]. At this place we meet the deepest motive, most significant for the further development of the Nirvāṇa-motive into Christianity. The quality of Isis, the Mystery of the Night, the 'consecration to the night' that also sounds so strangely in the Indian Sāmavidhāna-brāhmaṇa, we meet again in *Tristan and Isolde*. The name *Isolde* (Ishild, Eisholde) is connected to Isis and the Isis Mysteries of the ice-crystal, of the cold, 'virginal' light [H. Beckh. *From the World of the Mysteries*, Temple Lodge, forthcoming. Germ. ed. 71, 134]. With Novalis we find the quality of Isis further developed into the Christian quality of Mary, in such a way that we clearly recognize that we are dealing here with the light of Eternity, with that same being, who in Christianity is experienced only on a new level of consciousness, on the level of the 'I'. Novalis also experienced that Isis-quality, expressing maternal warmth, in the depth of the nocturnal, starry heavens in his *Hymns to the Night* [4].

Trägt nicht alles, was uns begeistert, die Farbe der Nacht – sie trägt dich müt-
terlich, und ihr verdankst du all deine Herrlichkeit. Du verflögest in dir selbst, ins
endlose, Raum zergingest du, wenn sie dich nicht hielte – dich nicht bände, dass
du warm würdest und flammend die Welt zeugtest. Wahrlich, Ich war, eh' du
warst, mit meinem Geschlecht schickte die Mutter mich, zu bewohnen deine Welt
und zu heiligen sie mit Liebe, zu geben menschlichen Sinn deinen Schöpfungen
'...Wahrlich, Ich war, eh' du warst' –
Does not everything that inspires us bear the colour of the night? She carries you, mother-like, and all your magnificence you owe to her. You would vanish into yourself – dissolve into boundless space – if she did not hold you, bind you tight, until you grew warm and in a sudden burst of flame begot the world. *Truly, I was before you were* – my Mother sent me with my brothers and sisters to inhabit your world, to hallow it with love so that it might become a monument to gaze at forever and plant it with the unfading flowers of your divine thoughts ... *Truly, I was there before you.*

Wondrously strange, these words of the archetypal Mother, Night, allow us to recognize that Mystery of the 'I' which is hidden in the night, which at the same time is the Christian Mystery. For the early Egyptians too, Isis was the one speaking maternally out of the depths of the nocturnal, starry heavens, the Ruler of Love, the Giver of Life and the Fashioner of Matter; at the same time, the Awakener of Consciousness, the Awakener of the 'I', whose full realization we then find in Christianity. In the picture in the Apocalypse, the Book of Revelation, of the Virgin in the Heavens who gives birth to the Son, the Child of the Sun, all these connections are profoundly indicated (Rev. 12).

In a great Address to Mary, the heavenly Queen, the *Hymns to the Night* concludes, which ultimately is given completely to the description of the Christian mystery and the Christ-Event. In the songs to Mary [*Geistliche Lieder*, 1802, XV], Novalis connected most inner heavenly experiences with Mary:

Ich sehe dich in tausend Bildern,	I see you in a thousand pictures,
Maria, lieblich ausgedrückt,	Portraying you, lovely Maria,
Doch keins von allen kann dich schildern,	But none of all can depict
Wie meine Seele dich erblickt.	How my soul sees you.
Ich weiss nur, dass der Welt Getümmel	I only know that the turmoil of the world

Seitdem mir wie ein Traum verweht,	Since then blows away like a dream
Und ein unnennbar süßer Himmel	And an indescribably sweet heaven
Mir ewig im Gemüte steht.	Remains forever in my heart.

Once again we hear at this point the critical objections of the Indologist asking what all this, especially the quotations from Novalis, has to do with the question of the Indian Nirvāṇa. He cannot imagine that it could also have a Christian aspect, that it could extend into Christianity. Just this here shows how the 'Mystery of the Night' presented in Novalis' *Hymns* carries in the most complete manner (to put it simply) the exact definition of the Indian Nirvāṇa. We have indeed heard what is essential with Nirvāṇa is the tearing to shreds of the fetters of existence, the dissolving of the bands of longing and desire binding the soul to repeated incarnation. Also the 'dissolving of the knots of the heart' is in this sense much discussed in Indian thought. In the same way in Novalis, even in the same words, the one who is now lonely describes in that passage that has remained prose in the *Hymns to the Night* — it forms almost their poetic climax — his experience of the night:

> *Einst, da ich bittre Tränen vergoss, da in Schmerz aufgelöst meine Hoffnung zerrann und ich einsam stand an dem dürren Hügel, der in engem, dunkeln Raum die Gestalt meines Lebens begrub einsam, wie noch kein Einsamer war . . . das kam aus blauen Fernen, von den Höhen meiner alten Seligkeit ein Dämmerungsschauer — und mit einem Male riss das Band der Geburt, des Lichtes Fessel — hin floh die irdische Herrlichkeit, und meine Trauer mit ihr. Zusammen floss die Wehmut in eine neue, unergründliche Welt — du Nachtbegeisterung, Schlummer des Himmels, kamst über mich . . .*

> Once, when I was shedding bitter tears, when I was distraught with suffering and all my hope had vanished, I stood alone by the barren mound which buried in its cramped, dark walls the figure of my life (Novalis is thinking here of his destiny so deeply determined by the death of Sophie [Sophie von Kühn, 1782–97, betrothed to Novalis, died of tuberculosis]), alone, as no man has been alone before, . . . — out of the blue distance, from the heights of my old salvation, there came a twilight shudder, and all at once the bond of my birth — the chain of light — was ripped. All earthly splendour flew away and with it my mourning — melancholy flowed into a new, unfathomed world — and you — inspiration of the night, the slumber of the heavens — came over me . . .

'Das riss das Band der Geburt — *the bond of my birth was ripped.*' This is after all what we have already heard about it, truly the most exact of all possible definitions in words of the Indian Nirvāṇa, and at the same time the most genially poetic expression. And the Christian-Johannine soul of Novalis receives this Nirvāṇa-experience at the same time as a Christian experience. The soul experiences this ripping apart of the fetters of birth like a standing above life while in its midst, being connected in love with everything earthly when no longing or desire is the driving force. As the Indian Buddhist looks from the Nirvāṇa that can already be experienced in the earthly realm towards the great Parinirvāṇa that can only be experienced in death, Novalis [HN, 4] also looks towards dying, but again, with a Christian feeling, characteristic for him:

Nun weiss ich, wenn der letzte Morgen sein wird – wenn das Licht nicht mehr die Nacht und die Liebe scheucht, wenn der Schlummer ewig und nur ein unerschöpflicher Traum sein wird. Himmlische Müdigkeit verlässt mich nun nicht wieder. Weit und mühsam war der Weg zum heiligen Grabe, und das Kreuz war schwer. Wessen Mund einmal die kristallene Woge netzte, die, gemeinen Sinnen unsichtbar, quillt in des Hügels dunklem Schoss, an dessen Fuss die irdische Flut bricht, wer oben stand auf diesem Grenzgebürge der Welt und hinübersah in das neue Land, in der Nacht Wohnsitz: wahrlich, der kehrt nicht in das Treiben der Welt zurück, in das Land, wo das Licht regiert und ewige Unruh haust.

Oben baut er sich Hütten, Hütten des Friedens, sehnt sich und liebt, schaut hinüber, bis die willkommenste aller Stunden hinunter ihn in den Brunnen der Quelle zieht. Alles Irdische schwimmt obenauf und wird von der Höhe hinabgespült, aber was heilig ward durch der Liebe Berührung, rinnt aufgelöst in verborgenen Gängen auf des jenseitige Gebiet, wo es, wie Wolken, sich mit entschlummerten Lieben mischt.

Now I know when the final morning will dawn — when night and love will no longer be afraid of the light — when sleep will last forever and be one unbroken dream. A heavenly weariness grows within me. Long and tiring was my pilgrimage to this holy grave and the cross weighs heavy upon me. Imperceptible to the common senses, the crystal wave wells up in the dark bosom of the mound at whose foot the earthly tide ebbs; he who stood above it, who has stood at the threshold Mount of this world and looked across into the new land, into *the dwelling of the night* — truly, he will never return to the labours of the world, to the land where the light is housed in ceaseless unrest.

On its heights he builds huts — huts of peace — with longing and love, and gazes across until the welcome hours draw him down to the source of the spring; then all earthly things float aloft, and are washed down from the bordering heights; but what was made holy by the touch of love flows, freely dissolved through hidden channels into the land beyond where, like clouds, it mingles with love falling asleep.

With all its depth of Christian feeling, many things also remind us of Indian pictures and ways of expression, especially the 'crystal clear wave', of the 'crystal clear mountain lake' which we shall meet with the Buddha in the pictorial expression of Nirvāṇa. Like a word-for-word translation of 'Nirvāṇa', the nocturnal *Hymns* [4] appear to us with the passage:

> *Einst zeigt deine Uhr das Ende der Zeit, wenn du wirst wie unsereiner und voll Sehnsucht* auslöschst *und stirbst.*
> — One day your clock will point to the end of Time, and then you shall be as one of us, and, full of ardent longing, shall be *extinguished* and die.

We may also be reminded of the '*Verwehen* — 'blowing away' (Nirvāṇa) of the tumult of the world' (Nirvāṇa = blowing/ drifting away of the world) in that song to Maria by Novalis, with which we may conclude:

> I only know that the turmoil of the world
> Since then blows away like a dream
> And an indescribably sweet heaven
> Remains forever in my heart.

Appendix Two

August Pauli

Memories of Hermann Beckh

My personal memories of our departed friend Professor Beckh begin with the Conference organized for Easter 1922 in Nuremberg to prepare for The Christian Community, which had not yet been founded. There I saw some of my later colleagues for the first time, including Prof. Beckh, who had agreed to give some lectures. I have forgotten the content; the immediate impression they made has remained — the streaming, hardly stoppable abundance of ideas, mostly new to me at that time, from the riches of his well-stocked knowledge that flowed over his audience. To lay hold of the details was only possible to a minimal extent, but the warmth, strength and fullness of the speech worked through itself.

I then saw Professor Beckh again in the summer of the same year [1922], as we assembled for the immediate preparations for the founding [of The Christian Community] in Breitbrunn on Ammersee, meeting to confer in the memorable cattle shed on the shores of the Lake. There one evening in Breitbrunn he told us for the first time of the discoveries he had made on the essence of the musical keys. For many it was a 'speaking in tongues'. People today experience a dismembered world whose separate bits and aspects have nothing to do with each other. The very concern with it divides and splits people. But here a relationship was presented and a highly surprising but thoroughly illuminating correspondence between things most people hitherto would not link together in that sense — the keys and the constellations. One felt that just on the periphery of appearances the world is dismembered. One had to penetrate from this periphery to the centre, to the spirit streaming out on all sides, in order to experience the world as one.

During the following winter I saw Prof. Beckh again in Munich. We sat with a group of friends one afternoon drinking coffee, and Prof. Beckh, who was speaking in a lively fashion, leant over to the side from time to time to scribble down something or other, as we have often seen him do when during a lecture some new thought or other came to him that he wanted to record, which he, without breaking the flow of his speech, quickly wrote down in a notebook. On another day it was revealed what Beckh had noted down that afternoon at coffee time. He had celebrated the Service and read the gospel, the first chapter of the Apocalypse, in a translation which streamed to him during that discussion. It was the first attempt in our circles to translate [this text], and I could only wonder at the might of speech revealing itself. It was able to shine from within with a brilliance illuminating world-depths, relighting the already paling concepts and expressions in Luther's translation.

On these occasions, looking from different sides at what met us, it came to me for the first time what Prof. Beckh's special gifts were and what gave a special note to his influence in The Christian Community, indeed what allowed him in his way to be unique. We heard him in all the ensuing years frequently speak on such things in Munich. Professor Beckh especially liked to come to Munich. He loved this city, in which in his day in the Maximilianeum, which only accepted specially gifted students, he graduated from his studies in law. The friendly atmosphere of Munich was especially agreeable; the assembled audience, eager to hear him, loosed his tongue and awoke all the sleeping forces of thinking. Here he unfolded his whole enthusiasm, which he could do, so that he very often didn't notice how the evening had advanced, and also didn't see the watch that we held towards him, when the lecture even at 10.30 or 10.45 still didn't want to come to an end.

Thus he spoke once for a whole week on his star-theme to an audience packed into the rooms of a private flat. His enthusiasm took his audience so strongly with him that they hardly felt the almost unbearable rising heat of the summer. The time will come when Beckh's 'Christened' star-knowledge, which signifies a basic overturning of today's decadent astrology, will be appreciated for its significance. Frequently and with ever-fresh joy, he attempted to supplement and illuminate unassisted on the piano what he had to say on the spiritual content of Wagner's works. He had discovered things that in this way probably no other living person had discovered and could record. Certainly, very much of what he presented may have passed not understood and was not retained, and yet everyone gained something. What he said didn't so much depend on the details. By speaking, he tuned the strings of spirituality in the soul, causing them to sound; he rehearsed his audience in a listening into a spiritual observation of the themes, and this rehearsing was what was essential and fruitful.

Die Christengemeinschaft, 15. Jahrgang, 12. März 1939. 331f.

A Memory of Hermann Beckh

Harro Rückner

On the occasion of the new edition [Urachhaus, 1960] of
Der Hingang des Vollendeten and *Der Hymnus an die Erde*

It was 1925. On the Dornach hill, in a truly paradisal garden full of trees, a group of mostly young theologians gathered. Seeing them sitting there on the grass in the Paryanka position, holding themselves upright with effort, the older ones using apple trees to support their backs, one could be reminded of the words of Gautama, with which the Tathagata greeted the meadow of Vesali. 'Charming, Ananda, is Vesali, charming the sacred meadows of the rising daylight, charming the sacred meadow of Gautama, charming the meadow of the seven mango trees ...'

But most of the theologians gathered there did not yet know these words, yet they were to get to know them now, for, after studying some serious questions of the history of religion a short breathing space appeared. Out of the group of 'apprentices of a new priesthood', appearing very young, there arose a man of middle age who, with a somewhat abrupt movement of his arms, pulled out of his voluminous pockets a bunch of papyrus leaves—well, no, they were printer's proofs of a book about to be published—and with a booming voice proclaimed he had to give us now some wisdom from a unique product of the human spirit, of a work of extraordinary beautiful language and primal power, of a document of highest wisdom and deepest humanity.

The leader of the gathering enthroned under an apple tree like a teacher of wisdom, a certain Lic. Emil Bock, allows a softly resigned, mildly excusing, yet friendly smile on his Jove-like countenance, commanding indulgence. Encouraged by this, without properly waiting until everybody had settled themselves on the grass and placed themselves again in Paryanka position, our dear Professor Beckh began, not in German but in resonant Pali, to recite the third chapter of the *Hingang des Vollendeten* ['The Passing of the Perfected One'] with the same booming voice with which he had made his announcement, bringing to sound the magic, mantric quality of this solemn text with its rhythmic emphases.

Whereas initially you understood not a word, apart from some names, you felt a mighty primal stream of words flowing over you; it was suddenly as if a veil were torn away. You realized the good fortune of witnessing a miracle of language; now the German translation had the effect of a direct unveiling of the original, and like a mysterious song, better said like a bardic song, sounded in our listening ears, 'Charming, Ananda, is Vesali, charming the sacred meadows of the rising daylight,...'

Suddenly Beckh's voice changed a little, without, however, losing the streaming rhythm. And so there sounded now a stern admonition, 'Whosoever, Ananda, awakens in themselves and develops the four elements of supernatural power through meditation, who knows how to move in them, realizes them essentially in themselves, who masters its methods, has become strong through exercise in them and has completely mastered them, if he only wanted, could constantly remain for an age of the world on the earth, or for the rest of the world ages ...'

Thus Prof. Beckh read the whole passage in order, speaking in the same intonation, to speak on as though he was allowing the Pali to sound, in order to show how at this place the Christ-Impulse and the Buddha-Wisdom meet very closely, but how precisely in this narration of Vesali the tragedy of Buddhism is revealed. The great world-teacher can point to the secret of change; he knows the law of renewing substance, but a Greater than him was to come, Who was not dependent whether an Ananda understood Him or not, but out of His divine freedom decides to sacrifice Himself on Golgotha.

Some of the 'Vesali-apprentices' on that occasion wanted a repeat of this reading with Prof. Beckh. And, after 35 years, as one hears of the announcement of a new edition of *Hingang des Vollendeten* from Urachhaus, there appears in recollection to the writer of these lines that image of the wish that this work would be available to relate to a later generation something of the Mystery: 'Buddha and Christ.' He rejoices to see that the publisher has included as an Introduction a substantial part of Beckh's *From Buddha to Christ*. Now it is up to the reader to create a Vesali-occasion, in which he can receive the key to understanding in the Introduction and Afterword, and to bring the [Pali] text of the Mahaparinibbanasutta itself to sound for himself and others.

This method of 'making it sound aloud', however, also applies to another work of Prof. Beckh's from the same publisher, appearing in time for Christmas, with the *Hymnus an die Erde* (*Hymn to the Earth*, Eng. tr. Temple Lodge, forthcoming). In this unique work, Beckh himself gives us an illuminating Introduction. And Dr Lauenstein takes the opportunity in an Afterword to sketch an exceptionally impressive picture of Prof. Beckh's personality and spiritual calibre. He also shows by comparing the translation of the Orientalist and the poet Friedrich Rückert, how Beckh's translation is a first-rate linguistic creation.

The present writer is impressed, alongside the *Hymn* itself, mostly by the deep devotion with which Hermann Beckh ponders on Christ's Being and Name [or rather, title], and how he finds in the Sanskrit a spiritually-related word, that expresses this title in Greek at a still deeper level. In truth, our dear, unforgettable Hermann Beckh has presented us for Christmas 1960 with the most beautiful gifts for which we could wish. They appear in a very beautiful outer dress, and it only rests with us to make use of this extraordinary gift.

Die Christengemeinschaft, 33. Jg. Nr. 1. Jan. 1961. 30f.

Appendix Three

Donald Francis Tovey

Wagnerian Harmony and the [possible] evolution of the *Tristan*-chord

Musical Articles from the Encyclopaedia Britannica, **Oxford: OUP 1944, pp. 67–68:**

Wagner's sense of key is exactly the same as Beethoven's; but it has hours in which to exercise itself whereas Beethoven's designs seldom stretch without a break over fifteen minutes, and always show their purport within five. But take, for example, the conflict between two major keys a tone apart. The jealous Fricka did hope (in F-major) that the domestic comforts of Valhalla would induce Wotan to settle down. Wotan, gently taking up her theme in E-flat, dashes her hopes by this modulation more effectively than by any use of his artillery of tubas and trombones.

But the most distinctive feature of Wagner's harmony is his use of long auxiliary notes in such a way as to suggest immensely remote keys, which vanish with the resolution. (Chopin anticipates Wagner in what Sir Henry Hadow finely describes as 'chromatic iridescence'.)

On [the next page] is the evolution of the wonderful opening of *Tristan and Isolde*:

Tr. note: As an ingredient of harmony, this 'most famous chord of all music', as it is called, has been discovered in several earlier composers; there it is in Beethoven's *Piano Sonata*, op. 31, 3, bb. 36 & 38. Wagner, however, made it thematic. This historically significant deed, Beckh shows, focusses human *longing*—a theme that is amongst the most valuable in a book teeming with insights. Beckh mentions Chopin's last composition (Chapter 5; see footnote 38), and in 1936 he may even have been one of the first to point to it. However that is, the unique moment in musical history clinched by Wagner with *Tristan and Isolde* also opened new possibilities to get beyond the romantic nineteenth-century ego. Developments, for example, in late Liszt, Bartok and Debussy show these composers were aware of the challenge of keeping

68 HARMONY

Evolution of the opening of Wagner's Prelude to *Tristan und Isolde*

Ex. 19 — Three concords (tonic, first inversion of subdominant, and dominant of A minor, a possible 16th-century cadence in the Phrygian mode)

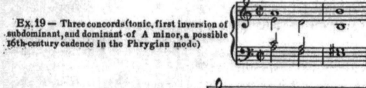

Ex. 20 — The same chords varied by a suspension (*)

Ex. 21 — Ditto, with the further addition of a double suspension (*) and two passing notes (††)

Ex. 22 — Ditto, with a chromatic alteration of the second chord (*) and an 'essential' discord (dominant 7th) at (†)

Ex. 23 — Ditto, with chromatic passing notes (**) and appoggiaturas (††)

Ex. 24 — The last two chords of Ex. 23 attacked unexpectedly, the first appoggiatura (*) prolonged till it seems to make a strange foreign chord before it resolves on the short note at ♮, while the second appoggiatura (†) is chromatic.

WAGNER

Ex. 25 — The same enharmonically transformed so as to become a variation of the 'dominant ninth' of C minor. The G♯ at * is really A♭, and ♮ is no longer a note of resolution, but a chromatic passing note.

WAGNER

Musical example: Tovey's analysis of the 'Tristan-chord' from Encyclopaedia Brittanica (11th edition), reprinted 1944.

one's feet on the ground. The gentle satirical allusion in Debussy's 'Golliwog's cake-walk' (*Children's Corner*) is, of course, not a literal quotation of the *Tristan*-chord. Debussy, however, may have smuggled it into the *Prelude, Footsteps in the snow* ... (with a pedal-point, b. 21) for the most tender, reflective passages. Again, it appears, for example, in passages of preparation in both *L'isle joyeuse* (bb. 61-3) and *Reflects dans l'eau* (around the Quasi cadenza, b. 18ff.). 'Splintered tonality' as such is

Musical Example: The first page of Chopin's Mazurka, op. 68, no. 4.

both symptom and challenge—the artistic challenge Beethoven had lived through during the seven 'years of silence' (that is, no major publication), before the late works revealed what he had been through of 'self-initiation', the challenge in spiritual development to keep whole—A. S.

Appendix Four

Book Reviews

Buddha's Life and Teaching, by Prof. Hermann Beckh

[*Die Christengemeinschaft*, 31. Jg. Heft 6. Juni 1959, p. 188f.]

When Hermann Beckh in 1916 published his Buddhismus in two small volumes (I. *Der Buddha*, II. *Die Lehre*) in the Göschen series, the young scholar in the University of Berlin experienced the great love of his life coming to fulfilment—love of heaven, of the spirit. He could lend expression to it not only with scholarly thoughts, but above all with words of an enthusiastic heart. The one who had enkindled this love in him was Rudolf Steiner.

Hermann Beckh had just caught fire for anthroposophy when he began to work on his Buddha book. Earlier he had sought the spirit of humanity in the early Oriental writings, which he penetrated with extensive scholarship. In those days he was private tutor for Indian philology at the University of Berlin and at the same time one of the few and best practitioners of Tibetan. Now he had found in Rudolf Steiner's anthroposophy a living spiritual cosmos which, although not transferable to the Eastern tradition—this Beckh never attempted—yet made him finely sensitive for the Eastern world of the spirit. The object of his scholarly studies suddenly shone in unusual clarity. This was also perceived by his colleagues.

During the Second World War the writer of these lines had to deal in professional matters as an Orientalist with a leading Orientalist at the University of Berlin. In this connection he touched on his relationship to Hermann Beckh and Rudolf Steiner. Immediately his partner in dialogue became involved and answered with a hidden yet clear warning: 'When the two little books on Buddhism by Beckh were published, we colleagues read them with great joy and benefit. They are the best that has been written hitherto on Buddhism in the German language. But when Beckh turned to Rudolf Steiner we did not read him any more.'

We today have no reason to continue this old feud about Hermann Beckh. We have every reason to stay with the factual evaluation of Beckh, which is also contained in the otherwise strange confession of H.H. Schaeder. And thus we are grateful to the publisher that it presents to us this treasure of comprehensive and reliable scholarship in a handsome one-volume edition, which nevertheless anyone can access, because it glows through with the fire of the heart.

Each feeling soul will gain stimulus from the first part of the book on Buddha's life, out of the pure incomparable pictures out of the realm of the spirit, in which the descent of the Buddha-soul to the Earth, his growth and his travels on the Earth are mirrored. But similarly there flows pure the astoundingly rich source of the sure historical traditions concerning this great man. We are in a strictly historical sense better instructed about the Buddha, who nevertheless lived 500 years earlier, than we are about Jesus of Nazareth.

The second part, 'The Teaching', is written for such readers who also with a contemplative understanding would penetrate into Buddhism. The Buddhist teaching is an ocean. As much as the poetic vein in Hermann Beckh helped him in presenting the fairytale-like pictures in the first part, so much is the living penetration into the teaching into a comprehensive inner ordering in the second part of the book, the actual great accomplishment of the author. The above-quoted witness, H.H. Schaeder, also thought mainly about this achievement, which he then expressed more exactly.

Diether Lavenstein

[*Die Drei*, Juni 1959. Heft 3. 158f.]

This book by Hermann Beckh, the well-known Indologist who died in 1937, is an unaltered reprint of the two-volume work that appeared in the 'Sammlung Göschen' in 1916 under the main title Buddhismus ('Buddhism'). It went through three editions from then, until 1928. I clearly recall the great impression the book made on us in the emancipated 'twenties. It belonged to those works that one had to read and took up eagerly. At this time I had the good fortune to make the personal acquaintance of the University Professor Dr. Hermann Beckh. I met him in connection with anthroposophy, which I was approaching at that time. In order to express his tremendous gratitude to Rudolf Steiner, he mentions the latter's *The Philosophy of Freedom* in a footnote to the Göschen volumes. As he related to me, this brief reference was sufficient to bring him into the gravest difficulties regarding his position at the University. But he did not regret it. In his unfettered urge for truth he knew no restraint, no compromise. This was repeatedly shown in his life.

The book carries unequivocal traces of the purity and greatness of his being. This work has also found the highest recognition in professional circles; indeed, one has to place it alongside the classical works on Buddhism. All the quoted passages are exactly verified. What the reading especially stimulates is [appreciation of] the exceptional beauty of the language, which he also demonstrates in the excerpts convincingly translated from the Sanskrit.

The most significant result of the researches on Buddhism recorded in this work is its close connection, first shown by Beckh, with ancient Indian Yoga, wherein the actual essence of Buddhism can be recognized. 'Through the Buddha and his disciples, Yoga, alongside the breakthrough of all the bounds of caste and nationality, is brought as a gift for the world in general.' In the 'teaching' as also in the 'legends' of the life of the Buddha, the decisive significance of Yoga is clearly to be seen. For Beckh, Yoga is no abstruse, antiquated affair. He certainly knows where to place it. He writes, 'Kant shows theoretically where, within the given consciousness, the boundaries of knowledge lie. Buddha teaches the practice, the path, how the given form of consciousness can be surpassed.' Beckh does not, for example, commend Yoga for our time. For him there is no doubt that there are degrees of higher knowledge, which, beyond all empty speculation are able to approach the 'mysteries of the world and the human being'. Thereby he shows his contemporary allegiance to anthroposophy.

The remarks on the relationships of Buddhism to Christianity are convincing and fruitful. On the one hand, Buddhism in its mystical element points back over a far past of human history; on the other hand, in its characteristics as the 'gospel of compassion and of love' it appears as a 'herald of Christianity'. Nevertheless, the basic differences are never ignored, which frequently happens in 'nuances of feeling'. Goethe's words in the 'Mysteries': 'From the power that binds all beings, the human being is freed who overcomes himself' could, according to Beckh, be seen as the quintessence of Buddhist 'truths'. And yet these words in their 'nuances of feeing' are fundamentally different from all Buddhism. Something similar is also valid concerning the central concept of Christian love. Whereas in early Buddhism compassion is the feeling that mostly appears in the foreground, *maitri*, love, is woven into the name of the *future* Buddha. His name will be, the Maitreya Buddha, the Buddha of loving-kindness. With the concept of *maitri* Buddhism is brought alongside that which is Christian. But here too the 'nuances of feeling' again divide and determine, resulting from that other conception of personality and the attitude to suffering.

Even if the unsurveyable quantity of more recent literature on Buddhism of more than 40 years may have increased, Beckh's work remains unaltered and valid. It is scholarly and at the same time in the highest sense human. This happens only in few cases. Consequently, it is most gratifying that the publishers, Freies Geistesleben, Stuttgart, brought out a new edition, for which we warmly wish the greatest success.

Hans Koester

[The English translation *Buddha's Life and Teaching* made by Dr Katrin Binder, is published by Temple Lodge 2019.]

Das Parsifal=Christus=Erlebnis
('The Parsifal=Christ=Experience in Wagner's Music Drama') by Prof. Hermann Beckh

[*Das Goetheanum* 25 May 1930, p. 166.]

The author, who already with his booklet *The Essence of Tonality* [Eng. tr. Anastasi 2008] extends his mythological and cultic researches on spiritual-scientific bases in the direction of the less-researched realm of the art of music, makes with the above publication a further advance with a study of the 'stage dedication festival play', Wagner's *Parsifal*. This little book recommends itself straight away through its warm red case with the golden lettering and pictorial motif drawn by Margarita Woloschin—reproduced for the English edition—in which the basic concept is meditatively concentrated.

In this work, Prof. Beckh in an impressive manner leads the reader into a deeper understanding of this final word-music drama crowning Wagner's life's work. Above all he seeks to awaken a *consciousness* of what is generally only felt, that is, the sounding drama of the musical and esoteric language of the seven scenes: the Swan, the Walk to the Grail Castle, Amfortas and the Grail, and so on. With this work, Beckh faces the light off-hand objection that with this work he has only added yet another to the many, sometimes quite good, explanations of this Christian Mystery play. Through the manner of spiritual-scientific research, he seeks with particular earnestness to fulfil Wagner's wonderful admonition to gain knowledge in the final words of Parsifal:

Nicht soll der mehr verschlossen sein:
Enthüllet den Gral, öffnet den Schrein!

No more shall it be hidden:
uncover now the Grail, open the shrine!

To meet this admonition to gain knowledge, Beckh's revelations convey important matters, originating out of meditative experience on the musical motifs and the dramatic, pictorial events of the work. Beckh does not proceed in the analytical, dissecting sense, as so often in the completely inadequate outer interpretation of the motifs and themes, whereby the spirit of the work of art is killed. But he proceeds in a synthetic, spiritually developed sense, so that in the soul of the engaged reader something can come to light of Parsifal's first experience of the Grail: 'I scarcely tread, yet seem already to have come far.'

Beckh observes the progress of the Mystery play that engages with the deepest Mysteries of the world-evolution and of human development, with the leitmotif of the Christ-Impulse, of the One who loves, who suffers, and who emerges victorious. How this leitmotif is woven by the other, how the Sun is surrounded by the round-dance of the stars—to establish this is particularly well achieved with the observations on the Prelude to *Parsifal*. This portrays the inner experience of the Last Supper in musical sound, the Mystery of metamorphosis, of transubstantiation.

The particularly valuable thing about this book is the manner how for not particularly musical people it personally, individually, leads the soul of the reader in a generally understandable way, to the threshold of this change from suffering to victory, from the Mystery of Golgotha to resurrection. Beckh concentrates his presentations especially on the Redeemer's look of love sounding from within, looking full of compassion outwards. This is the leitmotif and the suffering motif of the longing of Kundry's double nature:

Nun such' ich Ihn, von Welt zu Welt,	Now I seek Him from world to world
Ihm wieder zu begegnen . . .	to meet Him once again . . .

'From world to world', whereby Wagner wanted slowly to prepare his age for deeper realms of experience of the searching soul, for the intuitive consciousness 'from incarnation to incarnation', from the karma of the Christ-Impulse in the pattern of re-embodiments.

With these leading thoughts and leading feelings, Beckh takes the figure of Parsifal, the human being searching, suffering, and through the power of Christ emerging victorious, in whose metamorphosis he sees man's actual task. Through the already-mentioned seven scenes from the experience with the swan to the 'Good-Friday music', we are led, accompanying Parsifal on the path of transformation, to the transubstantiation of the human soul through the *will* symbolized by the Spear, in the striving to the Communion with the power of the victorious, resurrected One, the spiritually present Christ.

It lies in the essence of this work of art that it can be seen and interpreted from various sides. Beckh takes here the path into the inner realm of the human soul. The macrocosmic aspect of the starry script in *Parsifal*, which is no less great, he only touches on, although the author of *Mark's Gospel: The Cosmic Rhythm* would have had much to say.

The most important musical examples added with the sung text, give moreover an introduction to follow and check for oneself the author's explanations, and in meditation to deepen one's knowledge. The book does not intend to close off but rather to stimulate the reader's conscious deepening of the experience of *Parsifal* as a work of art, both poetically and musically. In many respects it can contribute something to reveal the present task of the consciousness-soul and its connection with Christ in the realm of aesthetic experience. For the sake of this task, the book should find its way to many souls whose hearts are set on this task.

Dr Bruno Krüger
[1887–1979]

[The English translation, *The Parsifal=Christ=Experience*, Anastasi 2015, contains in addition three remarkable studies: Hermann Beckh's essay 'Richard Wagner and Christianity' (1933), and two articles, Emil Bock, 'Twilight of the Gods and Resurrection: Wagner's Mythological Wisdom' (1926) and Rudolf Frieling, 'King Ludwig II of Bavaria' (1956). — *Tr. note.*]

The Language of Tonality in the Music of Bach
by Prof. Hermann Beckh

When listening to some sequence of notes or notes sounding at the same time, how does it happen that in the listener a specific 'musical' impression arises? This question has ever and again been the object of investigation.

There have been great musical cultures and a dying residue still exists today in which to the notes and to the manner of their sounding are attributed the greatest effects on the human constitution. The activity of the [human] organs, the harmony of one's breathing, the change in the life of the day and of the night, procreation and fertility, birth and death—all this is seen and described in tangible relationship to notes, rhythms, sounds and instruments. The connection one has in mind with such a way this is regarded, is a natural, magical one. Notes are played—effects appear. The personal experience of the individual listener plays no part, or only a subordinate one. A theory of music of the arcane cultures can be described as a theory of *magical* musical effects.

Beginning with ancient Greece a musical culture spread in Middle Europe, in which the effects of experiences of sound on the individual soul-life of the listeners gain ever greater meaning. The phenomenon of mood appears, that remarkable spectrum of soul-nuances that can be experienced in listening to music composed during the actual high flowering of this art from the sixteenth to the nineteenth century. A theory, or appreciation, of music that strives to describe and fathom the relationship of the sounding notes to the inner soul-experiences of the listeners, one could call a teaching of the aesthetic effects of the notes, the musical sounds.

The natural effects on the life-processes in listening of course play a certain role in Western music (breathing, movement of the body, sleep, and so on), yet compared to the aesthetic effects they remain more in the background. Characteristic of the aesthetic effect of musical sounds is the strange fact that the aural phenomena, for example of a symphony, need hardly, or not at all, live in the consciousness of the listener, and yet what is heard lights up as an immediate soul-experience so evidently that this soul-experience is completely identified with the 'music' without knowing what has been heard.

The magical effects of musical sounds presuppose a sleeping listening, whereas the aesthetic experience of musical sounds is the result of a dreaming listening. The question arises whether an awake experience of musical sounds exists. What is meant here is that neither the richness of soul-experience nor the many and beneficial harmonizing effects on life out of the experience of musical sound, have [of necessity] to dwindle. Something would be added which corresponds to what the human being in daily awakening gains in addition to sleeping and dreaming—the fully conscious knowing, an overview of the connections of the processes by which the notes, the tones, proceed with those processes taking place in the listening human being. An appreciation of music that strives towards such a total reception could be called a teaching of the spiritual musical sounds. It is based on the teaching of the magical and aesthetic notes, or musical sounds, indeed it includes them, but leads beyond them in striving to penetrate to that region where the spiritual essence of musical sound, the notes, can be found as the basis and true course of its sounding and of its experience.

With his book, *The Language of Tonality* (1st Germ. ed. 1938) Hermann Beckh made an important contribution towards training the teaching of the spiritual notes, or tones. However, it only deals with a partial aspect of this discipline, which cannot as yet be fathomed; it makes a start towards a comprehensive characterizing of all the keys on the basis of a key-synopsis in the work of Richard Wagner. Yet through this it gave the most permanent impulses in the direction of new experiences in the realm of the spiritual essence of musical sound. Connoisseurs of this subject know full well that it has to be carefully pursued; they know how great in this field the danger exists of speculative interpretation, presupposed fixations and mystical illusions. The spiritual essence of musical sound will not reach musical reality through mere labelling of zodiacal or planetary names. All the more encouraging that the original book is again available in all its freshness, completeness and joy of discovery.

I have written an introduction in the new edition [included as Appendix 2 in the English edition]. It gives a short overview regarding the importance of Beckh's work in the context of musical life today. In four further sections it develops suggestions for a further path of practice, which at certain points may be suitable to form a bridge from Beckh's viewpoint of the keys to a future, pure experience of musical sound. From the final section concerning the significance of Beckh's stimuli the concluding passage may be quoted:

Many signs point towards this, that music is in this process of becoming conscious of finding completely new tasks. Whereas in public concert life care of the muse of early music and the products of musical intellectualism still mainly, and satisfactorily, serve the aesthetic needs, music in out-of-the-way places becomes an immediate help for life. Thus the training of spiritual differentiation in musical experience becomes fruitful when the attempt is made to fashion consciously the sequence of human life. This happens, for example, in the religious life through ritual. Musicians involved in the rite of The Christian Community church are immeasurably grateful for Beckh's work. Besides this, with the breakthrough to a spiritual experience of musical sound, new possibilities open up to allow music's organizing power to work on people who are ill. The realm of tasks in the highly topical field of music therapy can draw as little from the old magical sources as from subjective moods and talents of helpful people. Here the disciplined and thorough study of the spiritual nature of musical sound becomes an essential prerequisite. And thus the language of tonality may be welcome to all those who tread the indicated path.

Lothar Reubke

At long last, several important books that explore the holistic nature of music and its cosmic origins have been made available in English—for the first time. We have Heiner Ruland's *Expanding Tonal Awareness* and Christoph Peter's *The Language of Music in Mozart's 'The Magic Flute'* (Anastasi 2015)—which at the same time is the definitive study of the opera. To these must now be added the substantial achievements of arguably the greatest figure of them all, Prof. Dr Hermann Beckh (1875–1937). His works have only been available in German (excepting his standard book on Buddhism, translated into Japanese and Dutch), and there is much treasure still to come. Anastasi, based in Leominster, Herefordshire, have now issued Beckh's *The Language of Tonality* in a handsome paperback edition, with helpful layout (a welcome advance on all the German editions). Alan Stott's concise and very readable translation is a true labour of love in which Beckh's clear but rather complicated German style has been successfully surmounted. The translator has even risen to the challenge to complete a *Collected Edition* of this legendary writer, one of Rudolf Steiner's closest pupils. In 2004 (rev. 2008) Anastasi issued Beckh's *The Essence of Tonality* (written in 1922). Now in *The Language of Tonality* Beckh takes his ideas considerably further, embracing the Western musical language from Bach to Bruckner. He concentrates, however, on Richard Wagner (1813–83) and the evolution of this composer's use of the musical keys in all the major music dramas, from *The Flying Dutchman* to *Parsifal*. In his introduction, Alan Stott puts Beckh's ideas into a clear modern context. The book includes an article by Beckh on 'The Mystery of the Night in Wagner and Novalis', an inspiring contribution on Beckh and music by Lothar Reubke, interesting memories by August Pauli and a survey of the author's career by Gundhild Kačer-Bock (Beckh's biographer).

The universal scholar Hermann Beckh, Dr. jur. et phil.—*ein Original* as the Germans would say—who gained his first doctorate with a work on Civil Law, worked as a judge before changing career to pursue independent studies in Eastern languages; in the process he mastered six ancient languages to add to his complete fluency in six modern languages! He lectured at the University of Berlin, where, hearing a lecture by Rudolf Steiner in 1911 on Elijah, changed his life. Resigning from academic life in 1921, he aimed to work as an independent scholar for anthroposophy. But in 1922 he heard of plans to found the Movement for Religious Renewal, The Christian Community. Beckh joined immediately as a founder priest, taking on the task of founding the Seminary in Stuttgart. Two monumental studies, *Mark's Gospel: The Cosmic Rhythm* and *John's Gospel: The Cosmic Rhythm—Stars and Stones* (1928 and 1930) are now both available in English from Anastasi by the same translator. These gospel studies contain several references to the musical keys—to a polymath like Beckh the subjects mutually correspond. This born educator, a very accomplished pianist able to illustrate his lectures at the piano with ease from memory, enjoyed playing piano duets of the Masters with his friends and colleagues, Lic. Emil Bock, Dr Rudolf Frieling and Dr Alfred Heidenreich.

Beckh's 1922-essay *The Essence of Tonality* pictures the twelve musical keys and their interrelationships in the form of a 'tone-zodiac', linking them to the course of the day, the seasons of the year and the human form, as a vast cosmic rhythm. Beckh understood the circle of fifths of the musical keys not merely as abstract theory, but as the deepest organizing principle, to be lived and experienced, that is, inwardly *heard*. These ideas, expounded in lectures over many years, appeared in later works, such as *Wagner and Christianity* (1933) and *The Parsifal=Christ=Experience* (1930, available in one volume from Anastasi, 2015), before finally coming to fruition in a crowning magnum opus,

The Language of Tonality. Beckh completed his book in 1936, though in considerable pain from a progressing cancer of the kidneys. The book was posthumously published in 1937; the terrible turmoil of World War II and the aftermath effectively buried it, certainly it did his other impressive works. Since those years Beckh has been known, if at all, predominantly in German editions—until now.

Although the title runs 'from Bach to Bruckner', the central core of the book is devoted to how Wagner, apparently totally intuitively, explored the cycle of key-relationships in his music dramas. Beckh's first chapter, 'The Circle of the Musical Keys' explains the deeper connections between, for example, C-major and its polar opposite in the circle, F#-Gb-majors, also G-major and Db-major, E-major and Bb-major, all of which also form triangles with other keys. The circle of keys moves, like the day and the year, progressively lighter and higher, then after the transition in F#-Gb-majors to the keys with flats, Db, Ab, Bb and F-majors. The minor keys normally depict the shadow side of the key-centre. The remaining chapters explore each of these key-centres in detail, constantly referring to examples from the masters; much of the music is quite familiar. Beckh moves on to specific passages in Wagner's *The Flying Dutchman, Tannhäuser, Lohengrin, The Ring, Tristan and Isolde, The Mastersingers* and finally *Parsifal*. No written musical examples are given—strictly not necessary as Beckh describes relevant passages from each work using Wagner's text, here printed with the original German and in English translation side by side. Wagner-lovers will have the advantage in recognizing passages and are encouraged to place them in the context of the whole work performed in one's mind. But this book is not only for musicians; the musical terminology is widely used but kept to a minimum. Music-lovers will find Beckh's insights a revelation, a stimulus to revisit this controversial, yet considerable artist.

At the time Beckh was writing (during the difficult 1920s and 30s), the language of music, like the visual arts, was passing through various stages: tonality, atonality, bitonality, polytonality, neo-classicism, dodecophony, et al. After the War, some music sank even deeper into the subterranean realms of 'organized noise', electronic 'music' and the rise of the 'avant- (but really *derrière!*) garde'. But music is not to be mocked; it has taken quite a time for the truer understanding of music and its mission to re-surface again. The 21st-century will expect from us a much more holistic re-membering of the source of music, often called the 'universal language'. In this respect, is could be that Hermann Beckh really was writing for the future, as Emil Bock, for one, maintained; his vision (or 'audition') is for a time when music's true destiny and purpose should re-awaken. That time is now; this is *the* book to assist in that process.

Michael Jones

[*New View*, Issue 76, Summer 2015, pp. 70f.]

The Language of Music in Mozart's The Magic Flute by Christoph Peter

In the original edition, *Die Sprache der Musik in Mozarts 'Die Zauberflöte'* (Verlag Freies Geistesleben, Stuttgart, 1983, corrected and augmented 1997), Christoph Peter set the standard for not only musical analyses of scores—lots of those exist—but also for life-changing training and education in understanding and responding to music. Born out of his profound commitment to teaching music in the Steiner-Waldorf School in Hanover for twenty-two years and then his work in the Stuttgart Teachers' Seminary, the text reflects the overriding concern that *The Magic Flute* is a gateway to an ongoing exploration of the ways by which music, at its best, reflects and stimulates those human capabilities that are higher than intellect, logic and the self-evident values of feeling. Ultimately, Christoph Peter realized that the direct apprehension and understanding of aesthetic qualities was something pre-eminently required today, and beyond that we enter the realm of moral intuitions with Mozart. And this can, perhaps should, start in the classroom.

When I was trying to 'teach' *The Magic Flute* (whatever that might mean) for The Open University I came to expect that all students would love it and take it to heart, and this always happened of course. But what was surprising was that everyone wanted to know more about the language of music. Whether it was keys, intervals, rhythms or orchestral harmonies people wanted to be able to appreciate it more deeply. What we all needed, in fact, was this book now in a lucid and natural English which belies the huge effort Alan Stott has made to make the text more accessible. This does not mean to say, however, that the book is simple. While it is invaluable for any general reader interested in progressing their knowledge of how music can be structured, or in the magic of the *Singspiel* itself, the text is especially designed to lead students at any level into ever more detailed and profound listening. A very great deal can be accomplished, Christoph Peter points out, by working in groups.

As the author well understood, as he continued to revise the text until his last days in the summer of 1982, *The Magic Flute* represents a path of initiation at three levels: the story itself of Tamino and Pamina as they tread the boards on stage; the education of the audience as we begin to understand; and finally what we might call 'the great mirroring' or ladder of ascent: from Tamino's flute in hand to the opera of the same name to music as a whole: we learn, we are moved, we are changed. Running through the many pages of meticulous analysis we are never far from the heart of the opera which is convincingly set forth on p. 464. In *Art as seen in the Light of Mystery Wisdom*, Rudolf Steiner describes (30 December 1914) 'the subjective side of the path of initiation' in a series of clear stages; Christoph Peter shows precisely how and where these occur in *The Magic Flute*.

The three degrees of Johannine Freemasonry, which Mozart entered in 1785, bear a striking resemblance to this particular course of education. One can usefully compare the traditional degrees to the learning programme spread through *The Language of Music*. What was simply learning about simple emblems, allegories and symbols in the 1° Apprentice has become a soul-filled excursus leading the reader into a rich understanding of 'The Elements of Music' (Part 1). This extends further, especially in Part 2 'Survey of the Opera', to help the reader recognize otherwise 'hidden' patterns in the opera—delicate echoes and inversions, the structuring of musical phrases according to the Golden Mean, how a subdominant chord in one location recalls a previous appearance ... these are open secrets, the alphabet of a language.

The traditional 2° Journeyman was called upon to study the Book of Nature. Here we now enter where phenomena (the music) relate to the worlds of soul and spirit. How do we experience the difference between a range of musical intervals? How does Sarastro's Aria '*O Isis und Osiris*' communicate our understanding that this moment reveals a knowledge and compassion that 'reach right into the depths'? (p. 373). How does the syncopated woodwind accompanying the Queen's '*Der Hölle Rache*' substantiate the 'nocturnal shine of this scene' (p. 397)? The Quintet between the Three Ladies, Tamino and Papageno, No. 5, includes 'would all change to love and brotherhood': the word '*Liebe*' is delicately underlain with the first inversion chord which communicates 'its tendency to strive upwards' (p. 327). Can we read this language of music? Are we moving from the alphabet towards words and sentences?

The 3° Master, also in Vienna, was symbolically slain, laid in a coffin, and raised by the hand of the Grandmaster of the Lodge thereby entering into a new life, one of self-knowledge. Probably for most of us the moment in the first Finale when Tamino is plunged into literal darkness and the key changes to A-minor then leading to the Choir's *'Pamina lebet noch'* is the most magical moment: 'Yes, Pamina is alive!' We are led to reflect on silence — and Peter does not fail to adduce the most helpful and extensive comments on rests. What happens in such silences? When the stream (of sound) 'comes to a standstill ... then we become aware of the significance and importance of an unnamed, creative force which streams out of this fundamental musical element' (p. 211). Out of the language of music, its elements, forms and movements, we cannot help but find ourselves, and thereby Meaning. We are finally reading the language of music.

It is one thing to analyse musical structures, then, but a different task to describe their effects — each listener has to seek within and an author has to find language that can convey and prompt. Fortunately Christoph Peter was able to call upon the vast literature already at hand which deals with the elements of music in *The Magic Flute*. This presence is never heavy, always tactfully introduced and often deeply rooted in anthroposophic research. Further, one is blessed with the original bibliography plus the translator's updating and meticulous cross-referencing (one of the several improvements to the German edition, along with a clearer layout). What clearly emerges here is that there is a need in the listener to find bridges between sound as a physical phenomenon, also represented in this meticulous analysis of musical techniques, to music as 'inner time, inner space and inner centring ... The perennial path of transformation' (cover material).

With this new translation for our guide a certain challenge is thrown down, again reminiscent of the old Masonic trials. Tamino has to pass the trials of silence, of water and of fire. First we have to confront the well-known, crucial problem of the libretto — is the *Singspiel* an incomplete botched piece of work, or does the Queen change her character, or is the story a *Bildungsroman* in which the audience, following Tamino, is progressively educated to overcome the initial illusory appearances? Secondly, what might be the relationship between the music and any one production? What role does a stage director have? Here, naturally, it is good to find the author calling up many of the known details of the first performance. Yet, should the Orphic animals be cuddly? Would we attempt to make Monostatos a chilling threat or a buffoon? Is the language of music affected thereby? Are we entering a realm of personal freedom here?

Finally, however, and I think this is the truly wonderful thing, if as teachers, musicians, eurythmists or music-lovers we find ourselves in unknown realms, feet leaving the ground, then we will hear the call of this invaluable publication. Its voice says as emphatically as possible: Listen! Study! Think! Above all, think with the utmost power of your intellect! What is displayed in the final Transformation scene in *The Magic Flute* as the 'iron gate' becomes for us the portal to higher knowledge. Yes, it is always enough to enjoy a performance or the music; yes we can quite comfortably appreciate the contrasts between Papageno's G-major and the Three Boys' E♭-major. But with each step further into analysis and reflection the rewards increase, not just for ourselves but for the opportunities we might have for teaching — Christoph Peter himself said in 1982 that *The Magic Flute* takes 'a decisive position' (p. 19) in the Waldorf School syllabus.

Consider the end of the Quintet No.5 where all voices sing 'So fare you well ...'. The passage 'leads into the full epilogue with all the voices, distinguished by the pure subdominant and the releasing leaps to the sixth degree. Like watchmen, the horns sustain the keynote; the prospect to the realm of the octave, the world of the Three Boys is open' (p. 334). Christoph Peter, Alan Stott and Anastasi have now provided the point of entry to this world for English readers. At all stages it has been a huge task, magnificently achieved.

Neil Franklin

[*New View*, Issue 75, April–June 2015. Pp. 72–74.]

Etymology and the Meaning of Speech Sounds in the Light of Spiritual Science by Prof. Hermann Beckh

[from *Das Goetheanum* 1. Jg. Nr. 11, 82f.]

Under this title Prof. Dr Hermann Beckh has published a work that is small in size but is very rich in content.[91] The well-known Orientalist, whose two-volume work on the Buddha caused a stir in influential circles, now joins the ranks of leading researchers of language. At the basis of his great knowledge, which even includes the Tibetan language, lies an inner, almost romantic, love of the word. For the reader who studies this little book, it is as if the destiny of language concerns his innermost being. It is as if his own development depends on it, how he makes as his own the discoveries that the author presents — a remarkable experience in the otherwise dry sphere of philology.

Beckh proceeds from a saying of Novalis, whom he venerates very much. Etymology is differentiated into the genetic and the pragmatic. He distinguishes two kinds of linguistics:

- pragmatic etymology which looks at the word as something that has *become* in its transformations and combinations. And
- genetic linguistics that attempts to lay hold of the *becoming* of the word, the original relationships between speech sounds and the meaning of speech sounds:

The expression 'genetic etymology' from the Greek γένεσις ('genesis, origin') points to that original becoming of the word, to the connection of speech sound and its meaning. 'Pragmatic etymology' (from πρᾶγμα 'that which has happened, the deed' = Indian 'karma') points to that destiny of what has become on its way through space and time, to the karma — so to speak — of the word, after it has been laid hold of by the forces of differentiation which obscures the spiritual origin of the word.

Beckh initially describes the path of pragmatic linguistics governing today. He shows how these linguists strive to reach the origins of the word, by tracing back (for example from New High German to Middle High German, Old High German, to Old Norse, Gothic, etc.); in that they draw on other languages in comparison, establish correspondences of sounds wherein laws can be found; they peel out equivalences, in order finally to arrive at what is called the root, out of which the respective transformations, changes of forms and combinations have fashioned the various categories of words and forms.

Many researchers—for example, the recently deceased Dr Finck,[92] who absorbed the 700–750 languages into the realm of research—came to the point of assuming a single original language existed, 'an original mother of the languages living today in Europe', the *Indo-European* language. But here they saw they had arrived at a dead point. They had to remain standing. Here they met the well-known borders of knowledge. People were satisfied with a philological *ignorabimus*, 'we do not know and shall never know'. Nobody was able to demonstrate that the original, root language was more than a hypothesis of the understanding. It only led a virtual life.

The pragmatic methods are indeed able to penetrate to the roots of words, but how these methods come to the speech sounds of these root remains veiled. It is the intellect that, with the web of concepts that it spins, veils the creative influence of the powers forming speech, of the genius of speech. It itself set up the limits to knowledge which it had formed around that which has become. It became itself a hindrance to a laying-hold of how the roots came about.

After Beckh in such a way has revealed the inadequacy of the pragmatic methods, he goes on to develop the genetic methods, 'with which we are concerned today within our anthroposophic endeavours'. He applies the manner of research that Rudolf Steiner has built up to the realm of linguistics. It consists therein that one lives inwardly and with the strength of thinking into the sounds of words, into the vowels and consonants, and so develops a sense in oneself that which in earlier epochs was instinctively creative, but which today has become buried under rubble, or still speaks today, yet only seldom, in a few poets. It is the *sense for speech* as such.

Indeed, the further back we go in the development of words, all the more the experience of the sounds and the meaning of words mutually approach. In the original language they must have been one and the same. Today, though, the experience of speech sounds has fallen into the subconscious; the sense for the word, for speech, has become superficial. Language, which earlier worked instinctively, falls to the might of the intellect and to that extent became a means for the understanding merely to convey information.

Beckh attempts to break through the trellis-work of the intellect and approach the genius of language. He wants to lay hold of the essential strength that governed in the human instincts and lies at the basis of the becoming of words, and to raise it to consciousness. And in actual fact, he manages to free the spirit out of the dungeon.

By taking his start from Sanskrit, Avestan and Hebrew, he comes to a genial overview. He discloses the kinship of the Indian language, Sanskrit, with the capacity of thinking, of Avestan with that of the feelings, and Hebrew with the will; thereby he goes over to the Germanic languages, wherein he glimpses the direct expression of the 'I'.

> Different from modern European languages (he writes), ancient Sanskrit, ancient Avestan and ancient Hebrew allow us to approach those living origins of the word, that genetic etymology which we can only find in the word of today in an incomplete manner. We are not led here by one-sided theoretical interests, but by the intention to make again practical and fruitful for the living word that which we have learnt from the word of the past.

In order to emphasize for the reader the path that Beckh suggests, we quote a passage that certainly must have pleased the brothers Schlegel and the brothers Grimm:

> The early Indians also possessed a clear concept of the super-sensory side of the word. In a quite different sense from the people of today, they were still able to feel the sacred side in the word and in language. In the element of language and of sound they venerated the eternal cosmic being, brahman, as that which is called 'sound-brahman' (*śabdabrahman*), and they called this super-sensory element, this aura of the word, the *sphoṭa*. Especially in Mimansa philosophy, this teaching of the super-sensory elements of speech, the *sphoṭa* has been developed. There it is identified with the sound-brahman, the etheric sound-element itself.
>
> But *sphoṭa* is more than an abstract concept. The word goes back to the root *sphuṭ*, lying etymologically as the basis of the German word *spalten* ('to split'), that also means, bursting open, breaking up, springing up, opening itself, etc. It expresses an *Imagination*, that conjures up before our spiritual eyes like the opening of a flower-chalice or something similar. The train of consciousness linking the speech sound and its meaning, for us today a subconscious activity of the sense of speech, the early Indian still experienced out of instinctive, atavistic clairvoyance in super-sensory Imaginations. When he heard the word, the sound, 'something took place within him', and he beheld that which arose in him in a delicate etheric picture. Such tangible pictures later became abstract concepts. Today in spiritual science we seek to get beyond abstraction to the tangible, concrete picture, to Imagination. Not only alongside the more abstract word does the pictorial element of Imagination appear, but with a corresponding living into language a stage exists on which the word and speech-sound themselves again become Imaginations.

In the outer world speech is increasingly sinking, increasingly descending to a merely conventional means of understanding. The connection with the spiritual content of the word is becoming increasingly lost, in particular in those languages that are destined to develop a future world-language. However, on the basis of spiritual-scientific attempts there will nevertheless be an ever-more intimate relationship to the word and speech. Speech will develop in a completely new sense towards the spirit. Speech will take on a magical-moral influence, still unimagined today; speech will again develop a real power that is called to turn human thinking to the heights of the spirit.

At the peak of the investigation, what goes on in the depths of consciousness with the individual experiences of the speech sounds, Beckh places the breath-sound *h*. In Tibetan *ha* is actually a word; it means the 'breath of air'. In the Indian dictionary the meanings for the sound *h* are 'divine, heavenly, most sublime soul'. In *h* one is divested of the physical. A dilation, an expansion, an excursion into the cosmos takes place. *Ātman* and *brahman* behave like a breathing-in and a breathing-out. A striving away from the earthly element is given in the *h*.

In Hebrew where the *h*-sound is differentiated in a variety of ways, Beckh shows how the earthly is mixed in. He develops a whole myth out of the metamorphoses of the sound.

> The spiritual *h* of the name Yahveh receives in the *ch* of the name Eve Ḥavâh a touch of the earthly element. From Eve we turn towards the snake, whose sound, the sizzling sound *s*, is the most earthly, physical sound, presenting as it were the counter-pole of the spiritual *h*. Still before the human being has physically descended to the Earth, the snake that had already become physical, uttered its *s*, whereas *h*, spiritually taken, lies on the border of the visible and the unutterable. *S* lies so to speak completely in the physical, sensory world — cf. the initial sound of the Germ. *sein* 'to be' (Skr. *sat*), [and both Germ. and Eng.] *sehen*, see, *Sinn*, sense — it is the backbone of the physical, purely earthly existence. In the Indian sound-meaning system, the snake-sound *s* indeed means 'snake'; one feels in it genetically the initial sound of the root *sṛp* 'to crawl', from this *sarpa* 'the snake', Lat. *serpens* 'serpent'. It is meaningful for genetic etymology that we also find in Hebrew *saraf*, 'the snake' and in late Egyptian *srrf*. The form of the letter for *s* also expresses the snake in many systems of writing.

To these two sounds *h* and *s* a certain importance is rightly attributed. In actual fact they correspond to the two main drives within the human being: *h* the drive towards the spirit, as flight from the Earth; *s* the drive towards the Earth, as a flight from the spirit. Schiller made these drives known as the 'form-drive' and 'material-drive'. Anthroposophy, by passing from the abstract expression to the pictorial, bases these drives on two significant powers, called Lucifer and Ahriman.

Albert Steffen

The Works of Prof. Hermann Beckh Dr. jur. et phil.

'An abundance of books came into existence whose significance perhaps will only be properly appreciated in the future.'
(Lic. Emil Bock, 'Hermann Beckh' in *Zeitgenossen Weggenossen Wegbereiter*, Stuttgart: Urachhaus 1959. p. 132)

*

Die Beweislast nach dem Bürgerlichen Gesetzbuch
'The Burden of Proof according to the Code of Civil Law'
Prize essay, awarded distinction from the Law Faculty the University of Munich
München and Berlin 1899. Download: http://dlib-pr.mpier.mpg.de/m/ kleioc/0010/exec/books/%22103926%22/

Ein Beitrag zur Textkritik an Kālidāsas Meghadūta
'A contribution for the text criticism of Kalidasa's Meghadūta'
Doctorate dissertation approved by the Department of Philosophy of the University of Berlin 1907.

Die tibetische Übersetzung von Kālidāsas Meghadūta
'The Tibetan translation of Kalidāsa's Meghaduta'
Edited and with a German translation, Berlin 1907/2011.

Beiträge zur tibetischen Grammatik, Lexikogaphie, Stilistik und Metrik
Habilitationsschrift. Berlin 1908.
'Contributions to Tibetan grammar, lexicography, style and prosody'
Inaugural dissertation.

Udānavarga
A collection of Buddhist sayings in the Tibetan language.
Berlin 1911 (also reprinted by Walter de Gruyter, 2013).

Verzeichnis der tibetischen Handschriften
'Catalogue of Tibetan MSS in the Royal Library in Berlin' (Vol. 24 of the Manuscript Catalogue). First division: Kanjur (Bhak-Khgur).
Berlin 1914/2011/14.

Buddha und seine Lehre
'Buddha and his Teaching.' Vol. 1: The Life. Vol. 2: The Teaching.
Sammlung Göschen. Berlin and Leipzig 1916. Third edition 1928.
Later one-volume editions, Stuttgart: Urachhaus 1958/98/2012. Tr. into Dutch and Japanese. Eng. tr. *Buddha's Life and Teaching*, Temple Lodge, 2019.

'Rudolf Steiner und das Morgenland'
in *Vom Lebenswerk Rudolf Steiners*
Ed. Friedrich Rittelmeyer, München: Chr. Kaiser 1921
Reprint by HP, Univ. of Michigan (www.lib.umich.edu) (download: www.archive.org).
Eng. tr. in *Hermann Beckh and the Spirit-Word*, Anastasi 2015. pp. 33–65.

[1] *Der physische und der geistige Ursprung der Sprache*
The physical and the spiritual origin of language. Stuttgart 1921.
[2] *'Es werde Licht!'*
'Let there be light!'
The primal biblical words of creation and the primal significance of the sounds in the light of spiritual science. Stuttgart 1921.
[3] *Etymologie und Lautbedeutung*
Etymology and the significance of speech sounds in the light of spiritual science.
Stuttgart 1922/2013.

All three essays on language (above) reprinted in
Neue Wege zur Ursprache, Stuttgart 1954
Eng. tr. *The Source of Speech*, includes two extra essays 'Indology and Spiritual Science'. Temple Lodge, forthcoming 2019.

Anthroposophie und Universitätswissenschaft
'Anthroposophy and University Knowledge'
Breslau 1922. Eng. tr. in *Hermann Beckh and the Spirit-Word*, Anastasi 2015. pp. 71–101; also included in *The Source of Speech*, Temple Lodge 2019.

Vom geistigen Wesen der Tonarten
The Essence of Tonality: An Attempt to view musical Problems in the Light of Spiritual Science. With diagrams. Breslau 1922. Third edition 1932. Eng. tr. Anastasi 2008.

Der Ursprung im Lichte
Our Origin in the Light: Pictures from Genesis. Stuttgart 1924. Eng. tr. Temple Lodge, 2019.

Von Buddha zu Christus
From Buddha to Christ
Stuttgart 1925 (tr. in Norwegian, Oslo 1926); Eng. tr. selections Floris Books 1978.
Eng. tr. of full text, with 'Steiner and Buddha' (1931), Temple Lodge, 2019.

Das neue Jerusalem
'The New Jerusalem'
A poetic work, in the collaborative work *Gegenwartsrätsel im Offenbarungslicht*

('Problems of the present in the light of revelation'), Stuttgart 1925. Eng. tr. in *John's Gospel: The Cosmic Rhythm – Stars and Stones*, pp. 459–77. Anastasi 2015; Temple Lodge, forthcoming.

Der Hingang des Vollendeten
'The Passing and Nirvana of the Perfected One (Mahaparinibbana Sutta of the Pali canon).'
Translated and with an Introduction. Stuttgart 1925/60. Eng. tr. *Buddha's Passing*. Temple Lodge, forthcoming.

Zarathustra
Stuttgart 1927
Eng. tr. in *Collected Essays and Articles*, Temple Lodge, forthcoming.

Aus der Welt der Mysterien
From the World of the Mysteries
Seven articles (reprinted). Basel 1927. Eng. tr. Temple Lodge, forthcoming.

Der kosmische Rhythmus im Markus-Evangelium
Mark's Gospel: The Cosmic Rhythm
Basel 1928/60/97. Eng. tr. Anastasi 2015; Temple Lodge, forthcoming.

Der kosmische Rhythmus, das Sternengeheimnis und Erdengeheimnis im Johannes-Evangelium
John's Gospel: The Cosmic Rhythm – Stars and Stones
Basel 1930. Eng. tr. Anastasi 2015; Temple Lodge, forthcoming.

Das Christus-Erlebnis in Dramatisch-Musikalischen von Richard Wagners 'Parsifal'
The Parsifal=Christ=Experience in Wagner's Music Drama
Stuttgart 1930. Eng. tr. with 'Richard Wagner and Christianity' (1933) and essays by Emil Bock (1928) and Rudolf Frieling (1956), Leominster: Anastasi 2015; Temple Lodge, forthcoming.

Vom Geheimnis der Stoffeswelt (Alchymie)
Alchymy: The Mystery of the Material World
Basel 1931/37/42/2007/13. Eng. tr. Temple Lodge, 2019.

Der Hymnus an die Erde
The Hymn to the Earth: From the Old Indian Atharvaveda: A memorial to the oldest poem and to the early Aryans.
Germ tr. and commentary. Stuttgart 1934/60. Eng. tr. Temple Lodge, forthcoming.

Psalm 23 aus der Heiligen Schrift
Psalm 23: Newly translated from the original text and set to music, op. 7.
Stuttgart 1935.
Die Rosen von Damaskus
The Roses of Damascus. 'Thibaut von Champagne'. The ballad by Conrad Fer-

dinand Meyer. For solo high voice with piano accompaniment set to music, op. 8. Stuttgart 1937.

Die Sprache der Tonart
The Language of Tonality in the Music from Bach to Bruckner with special reference to Wagner's Music Dramas
Stuttgart 1937/87/99. Eng. tr. Leominster 2015; Temple Lodge, forthcoming.

Richard Wagner und das Christentum
Richard Wagner and Christianity
Stuttgart 1933. Eng. tr. incl. in *The Parsifal=Christ=Experience in Wagner's Music Drama.* Anastasi 2015; Temple Lodge, forthcoming.

Indische Weisheit und Christentum
Indian Wisdom and Christianity
Articles: 10 reprinted and 9 from the literary estate.
Stuttgart 1938. Eng. tr. in *Collected Essays and Articles*; Temple Lodge, forthcoming.

Das Mysterium des musikalischen Schaffens; Der Mensch und die Musik
The Mystery of Musical Creation: Human Being and Music
A recently discovered history of music in Ms:
Five chapters pub. in three articles in *Der Europäer*, Basel 09.2005/09.2006/02.2007–08.
http://www.perseus.ch/archive/category/europaer/europaer-archiv
Eng. version (first pub.) Temple Lodge, 2019.

Collected Articles, on Eastern religions, Yoga, Christianity, 'Snow-white', language, etc. (Temple Lodge, forthcoming)

Biography:

Hermann Beckh: Leben und Werk
Hermann Beckh: Life and Work
by Gundhild Kačer-Bock
Stuttgart 1997. Eng. tr. Anastasi 2016; Temple Lodge, forthcoming.

Hermann Beckh and the Spirit-Word:
Orientalist, Christian Priest and Independent Scholar (Anastasi 2015)

- A. S. 'Hermann Beckh and the Twenty-First Century'
- H. B. 'Rudolf Steiner and the East'
- H. B. 'Anthroposophy and University Knowledge'
- H. B. 'Meeting Rudolf Steiner'

- Numerous appreciations by Beckh's colleagues and his biographer;

introducing the *Collected Works of Hermann Beckh* (Temple Lodge, forthcoming).

Notes

1. Rudolf Steiner's *Collected Works* (GA = Gesamtausgabe, CH-Dornach) are available online. Most of GA 283 (excluding answers to questions) is translated as *The Inner Nature of Music and the Experience of Tone*. Spring Valley, New York: Anthroposophic Press 1983; the lecture of 2 Dec. 1922. pp. 30–45.
2. See *Festschrift: Essays in honour of Hermann Beckh*. Leominster: Anastasi 2016.
3. 'Hermann Beckh's spiritual manner' in *Hermann Beckh & the Spirit-Word*. Leominster: Anastasi 2015, pp. 131–144.
4. Hermann Beckh, *Indische Weisheit und Christentum*. Ed. Robert Goebel & Rudolf Meyer, Urachhaus 1938, p. 132–40. Eng. tr. in *Collected Essays and Articles*, Temple Lodge, forthcoming.
5. Prepared by Helga and ingrid Paul. *Die Europaer*. Jg. 9/Nr. 9/10 Juli/Aug. 2005; Jg. 10/Nr. 9/10 Juli/Aug. 2006; Jg. 12/Nr. 2/3 Dez./Jan. 2007/08; download: http://www.perseus.ch/archive/category/europaer/europaer-archiv/
6. Eng. tr. by A. S. *Interpreting Melos*, in Rudolf Steiner, *Eurythmy as Visible Singing*, RSP, 2019. pp. 497–530. Steiner refers to this manifesto in Lecture 5. Hauer, who 'discovered' the twelve-note concept independently of, and shortly prior to, Schönberg, speaks on the one hand of the inner voice, the 'spiritual melos' that needs 'interpreting'. In contrast to the prevailing ignorance, he recognizes Goethe's *Theory of Colours* and devotes another chapter to the sounds of speech. On the other hand, Hauer, a sensitive musician, scorns the sensory world; harmony is 'noise'; especially with and after Beethoven, music became thematic, a sensual whipping-up of emotions, materialistic—in short, prostituted. Wagner is 'utterly decadent'. In an attempt to 'reach for the stars', Hauer champions the atonal, twelve-note concept that excludes the diatonic, 7-note level in the tonal system.
7. Professor Hermann Beckh, Dr jur. et phil., *Anthroposophie und Universitätswissenschaft*. Breslau: Verlag von Preuß & Jünger 1922; see also Hermann Beckh, 'Rudolf Steiner und das Morgenland', in *Vom Lebenswerk Rudolf Steiners*. Ed. Friedrich Rittelmeyer. 1921, pp. 273–304 (https://archive.org/details/vomlebenswerkru00bauegoog); Eng. trs. A. S. 'Anthroposophy and University Knowledge' and 'Rudolf Steiner and the East', both in: *Hermann Beckh and the Spirit-Word*. Leominster: Anastasi 2015, pp. 67–101 and 33–65 and *The Source of Speech*, Temple Lodge, 2019, pp. 16–42, 183–207.
8. Beckh's association with important events in Rudolf Steiner's life is traced

by his biographer: Gundhild Kačer-Bock. *Hermann Beckh Leben und Werk.* Stuttgart: Urachhaus 1997. Eng. tr. *Hermann Beckh: Life and Work.* Leominster: Anastasi 2016.

9. Ian Dall, *Sun Before Seven.* Introduction by Walter de la Mare. London & Edinburgh: Thomas Nelson, 1936, p. 114. To 'birds' cries and the frogs', mentioned by Dall, other animal cries could be added, including the song of the whales.

10. In every ancient language one undifferentiated word meant 'spirit' and 'wind'. Beckh also writes on John 3:8: '... we are allowed to feel in the revelatory cosmic-symphonic language of John's Gospel that in the cosmic wind, as in the blowing earthy wind, we perceive the secret of the cosmic music. This, though, is at the same time the secret of the sound-ether in the world ... the secret of the life-ether is hidden in the wind of life of the magical sound-ether' (Hermann Beckh, *John's Gospel: The Cosmic Rhythm — Stars and Stones.* Leominster: Anastasi 2015, p. 222).

11. See Hermann Beckh, 'Von meinem Leben', in *Die Christengemeinschaft,* 14. Jg. Nr. 12. März 1938, pp. 325–27; the whole account reprinted in Gundhild Kačer-Bock, *Hermann Beckh Life and Work,* pp. 55–101; quotation from p. 68.

12. Cf. Jim B. Tucker, *Life before Life.* New York: St Martin's Griffin 2005; the bibliography includes much of Ian Stevenson's work, the first head of department devoted to this empirical research at the University of Virginia.

13. The poet, novelist and writer Walter de la Mare (1873–1956), in a lecture 'Rupert Brooke and the Intellectual Imagination', Harcourt, Brace and Howe, New York 1920 [https://archive.org/details/rupertbrookeinte00de], also in *Pleasures and Speculations.* London: Faber 1940 pp. 172–199, makes a fruitful distinction between writers who through their imagination draw on remembrance of early consciousness experienced as children, or, through intuition, even as infants. The latter (Blake, Vaughan, Traherne...) develop mysticism and insight. 'The greatest poets — Shakespeare, Dante, Goethe, for instance — are masters of both. There is a borderland in which dwell Wordsworth, Keats and many others. But the visionaries, the mystics, Plato, Plotinus, the writer of the Book of Job, Blake, Patmore, and in our own day, Flecker, and Mr. John Freeman, may be taken as representative of the one type; Lucretius, Donne, Dryden, Pope, Byron, Browning, Meredith, and in our own day, Mr. Abercrombie, may be taken as representative of the other...' Walter de la Mare's celebration of childhood, *Early One Morning in the Spring.* New York: Macmillan 1935; London: Faber 1935/2010, like his other 'anthologies', is a liberal education.

14. Donald Francis Tovey, *A Companion to Beethoven's Piano Sonatas.* London: The Associated Board 1931 (reprinted 1948/76/99). Tovey's *Essays in Musical Analysis* (OUP), too, are read as much for the quality of the author's

prose as for the musical insights. Pianists, too, who know the study editions of Alfred Cortot especially devoted to the romantic repertoire (Editions Salabert, Paris), appreciate the poetic hints as well as the author's expressive fingerings, and so on — all designed to help the player to access and release the music.

15. Rudolf Steiner, *Eurythmy as Visible Singing*. Lecture 4. GA 278. Tr. A. S., Leominster: Anastasi 2012; corrected ed. RSP, 2019.

16. See Christoph Peter, *The Language of Music in Mozart's 'The Magic Flute'*, tr. A. S. Leominster: Anastasi 2014, Temple Lodge, forthcoming. Peter, an exemplary all-round musician, investigates here all the categories of music by concentrating on one acknowledged masterpiece, KV 620. He summarizes the essence of Beckh's approach in his chapter devoted to Mozart's use of the musical keys.

17. The philosopher and historian R.C. Collingwood (1889-1943) argues with clarity for the 'original language', in a book becoming increasingly relevant in the twenty-first century, *The Principles of Art*, OUP 1938/58, p. 246f.):

> I said that 'the dance is the mother of all languages'; this demands further explanation. I meant that every kind or order of language (speech, gesture, and so forth) is an offshoot from an original language of total bodily gesture. This would have to be a language in which every movement and every stationary poise of every part of the body had the same kind of significance which movement of the vocal organs possess in a spoken language. A person using it would be speaking with every part of himself. Now, in calling this an 'original' language, I am not indulging (God forbid) in that kind of *a priori* archaeology which attempts to reconstruct man's distant past without any archaeological data. I do not place it in the remote past. I place it in the present. I mean that each one of us, whenever he expresses himself, is doing so with his whole body, and is thus actually talking in this 'original' language of total bodily gesture... This 'original' language of total bodily gesture is thus the one and only real language, which everybody who is in any way expressing himself is using all the time. What we call speech and the other kinds of language are only parts of it which have undergone specialized development; in this specialized development they never come altogether detached from the parent organism.

Rudolf Steiner also claimed 'there is no doubt that this primordial language did exist'. See Lecture 2, Dornach 25 June 1924, in *Eurythmy as Visible Speech*, tr. A. S. Anastasi 2005, and RSP 2019; and Hermann Beckh, *The Source of Speech*, tr. A. S., ed. Neil Franklin and Katrin Binder, Temple Lodge 2019.

18. Original German available online: www.archive.org

19. GA 10, published under slightly different titles by Rudolf Steiner Press, London and Anthroposophic Press, New York; also available from: www.rsarchive.org

20. Beckh explains the Paradisal Trees in a number of works. See, e.g., 'The

Name Isis' and 'The Tree of Life' (1927) in: *From the World of the Mysteries*, Temple Lodge, forthcoming. *Our Origin in the Light: Pictures from Genesis*, Temple Lodge, forthcoming. *John's Gospel: The Cosmic Rhythm-Stars and Stones*, Anastasi 2015; Temple Lodge, forthcoming.

21. Günter Wachsmuth. *Die Ätherischen Bildekräfte in Kosmos, Erde und Mensch.* Stuttgart 1924. *The Etheric Formative Forces in Cosmos, Earth and Man.* Eng. tr. by Olin D. Wannamaker. London & New York 1932. Sacred Science Institute 2006; also to download from <www.scribd.com>—*Tr. note.*

22. Rudolf Steiner. *Karmic Relationships.* Vol. 2. GA 236, London: RSP, 1974.

23. Hermann Beckh. *Alchymy, the Mystery of the Material World*, Temple Lodge, 2019 (Eng. tr. of *Vom Geheimnis der Stoffeswelt: Alchymie*, Basel: R. Geering Verlag, 1931). [The quaint spelling of 'alchymy' and 'chymical' is no doubt an attempt by the author to differentiate the subject, pointing to the genuine tradition—*Tr. addition.*]

24. See Rudolf Steiner. *Mystery Centres*, Dornach, 23 Nov.–23 Dec. 1923. GA 232, Lecture 11, 15 December 1923.

25. Hermann Beckh. *John's Gospel: The Cosmic Rhythm – Stars and Stones.* Leominster: Anastasi 2015; Temple Lodge, forthcoming (Eng. tr. of *Der kosmische Rhythmus: das Sternengeheimnis und Erdengeheimnis im Johannes-Evangelium*, Basel: R. Geering Verlag, 1930).

26. Rudolf Steiner. *The Inner Nature of Music and the Experience of Tone.* GA 283. Dornach, 7 March 1923. Germ. ed. 131. In the Eng. tr. 53, with its re-cast version of the whole passage, the actual phrase seems to have been lost in translation. The passage runs: '... *Musik im Grunde genommen nur innerlich im Menschen lebt, im Ätherleibe, wobei dann der physische Leib natürlich mitgenommen wird für die unteren Skalentöne ...*' – 'Basically music is experienced inwardly by the human being, in the ether-body, whereby the physical body is, of course, taken along for the lower notes of the scale ...'

27. The instruments of the orchestra, Steiner explains, derive from spiritual archetypes [GA 283. Stuttgart, 8 March 1923. 75]; the piano is a string-and-percussion hybrid, appearing in orchestral scores with the percussion, but next to the strings. As a keyboard instrument, furthermore, it visibly shows its category as an instrument of 'fixed tuning'. With good string players, whose ears are finely attuned, intonation is more 'variable' and can be made audible with their unfretted fingerboard (e.g. leading-notes can be slightly sharper and fourths slightly flatter than is possible in tempered tuning); tuning is somewhat more fixed with the Böhm system on wind instruments, while actually playing. (The issue of tempered tuning and 'expanding the tonal system' is another subject altogether.) Steiner's joke about the piano as a 'Philistine' instrument—hereby the fact of the *keyboard* surely partly contributes, though the remark could also have a domestic, social meaning—has been mistaken by too many people who should know better. Steiner was not being disrespectful.

The piano is clearly a useful instrument for a single player — from great composers to the aspiring amateur — to command the range and extent of the whole orchestra. This is precisely why, in the cited passage, Steiner mentions 'Bruckner played on the piano' (recordings of this orchestral writer hardly existed in his day) for everyday consumption. As a labour of love Liszt transcribed all of Beethoven's symphonies for the piano (superior to all other versions; Liszt's Preface signed 1865) — to help make them known, obviously before the age of aural recordings. The 'piano disappears from the room,' Steiner continues — if it doesn't quite with every player on every occasion, this shows there are essentially no bad pianos, but only inadequate players.

The implied point here about the *piano* is its supreme ability to *suggest* any instrument under the hands of imaginative and sensitive players, a fact exploited by the great composers. The player, too, is continually 'juggling' to overcome the mechanical aspect of keyboard and the percussion of tone-production and its rapid 'decay' in order to 'sing' a melodic line. (That it is eminently possible one need only mention the word 'Chopin', who wrote his lyrical and heroic compositions almost *solely* for the piano, and Schumann, who for his Lieder composed codas for the accompanist, solo, *because* — as the composer himself explains — of the expressive possibilities of the instrument.) The *ear*, moreover, *adjusts* to the apparent 'black-and-white' sound, as opposed to the 'full colour' of the orchestra, just as (provisionally to complete the above observations) the *ear adjusts* also to the differences of the musical keys *despite* tempered tuning — because music comes from the composer's aural imagination through musicians, via instruments *of whatever sort*, to the musical listening of the audience. The activity of *all* parties involved is creative. And the circuit is closed, completed. In this sense, the piano is pre-eminently an instrument of the present age of the consciousness-soul. Chesterton's Father Brown is proved once again correct in essential principles in (q.v.) the detective story 'The Mistake of the Machine' (in G.K. Chesterton, *The Wisdom of Father Brown*, Create Space 2014; also in *The Complete Stories of Father Brown*, Ware: Wordsworth Editions 2006; Penguin Books, 2012) — *Tr. note.*

28. Beckh clearly refers to live music. Recordings have brought mixed blessings. According to Hermann Pfrogner, music has been torn apart in the twentieth century ('Der zerrissene Orpheus', in *Zeitwende der Musik*, München u. Wien: Langen Müller, 1986, 180–199). He analyzes musical sound (*Lebendige Tonwelt*, München 1981, 194) into *Tonkern* = 'musical essence', *Klanghülle* = 'mantle of resonance', *Schallhülle*, or 'mantle of acoustic sound', cutting right across conventional categories of genre. Pfrogner pursues his analysis of phenomena in more detail, finally concluding that there is a corresponding art of music, an art of resonance, and art of noise in the world today — *Tr. note.*

29. On this see Friedrich Creutzer, *Symbolik und Mythologie der alten Völker* [free downloads from various internet sites].

30. GA 278, Lecture 3. Tr. A. S., RSP 2019, p. 63. See also footnote 54 below — *Tr. note.*

31. No doubt the 'Pythagorean comma' known to all tuners. This slight discrepancy that arises out of 'perfect intervals' over a range of several octaves has to be distributed in a manner acceptable to the ear (today's tempered tuning of 'equal semitones'), in order to make it possible for instruments of fixed tuning to engage in music-making in every key — *Tr. note.*

32. The modes are the musical system in use in Europe and elsewhere before the arrival of the major-minor system. Tradition relates the main seven medieval, 'ecclesiastical' modes to the seven (visible to the unaided sight) planets of Ptolomaic cosmology. (Historically, the name of the Greek modes were changed during the Middle Ages; the experience, too, seems to have changed, reflecting the fact that consciousness evolved. Scales, earlier described by the Greek theorists as descending, are increasingly felt to ascend from a keynote.) The arrangement of the semitones, being unique for each mode, certainly creates varying moods. Though today for practical purposes carols and songs in the traditional modes are also transposed, the pitch does seem to belong with this musical system — e.g., the tune *Greensleeves* in the Aeolian mode (A), except from the cadences where it becomes A-minor; *Drunken Sailor* in the Dorian mode (D), and so on. The one scale where the tones and semitones reflect exactly — the Dorian mode — is appropriately ascribed to Mercury in the evolutionary sequence, which, of course, is retained today in the names for the days of the week. The number seven is specifically a human creation; the cosmic names point to extra-mundane creative influences — *Tr. note.*

33. Rudolf Steiner. *The Inner Nature of Music and the Experience of Tone.* GA 283. Stuttgart, 8 June 1923. Spring Valley, New York: Anthroposophic Press. 1983, p. 68.

34. Archimedes is reputed to have said, 'Give me a place to stand and I will move the Earth'. — *Tr.*

35. Erich Schwebsch, *Anton Bruckner*, Bärenreiter, 1921/25 [new edition, *Bruckners Symphonien*, Stuttgart: Freies Geistesleben, o/p].

36. Friedrich Doldinger, *Alter, Krankheit, Tod.* Stuttgart: Urachhaus. 1930/51, p. 85f.

37. Chopin's highly original A-minor *Prelude* of 23 bars, as part of the *cycle* (emphatically not a collection), op. 28, links to the previous, opening C-major *Prelude*, taking over the final note E (b. 3 in the treble) and, with its quasi *Dies irae*-motif in the tenor, after 14 bars of modulating transition — like a written down 'improvisation' — it finally arrives at the chord of A-minor in b. 15. On Chopin's cycle op. 28 as a homage to Bach, see A. S.

'Celebrating the Musical System' in *Festschrift: Essays in Honour of Hermann Beckh*, Leominster: Anastasi 2016, pp. 165–181 — *Tr. note.*

38. An interesting piece of research goes into Wagner's knowledge of Chopin. Though not the first to notice the fact — for example, Beckh writing in 1936 — Maciej Gołąb ('Über den *Tristan*-Akkord bei Chopin', *Chopin Studies* 3. 1990, pp. 246–256) notes the similarity of the *Tristan*-chord to Chopin's *Mazurka*, op. 68, no. 4. L. Hofmann-Engl concludes his article (Chameleongroup online publication Mach 2008)

    <www.chameleongroup.org.uk/research/wagner.html>:

    'We set out to show that a few isolated forerunners exist for the *Tristan*-passage. We further established that op. 68, no. 4 by Chopin underwent a long editorial process. However, the *Tristan*-passage can be found [with] high similarity in the sketch to op. 68,4. We then established that Wagner was very familiar with Chopin and that the similarity between the *Tristan*-chord passage and op. 68, no. 4 are related beyond reasonable doubt. Finally, taking Wagner's general conduct and attitude into account, we conclude that Richard Wagner had access to op. 68, no. 4 — probably in [the] form of Franchomme's edition [1852] — and that Wagner copied the passage by deleting two chords and a melodic embellishment. Considering the enormous impact the *Tristan*-passage had over more than 150 years, we might be willing to view this as one of the greatest thefts in music history' — *Tr. note.*

39. The *Tristan*-chord, Beckh suggests, only nominally belongs to A-minor. In *The Language of Tonality*, with further discussion on the subject (p. 93ff.), he also suggests this key readily lends itself to chromatic writing that can tend to 'dissolve' into the atonal idiom ('a-tonal', a word deriving from journalism, originally meant 'not sounding' — music [in particular with J.M. Hauer's] 'conceived' in a pure spiritual manner, yet finding it difficult or unable to compromise with the grubby, physical world of correct tuning and so on. Soon, though, the word 'atonal' referred to music with no specific keynote; all twelve notes are conceived as equally significant, in fact abstracted, that is, the seven-note level in the musical system was abolished, at least theoretically. Hence the importance Prof. Beckh felt to uphold the spiritual essence of tonality.) The *Tristan*-chord is variously explained by musicologists, including Prof. Tovey. In musical notation, the evolution is traced from a possible sixteenth-century cadence in the Phrygian mode, with the addition of suspensions, passing notes, chromatic passing notes and appoggiaturas (see Appendix 3) — *Tr. note.*

40. Rudolf Steiner, *Four Mystery Dramas*. North Vancouver: Steiner Book Centre. 1973. Tr. Pusch, p. 107f.

41. See Rudolf Steiner, *Eurythmy as Visible Speech* [GA 279], Lecture 15, Dornach, 12 July 1924, tr. A. S. Anastasi 2013; RSP, 2019.

42. GA 279, Lecture 2, Dornach, 5 June 1924.

43. Rudolf Steiner, *Eurythmy as Visible Singing*, p. 48; GA 278. Lecture 2, 20 Feb 1924. Anastasi 2013; RSP, 2019, Rudolf Steiner, *The Inner Nature of Music...*, GA 283. Stuttgart, 7 March 1923. Spring Valley 1983, p. 51. Heiner Ruland, *Expanding Tonal Awareness*, London: RSP 2014. Chap XXVI, suggests the natural seventh 7/4 formed the basis of the Atlantean pentatonic scale, which is formed (as all scales are) by octave transposition — *Tr. note.*

44. See Rudolf Steiner's lecture-courses on *The Gospel of St John*, 18–31 May 1908 (GA 103), and Cassel, 23 June–7 July 1909 (GA 112).

45. See the two remarkable essays: Hermann Beckh, 'Wagner and Christianity' (1930), and Emil Bock, 'Twilight of the Gods and Resurrection' (1928), included in the Eng. tr. of Hermann Beckh, *The Parsifal=Christ=Experience in Wagner's Music Drama*, pp. 11–26 and 101–110, Anastasi Ltd, 2014; Temple Lodge, forthcoming — *Tr. note.*

46. The MS has '19. März 1907'. No lecture was traced for this date. However, on 25 March (in GA 96, p. 269) a passage reads very similar to that given by Prof. Beckh, translated here — *Tr. note.*

47. All the published translations of this lecture-course are inaccurate when it comes to this important final section; the translators have not completely understood the musical subject matter. An accurate translation appears in Lea van der Pals, *The Human Being as Music*, Anastasi, Leominster 2014, pp. 119–22 — *Tr. note.*

48. This is explained in detail by the author in footnote 3 of *The Parsifal=Christ=Experience*, p 29ff. Anastasi 2014; Temple Lodge, forthcoming.

49. A possible allusion in the subtext here: Germ. *Tor*, 'simpleton, fool', is also close to *Tür*, 'door, gate' — *Ed.*

50. Instrument builders have been working with Rudolf Steiner's indications for constructing new musical instruments: string instruments, percussion, the lyre, and so on — *Tr. note.*

51. The author plans a detailed study in the foreseeable future. [The Professor's study of Wagner's use of the musical keys appears as separate sections appended to each chapter devoted to every key in the posthumous publication *Die Sprache der Tonart in der Musik von Bach bis Bruckner mit besonderer Berücksichtigung des Wagner'schen Musikdramas* (1937, latest 3rd ed. 1999), Eng. tr. *The Language of Tonality*, tr. with Introduction by A. S. Anastasi 2015; Temple Lodge, forthcoming — *Tr. additional note.*]

52. Compared to this the Prelude to Act I is much more 'tonal'.

53. Prof. Beckh seems to be describing what Prof. Hermann Pfrogner terms the attained freedom of the 'the enharmonic level', the third level in the tonal system following the diatonic and diatonic-chromatic levels. Towards this level in the tonal system the art of music is developing out of inner listening. The atonal conception that, despite the theory that makes the 12 well-tempered notes absolute, has impressive musical achievements to its credit, is nevertheless the abstract shadow of what in the distant future

could be the bright reality of a fully 'owned' unity of 12 tonal centres. See Hermann Pfrogner, *Lebendige Tonwelt*, Münich: Langen Müller (1981), and relevant articles from the collection, *Zeitwende der Musik* (1986), Eng. tr. forthcoming — *Tr. note.*

54. The zodiacal figure of the 'circle of keys [circle of fifths]' in *The Essence of Tonality* [and as later developed in *The Language of Tonality*] can easily be supplemented in this direction, if it is known that in order to find what are called the 'houses', that means, the main ruling realms of the individual planets, proceed from:

- the Sun as the ruler of the Lion (of the heart), and from
- the Moon as the ruler of the Crab. On the simple basis of the astronomical sequence, the planetary 'houses' are arranged in the zodiac so that
- Mercury belongs to the sign of the Virgin and the Twins,
- Venus to the sign of the Scales and the Bull,
- Mars the Scorpion and the Ram,
- Jupiter the Archer and the Fishes, and
- Saturn belongs to the Goat and the Waterman.
- To the Waterman there also belongs the outer [= beyond Saturn] planet Uranus, the starry planet that indicates the realm of the fixed stars (whereas the other planets, as far as Saturn, still belong to the earthly viewpoint).
- C-major as the beginning of the circle of keys, the transition from the darkness to the light (from the lower keys with flats to the upper keys with sharps), as the key of the Ram would belong to Mars;
- Db-major (with Bb-minor) as the key of the Scorpion also belongs to Mars.
- G-major (with E-minor) as the key of the Bull, belongs to Venus, as does the key of the Scales, F#-major = Gb-major with Eb-minor;
- D-major (with B-minor) as the key of the Twins (it has two sharps!) belongs to Mercury, as does the Virgo key B-major:
- A-major, as the key of the Crab belongs to the Moon;
- E-major as the key of the Lion belongs to the Sun.
- The Jupiter-keys are Ab-major (F-minor) the Archer, and F-major (D-minor) the Fishes;
- Saturn keys are Eb-major (with C-minor) the Goat, and
- Bb-major (with G-minor) the Waterman. That the latter is also the 'starry key' in a higher sense, the Uranus-key, has already been noted.

Uranus is present here as the outer planet reaching into the actual realm of the fixed stars, into the highest starry realm. It is regarded as the starry planet. It will be shown below how in this certain viewpoints lie for some purposes of the music of *Tristan and Isolde.*

Anyone looking for an anthroposophical expression of these things is directed to Rudolf Steiner's [poetic work] 'The Twelve Moods' in the *Wahrspruchworten* [GA 40. The tr. by Ruth & Hans Pusch is pub. by Mercury Press, Spring Valley, New York, also included in Rudolf Steiner, *Eurythmy: Its Birth and Development*, p. 75, GA 277a. 2015; RSP, 2019. In their arrangement to the rhythm of the earthly zodiac, each of their 7 lines corresponds to the planetary septenary (Sun, Venus, Mercury, Mars, Jupiter, Saturn, Moon). The Uranus-mystery manages to be expressed in the Waterman verse, with its differentiation of the '*Grenzenlosen*' from the '*Begrenzten*' — of the 'boundless' from 'that which is bound'.

55. Hermann Beckh, *Der Hingang des Vollendeten — Die Erzählung von Buddhas Erdenabschied und Nirvana (Mahāparinibbānasutta des Pali-Kanons), übersetzt und eingeleitet*. Velag der Christengemeinschaft, Stuttgart, 1925.

56. Rudolf Steiner, Lecture 3, Dornach 21 Feb. 1924, in *Eurythmy as Visible Singing*, p. 64 (GA 278), Anastasi 2015; RSP, 2019. We *hear* the notes of a melody, but we *experience* the intervals between them and their relation to the keynote; thus a melody acquires meaning. Steiner also points out that all musical listening lives 'between recollection and anticipation'; the 'melody in the single note' is a supersensible, etheric experience of inner listening, making sense of the simplest melody, as well as the greatest musical works. Applying the indication to a series of such experiences in any given melodic phrase explains the performer's and the eurythmist's aim, to reveal the inherent music as an *act of creation*. In the lecture-course other inaudible — though experienced — musical phenomena of phrasing are discussed, summarized in the phrase 'the life of melos'; Beckh's preferred phrase is the 'sound-ether'.

Steiner goes into more practical detail for the *eurythmical performer*: what happens during rests; the *Schwung*, or 'spirited swinging-onwards' between motifs and phrases; the *Ruck*, or 'sudden jerk' of consciousness between changes of pitch ('up/ down'), and also of rhythm — the change from short to longer time-values and vice versa ('forward/ backwards'); expressing the bar line (between 'left and right'), the 'holding-on' between bars, 'anterior' to the first beat of the next bar/measure, and so on. These are all flashes of consciousness, strictly speaking inwardly heard anteriorly, in anticipation, preparing for what then comes to sound. The *melody*, in Steiner's words,

> takes up the actual spirit and carries it on. Fundamentally speaking, everything else does not add the spirit of the musical element, being at all events a more or less illustrative element (p. 73).

Beckh, who knew this lecture-course on music, also attempts to lead his readers beyond regarding music as a product to 'illustrate' something or other; he mentions the conception of 'programme music'. The Professor's approach to the 'primary', anterior musical element is made in the face of misunderstandings and the insistent caricatures of this aim. Self-appointed critics, following the composer J.M. Hauer (1923; see Introduction), point to soundtracks, background 'music', recordings, and so on, as 'evidence' of decadent developments, largely fathered, it is often claimed, by a 'Wagnerian' influence. Beckh, like Steiner, raises a voice for 'the life of melos' leading in the opposite direction from a comfortable materialism in the musical realm, from the *product* to the anterior, creative *process* of inner listening.

Wagner is Beckh's courageous choice in his likewise courageous endeavour to raise awareness of the *act of creation*, of expressing the inner voice, of revealing what is inaudible within and between the audible notes. Wagner, Beckh tries to show, remained open to those very spiritual influences championed by Hauer, the 'discoverer' of twelve-tone/-note music. Hauer's sweeping diagnosis of materialism in music, or a subjective consumerism causing a cheap whipping-up of emotion, may indeed be a largely correct *social comment*. However, an exclusive insistence on a scheme of 12 *notes* — Hauer excludes the diatonic level as such — does not actually remove the offending all-too-human appetite. Ultimately the atonal concept spells our de-humanization — unless fully 'owned', which is the aim of initiation (Pfrogner's 'enharmonic realm' beyond the diatonic and diatonic-chromatic levels in the tonal system).

Prof. Beckh, by investigating the 12 *keys* remains holistic. He brings to light the cosmic source of inspiration, as manifested in the earthy realm. We may summarize by saying, Wagner in particular uses the very 'intuition' championed by Hauer. To lead by his example beyond the turbid, controversial arena caused by 'theorizing', Beckh, following Steiner, proposes a phenomenological research of 'what is' — *Tr. note*.

57. Cf. on this Adolf Arenson's delightfully written and seminal *Musicalische Plaudereien*, Dornach 1930.

58. The MS of this section contains several additional passages. These are included here, perhaps slightly affecting the flow of the exposition — *Tr. note*.

59. Rudolf Steiner, *Eurythmy as Visible Singing* [GA 278], Lecture 3, 63. Cf.: 'The human being is a musical scale' (p. 65); and Lecture 4: 'Music is the self-creating [power] in the human being' (p. 79); R. Steiner, *The Inner Nature of Music* (GA 283), Spring Valley, New York, Anthroposophic Press, 1983. p. 33: 'The human organism ... is really a musical instrument.' R. Steiner, *Art as seen in the Light of Mystery Wisdom* [GA 275], Lecture 2, Dornach 29 Dec. 1914: 'Music contains the laws of the "I", the ego ... [which] dives down into the astral body' — *Tr. note*.

60. Beckh bases his account on Steiner's lecture, Stuttgart 8 March 1923 (GA 283) in *The Inner Nature of Music*, Spring Valley, New York: Anthro-

posophic Press, 1983. p. 74. Some commentators ascribe the *woodwind* to the thinking, the *string family* to the feelings and the *brass* to the will. Cf. also the chapter on instrumental 'Tone Colour' – in: Chr. Peter, *The Language of Music...*, pp. 253–275, Anastasi 2014; Temple Lodge, forthcoming. – *Tr. note.*

61. Felix [von] Mittl [(1856–1911) Austrian conductor and composer] added a contrabassoon to *The Ring* operas. When one knows how strictly inwardly meaningful, with what inner necessity instrumentation is decided by Wagner, one would never be able to come to such a lapse.

62. Concerning E-major as the warmest key of all, see the author's works on music, especially the ending of *The Language of Tonality* – *Tr. note.*

63. The concluding, unfinished fourth movement of Bruckner's *Ninth Symphony* has been painstakingly reconstructed by John A. Phillips and published in the *Bruckner Complete Edition*. Wikipedia devotes an article to it. The performing version by Nicola Samale, John A. Phillips, Benjamin-Gunnar Cohrs and Giuseppe Massuca (1983–91, rev. 1996) is played by Johannes Wildner and the New Philharmonic Orchestra of Westphalia (recording issued by Naxos). Sir Simon Rattle has also recorded it with the Berlin Philharmonic Orchestra – *Tr. note.*

64. Erich Schwebsch, *Anton Bruckner*. Bärenreiter, 1921/25 [new edition, *Bruckners Symphonien*, Stuttgart: Freies Geistesleben, o/p].

65. Marginal note H.B.: This follows after the other passage, but stands inwardly related. [From 'The Drunken Song', 5, in 'Fourth and Last Part' of Friedrich Nietzsche, *Thus Spoke Zarathustra*. Tr. Graham Parkes. OUP, 2005, p. 280f. – *Tr. addition.*]

66. Pencil note, difficult to read: ??Dr Schoder [perhaps Dr Schwebsch?] – *Tr. note.*

67. Albert Steffen. *Wegzehrung*. Rhein, Basel 1921/augmented edition, Dornach 1927/1964[5], p. 75.

68. One cannot 'prove', only experience such a connection. Instead of immediately denying, one can examine Bruckner's music against the poem by [Albert] Steffen [1884–1963], word for word [*as if* it had been set]. One should seek to experience it pictorially in colours and might ask oneself, whether one cannot recognize in it much 'play of flaming colours, greens and blues', whether one does not recognize in the D-minor motif that appears in between the 'dark clouds that devour the light', and in the tender A-major episode, whether one cannot divine the bright heavenly blue, which then takes up motifs that are more closely described by Steffen. [See further, Hermann Beckh, *The Language of Tonality...*, pp. 166f., 101f., also 163, 270, 330ff. Anastasii 2015; Temple Lodge, forthcoming. – *Tr. addition.*]

69. *The Gospel of St John in relation to the three other Gospels* (GA 112), Lecture 13.

70. Regarding this lecture-cycle (GA 153), Steiner said: 'It gave me particular pleasure to be told one day by one of our artistically gifted friends that

some of the lecture-cycles I have given could be transcribed into symphonies purely on the basis of their inner structure. Some of the courses are indeed based in their structure on something very like this. Take, for instance, the lecture-course given in Vienna on life between death and a new birth: you will see that you could make a symphony of it' (R. Steiner, lecture, Stuttgart 28 Aug. 1919, in *Practical Advice to Teachers*. GA 294) — *Tr. note.*

71. Oswald Spengler (1880–1936), author of *The Decline of the West* (Germ. ed. 1922, Eng. tr. 1926) — *Tr. note.*

72. *Plays by August Strindberg*. Tr. Edwin Björkman. London: Duckworth & Co. 1912. https://archive.org/details/playsstrindbjork00striuoft/ Hermann Beckh also considers the following episode in the 1921 essay 'Let there be Light'. English translation in *The Source of Speech*, Temple Lodge, 2019 — *Tr. note.*

73. Translation into English from the German, probably Beckh's own translation — *Tr. note.*

74. Trans E. Sprigge, *Six Plays of Strindberg*, Anchor Books, N.Y., 1955, p. 244.

75. Emil von Reznicek (1860–1945), an Austrian late Romantic composer of Czech ancestry, composed five symphonies and a whole series of orchestral, vocal and stage works, chamber music, piano and organ music.

76. A category of music that is given titles, or descriptions; examples range from Vivaldi's *Four Seasons* to elaborate tone-poems of the romantic nineteenth century. A literary stimulus, Beckh is suggesting, may be a mere help to the aural imagination (Beethoven wrote on the score of the first movement of his *Pastoral Symphony*, '*Erwachen heiterer Empfindungen bei der Ankunft auf dem Lande* — The awakening of cheerful *feelings* on arriving in the countryside'), or precisely a detailed course of events that threatens to leave the purely musical realm. 'Absolute' music carries its own drama in the tension and release between the notes, phrases and harmonies themselves. The grey area between these poles is subject to debate: today, for example, scholars are able to say why Debussy, a master of form and proportion, claimed he was *not* an 'impressionist' — *Tr. note.*

77. There is a composition from a modern Russian composer, which intends to show in music the individual stalls and attractions of a fair-ground; from a French composer a piece that wants to convey in sound the picture of an outdoor restaurant with the chaotic commotion of chairs and tables — whereby this musician still claims that this picture actually releases certain poetic impressions in him, fully enabling him to translate it into music.

78. A long oblong wooden box, inside of which tuned strings could be caused to vibrate by the draft at an open window. The only stringed instrument that plays solely harmonic frequencies. Much favoured by the early romantics, to whom the idea of the 'wind' or 'spirit, blowing where it wills' (John 3:8) was attractive — *Tr. note.*

79. Can this surprising sentence be justified from a study of Steiner's lectures? In the cited lecture – describing *one* of the three 'order of the arts' Steiner gave from different viewpoints during his lecturing career – 'experience of colour' exists as the middle art between the pictorial, or spatial, fine arts (architecture, sculpture) inspired by pre-earthly experience, and the musical performing arts, or time arts (speech and music) that prepare after-death experience (see also, Munich, 5 and 6 May 1918; Dornach, 9 April 1921, in GA 271. No Eng. tr. to date). However, no phrase suggesting 'the foremost art' is made.

Does the author's sentence rather refer to the *social situation* of the time when the Goetheanum was under construction and the visual arts were particularly evident? The visual arts of the 'Goetheanum impulse', nevertheless, were conceived *musically*; indeed, all the arts are to become more musical.

> For centuries another impulse [than the sculptural, pictorial arts] has developed and this is the impulse towards the art of music. For this reason the pictorial arts are also taking on a more or less musical form. In the artistic sphere the musical element belongs to the future of humanity and this includes everything of a musical nature that can also appear in the other performing arts (R. Steiner, Torquay, 22 Aug. 1924, tr. A. S. *True and False Paths*... GA 243).

Compared to his engagement as architect, painter, playwright, and so on, music seems to be the one art that Rudolf Steiner did not engage in as a composer or player. But this is only apparent. In connection with speech-sounds, Beckh himself refers to Steiner's musical ear. Perhaps Beckh was unimpressed with the humble artistic achievements in music of those early years; in this respect the Goetheanum as a musical centre could clearly not compete with, say, Bayreuth.

Did Steiner practice his own advice? The evidence of Steiner's musicality certainly includes the creation of eurythmy itself – Steiner's favourite 'daughter'. During the early years speech eurythmy was developed – though it tends to be overlooked that the *musical element in speech* is the main object of study. Music eurythmy itself developed a little later. Rudolf Steiner's exemplary music-eurythmy forms (1921–24), and not least the memoirs of the early eurythmists and musicians themselves, witness to Steiner's astonishing musicality (Ralph Kux describes how the eurythmy forms were created: Ralph Kux, Willi Kux, *Erinnerungen an Rudolf Steiner*, p. 14, Stuttgart: Mellinger Verlag 1976). Moreover, the phenomenon of the simultaneous presence of a chiasmic 7-sentence rhythm *and* a 12-sentence prose rhythm on every page of every published work, suggests that only a musical genius could consistently write like that (for a summary, with Steiner's clues and references to initial studies, see *Hermann Beckh & the Spirit-Word*, Leominster 2015, p. 25; *Festschrift: Essays in Honour of H. B.*

pp. 137–40, and in further details in the proposed *Yearbook*, forthcoming). Moreover, the evidence of his astonishing lecturing career shows where Steiner poured his musicality, sowing seeds for the future. Cf. Michael Kurtz, *Rudolf Steiner und die Musik*, Dornach 2015. For what it is worth, experience of a working life in the performing arts prompts me without any doubt to claim Steiner as a major unsung musician of the twentieth century — *Tr. note.*

80. Another verb used (GA 271, p. 198) is *schnappt hinauf*. 'After death we lay aside our astral body; then — please excuse the banal expression — our musical [experience/ personality] "snaps up" [*or* "switches over"] into the music of the spheres. In music and poetry we pre-experience that which after death is our world, our existence....' — *Tr. note.*

81. The context is the lecture-course on music eurythmy. Rudolf Steiner mentions three musicians, R. Wagner, J.M. Hauer and W.A. Mozart (from whom he quotes a few bars of a piano sonata). Hauer, in his outspoken manifesto (1923) — an exoteric stimulus to the lecturer — criticizes Wagner for degrading music by making it serve the drama. Steiner is less severe. By claiming Wagner's music is 'unmusical music' (*Eurythmy as Visible Singing*, p. 56, tr. A. S. Lecture 2, Dornach, 20 Feb. 1924, GA 278. Anastasi 2014/ RSP, 2019) he is saying three things. This music is (i) music, (ii) 'unmusical' — words are sung, and the thematic content (in the orchestra of Wagner's mature style) also takes the place of words — and (iii) is 'justified in our age'. The art of singing is complete; what enhancement is still required to be revealed in eurythmy? To attempt this would simply be a duplication (GA 278, Lecture 6, p. 103). Eurythmy, a new artistic chapter, is not there to illustrate anything. It attempts to *reveal*, that is, create with the player/s, the inner tensions and their release inherent in absolute music. Steiner spoke many times on Wagner's work, in particular he speaks of Wagner's revival of Teutonic mythology. Wagner's work is something that 'humanly, is obviously a significant cultural phenomenon' (*The Course of my Life* [GA 28], Chapter IV) — *Tr. note.*

82. Beckh made good his claim in *The Language of Tonality*, tr. A. S. Anastasi, 2015; Temple Lodge, forthcoming — *Tr. note.*

83. The definitive study on the music is Christoph Peter, *The Language of Music in Mozart's The Magic Flute*, tr. A. S. Anastasi, 2015; Temple Lodge, forthcoming — *Tr. note.*

84. Also in *Tristan and Isolde*, at the place where Isolde's healing power of love is mentioned, we find the characteristic key of G-major. Further details in the author's *The Essence of Tonality*, tr. A. S. Anastasi 2008 [and the fuller account, *The Language of Tonality*, tr. A. S. Anastasi 2015; Temple Lodge, forthcoming].

85. 'Frau Holda' in German legends is the protectress of agriculture and women's crafts, cf. 'Mother Holle' in the Grimms' *Fairy-Tales* — *Tr. note.*

86. The Professor quotes from the libretto, *'webende Lohe'* ('weaving flame'). The connection with Beckh's discussion of √*vā* is also important here.

87.

- *Parsifal* with Jupiter, the spiritual and Christ-planet;
- *Twilight of the Gods* with Mars;
- *Siegfried* with the Sun;
- The Mastersingers with Mercury;
- *Tannhäuser* with Venus (see what was discussed concerning the 'Mystery of St Elisabeth');
- *Lohengrin* with 'Neptune', the 'sound out of cosmic distances', that played such a role in Wagner's own stars;
- *Tristan and Isolde* then with Uranus, not in the sense of the single planet beyond Saturn, but of the starry world, the actual starry heavens indicted by this planet.

[On this suggestive theme, cf. Jean Seznec, *The Survival of the Pagan Gods: The Mythological Tradition and its Place in Renaissance Humanism and Art.* Bollingen Series XXXVIII. Princeton Univ. Press, 1953/72. For the planetary inspiration in the sevenfold Narniad of C.S. Lewis: Michael Ward, *Planet Narnia*, OUP 2008, and the fine, popular account *The Narnia Code*, Paternoster 2010. A BBC documentary of interesting interviews is available as a DVD (same title); snippets appear on Youtube. Cf. also C.S. Lewis, *That Hideous Strength*. London: Macmillan 1968; HarperCollins 2005. — *Tr. addition.*]

88. Torquay, 22 Aug. 1924, in GA 243. The last third of the final lecture is inadequately translated in all the published versions of this lecture-course. An accurate translation is contained in Lea van der Pals, *The Human Being as Music.* Anastasi 2014. Endnote 40, pp. 120–23 — *Tr. note.*

89. Hermann Beckh, *The Parsifal=Christ=Experience in Wagner's Music Drama*, footnotes 2 and 3, pp. 29–31, tr. A. S. and Anneruth Strauss. Anastasi, 2015; Temple Lodge, forthcoming.

90. The obscure words seem to refer to an Easter-lecture, probably 25 March 1907. Cf. a paragraph from the author's book on *Alchymy* (chap. V). (JG = H. Beckh, *John's Gospel: The Cosmic Rhythm*.):

> That which in the *wine of the Marriage at Cana* as the *chymical mystery of the Earth's future* is prophetically placed by Christ before people, then in the Mystery of Golgotha, in the blood streaming from the wounds of the Crucified that sinks directly into the Earth, becomes the seed for this future. In Christ's blood starry forces of cosmic life give themselves to the dying Earth. Nowhere do we feel so close to the mystery of the *red tincture* and its power to metamorphose the earthly, material world, than in the Mystery of the Blood of Golgotha. It appears in the Manichean picture of the self-sacrifice of the *tincture of light* (JG. pp. 388, 407, etc.), sacrificing itself into the darkness of the earthly element, also

repeatedly mentioned by Jakob Böhme. Rudolf Steiner has shown how for the clairvoyant vision the Earth started to shine as in a new starry light, began to shine as a star amongst stars when it received the seed of the Sun of the future, the seed of its own Sun-becoming (JG. p. 387ff.). Rudolf Steiner expressed the conviction (Lecture, Berlin. 25 March 1907. GA 96; and similarly in *From Jesus to Christ*. Lecture, Karlsruhe. 8 Oct. 1911. GA 131) that nobody has come exoterically closer to this esoteric (chymical-esoteric) mystery than Richard Wagner in his music drama *Parsifal*. In modern times this has been placed before humanity for the first time. And what was presented above (Chapters 2 and 3) of the connections of the *chymical* and of the *musical element* is nowhere to be experienced so directly than in Wagner's *Parsifal*. Already at the end of the Prelude and then again in Acts 1 and 2, in the vision of Amfortas and of Parsifal, the glowing of the sacred Blood is spoken of in their beholding the Grail. Something like starlight twinkling within streaming blood, of 'blood turning itself into ether' (Steiner's expression) is eloquently expressed in the instrumental music. (On this, see the author's *The Parsifal=Christ=Experience in Wagner's Music Drama*, pp. 41, 65f. etc. Anastasi 2015; Temple Lodge, forthcoming.) At this point the chymical mystery becomes the Mystery of the Holy Grail.

91. The content was delivered as a lecture by Prof. Beckh at the Goetheanum, CH-Dornach, in spring 1921.
92. Franz Nikolaus Finck (1867–1910), German philologist, a professor of General Linguistics at the University of Berlin.

A note from the publisher

For more than a quarter of a century, **Temple Lodge Publishing** has made available new thought, ideas and research in the field of spiritual science.

Anthroposophy, as founded by Rudolf Steiner (1861-1925), is commonly known today through its practical applications, principally in education (Steiner-Waldorf schools) and agriculture (biodynamic food and wine). But behind this outer activity stands the core discipline of spiritual science, which continues to be developed and updated. True science can never be static and anthroposophy is living knowledge.

Our list features some of the best contemporary spiritual-scientific work available today, as well as introductory titles. So, visit us online at **www.templelodge.com** and join our emailing list for news on new titles.

If you feel like supporting our work, you can do so by buying our books or making a direct donation (we are a non-profit/charitable organisation).

office@templelodge.com

※ TEMPLE LODGE

For the finest books of Science and Spirit